The
10 Big Lies
About America

The 10 Big Lies About America

Combating Destructive Distortions About Our Nation

Michael Medved

CROWN
FORUM
NEW YORK

For Sarah, Shayna, and Danny—
appreciative heirs to American truths

■ ■ ■

Grateful acknowledgment is made to the following for the illustrations used in this book:

p. 1: *The First Thanksgiving, 1621* by J. L. G. Ferris (reproduction of oil painting from series "The Pageant of a Nation"), courtesy of the Library of Congress; *p. 11*: *Indian War Council*, provided by HistoryPicks.com; *p. 46*: *Emancipation* (detail), by Thomas Nast (c. 1865), courtesy of the Library of Congress; *p. 72*: *Freedom of Religion,* from the pamphlet "The Four Freedoms" (Office of War Information, 1942), courtesy of the Library of Congress; *p. 95*: *The Great Bartholdi Statue, Liberty Enlightening the World—The Gift of France to the American People* (Currier & Ives, c. 1883), courtesy of the Library of Congress; *p. 119*: *The Road to Dividends* (c. 1913), courtesy of the Library of Congress; *p. 139*: *Work Pays America! Prosperity* (Works Progress Administration, 1936–1941), courtesy of the Library of Congress; *p. 162*: *Another Explosion at Hand* (detail) by Udo J. Keppler (J. Ottmann Lith. Co., Puck Bldg., New York, NY, 1900), courtesy of the Library of Congress; *p. 189*: "Nader/Camejo 2004," "Proud to be a Libertarian," and "Vote Your Hopes, Not Your Fears—Vote Third Party," provided by PoliticalGifts.com; *p. 209*: Photo courtesy of the James D. Wilson family; *p. 232*: *Woman's Holy War: Grand Charge on the Enemy's Works* (Currier & Ives, c. 1874), courtesy of the Library of Congress; *p. 257*: Photo of President Reagan (Endicott, NY, 9/12/84), courtesy of the Ronald Reagan Library.

Library of Congress Cataloging-in-Publication Data

Medved, Michael.
The 10 big lies about America / Michael Medved.—1st ed.
p. cm.
Includes index.
1. United States—Civilization—Historiography. 2. National characteristics, American.
3. Culture conflict—United States. 4. Values—United States. 5. Anti-Americanism.
I. Title. II. Title: Ten big lies about America.
E169.12.M427 2008
973—dc22   2008034131

ISBN 978-0-307-39406-4

Printed in the United States of America

Design by Lauren Dong

10 9 8 7 6 5 4 3 2 1

First Edition

Contents

What's the matter with us anyhow? If America ever loses confidence in herself, she will retain the confidence of no one, and she will lose her chance to be free, because the fearful are never free.

—ADLAI STEVENSON, 1954

We've got to teach history based not on what's in fashion but what's important. . . . If we forget what we did, we won't know who we are. I'm warning of an eradication of the American memory that could result, ultimately, in an erosion of the American spirit.

—RONALD REAGAN, FAREWELL ADDRESS,
JANUARY 11, 1989

A Tainted Legacy

NO CAUSE FOR CELEBRATION

Why do so many Americans find it so difficult to celebrate their nation's achievements and blessings?

How did cherished occasions of joy and gratitude become the focus of anguish and controversy?

I confronted these uncomfortable questions in my own backyard when Seattle's notorious "Thanksgiving Letter" became a brief, embarrassing media sensation.

On November 8, 2007, the stern missive went out to all teachers and staff of the city's public schools insisting that they should "struggle with these complex issues" surrounding the yearly celebration and avoid, at all costs, "teaching about Thanksgiving in traditional ways." The bureaucrats who signed the letter worried that without their timely intervention, thoughtless educators might arrange precisely the sort of outmoded, one-dimensional observance of Turkey Day that emphasized inappropriate elements such as pride and reverence.

"With so many holidays approaching we want to again remind you that Thanksgiving can be a particularly difficult time for many of our Native students," warned the officials (led by a school district honcho who identified herself with the intimidating title of "director of equity, race, and learning support"). To achieve a more appropriate perspective, they directed all staff in the Seattle public schools to consult a list of "Eleven Thanksgiving Myths" prepared by the radical "Native" Web site Oyate.org. The letter urged the educators to "take a look . . . and begin your own deconstruction," specifically citing Myth #11:

> **Myth:** Thanksgiving is a happy time.
> **Fact:** For many Indian people, "Thanksgiving" is a time of mourning, of remembering how a gift of generosity was rewarded by theft of land and seed corn, extermination of many from disease and gun, and near total destruction of many more from forced assimilation. As currently celebrated in this country, "Thanksgiving" is a bitter reminder of 500 years of betrayal returned for friendship.

As soon as I read this alarming letter, I began to wonder how earnest teachers might take its suggestions to heart and begin to commemorate this festival of destruction and betrayal with, say, their kindergarten charges. My own appallingly innocent 1950s childhood offered shamelessly sentimental Thanksgiving pageants, complete with tacky Pilgrim and Indian costumes and, on one occasion, a live turkey. On my nationally syndicated radio show I speculated on the way such sweet but silly extravaganzas might be updated to accommodate the hip sensibility of contemporary Seattle. Perhaps the nervous kiddies could now parade onto the stage, appropriately costumed as little Pilgrims and Pilgrimettes, and then, after enumerating the countless crimes of their forebears, they could lash themselves (or each other) with miniature leather whips and wail together in regretful agony. The proud parents would no doubt rise and applaud in tearful, self-righteous appreciation.

Much to the humiliation of those of us who choose to raise our children in the Great Northwest, the story of Seattle's idiotic effort to turn Thanksgiving into a "day of mourning" became a subject for national debate. After I discussed the issue on the air, the Fox News Channel contacted me to provide a local perspective, and they also sent camera crews to interview local Indian tribes. The Tulalips, who occupy a prosperous, well-organized reservation about a half hour north of downtown (complete with high-end shopping center, resort hotel, and, inevitably, casino), emphatically affirmed their pride in the annual November holiday. Tribal spokesman Daryl Williams explained that "most Native Americans celebrate Thanksgiving in the same way that many other Americans do— as a way to be thankful for abundance and a chance to spend time with families." The Tulalips love to stage festive communal Thanksgiving feasts at which, in a bow to regional traditions, they serve alder-smoked salmon rather than turkey. Williams told the press: "The spirit of Thanksgiving, of people working together to help each other, is the spirit I think that needs to grow in this country, because this country has gotten very divisive."

He's right, of course. The divisiveness, shame, and self-hatred have spread far beyond the damp and moody precincts of Seattle. In fact, the year before our "Emerald City" launched its controversial assault on Thanksgiving, the Associated Press featured an account of an innovative educator at an elementary school in San Francisco, yet another city known for brain-dead trendiness:

> Teacher Bill Morgan walks into his third-grade class wearing a black Pilgrim hat made of construction paper and begins snatching up pencils, backpacks and glue sticks from his pupils. He tells them the items now belong to him because he "discovered" them. The reaction is exactly what Morgan expects. The kids get angry and want their things back.
>
> Morgan is among elementary school teachers who have ditched the traditional Thanksgiving lesson. . . . He has replaced it with a more realistic look at the complex relationship between Indians and white settlers.

Stealing backpacks and glue sticks provides a "realistic look" at a "complex relationship"?

Across the country, too many Americans have developed a complex, even tortured relationship with their own past. And like all deeply dysfunctional bonds, this frayed connection rests on a series of destructive lies—sweeping distortions that poison our sense of who we are and what our country means.

Consider, for example, the oddly apologetic May 2007 commemoration of the four hundredth anniversary of the first permanent British settlement in the New World. With both the queen of England and the president of the United States journeying to Virginia to mark the occasion, federal officials took grim pains to tamp down any sense of merriment in the festivities. The National Park Service invested taxpayer money in new exhibits at its "Historic Jamestowne" visitor center, and these displays explicitly shunned the congratulatory messages of prior tributes. "Past Jamestown anniversaries were referred to as 'celebrations,' " warned a prominently posted introduction to the Park Service exhibition. "Because many facets of Jamestown's history are not cause for celebration, like human bondage and the displacement of Virginia Indians, the Jamestown 400th Anniversary is referred to as the Jamestown 2007 Commemoration."

Another display in the same facility struck Edward Rothstein of the *New York Times* with its remarkably unbalanced approach: "The Indians, we read, were 'in harmony with the land that sustained them' and formed 'an advanced, complex society of families and tribes.' English society— the society that gave us the King James Bible and Shakespeare along with the stirrings of democratic argument—is described as offering 'limited opportunity' in which a 'small elite' were landowners; in London, we are told, 'life was difficult,' with social dislocation, low wages, unemployment, etc."

While official observances scrupulously avoided any overtly festive messages, small crowds of protestors denounced even the subdued themes of the "commemoration." Demonstrators from groups such as Black Lawyers for Justice and the New Black Panther Party announced their intention to "crash this illegitimate party and pursue the overdue case for Reparations and Justice for the victims of slavery, mass murder and genocide." The protest leader, Malik Zulu Shabazz, cited "crimes committed at Jamestown which resulted in America being originated on the corrupt foundation of racism, population removal, mass murder, slavery and a litany of crimes against divine law and humanity."

Mr. Shabazz not only rejects the long-cherished view that American society arose in fulfillment of some powerful, providential purpose but proudly advances the opposite perspective: that the nation's origins involved a "litany of crimes against divine law and humanity."

"It's not just Jamestown," he told the Associated Press. "It's what started in Jamestown."

And what started in Jamestown? Our distinctive civilization. Malik Shabazz and other America haters view the nation itself as a vicious, criminal enterprise that requires radical transformation if not outright termination. In June 2006, Jake Irwin, a student at Evergreen State College in Olympia, Washington, and an outspoken supporter of Venezuelan demagogue Hugo Chávez, told the *Wall Street Journal:* "My political belief is that the U.S. is a horrendous empire that needs to end."

POISONING THE PRESENT

Though few of our fellow citizens share this overt hostility to our national project, the big lies about America still circulate so widely that they feed an insecure and angry public mood. Grotesque distortions about the nation's origins and institutions poison our present and threaten our future. But any attempt to challenge the prevalent slanders will draw scorn as a sign of simple-minded jingoism, while those who teach or preach the worst about America earn fulsome praise for their "sophistication" or "courage." As a result, our universities and public schools eagerly endorse the cynical assumptions about the country, and alarmist mass media recycle hysterical accounts of imminent doom and corruption.

We worry over anti-Americanism abroad but parrot its primary charges here at home. While objective indications identify residents of the United States as among the most fortunate people in human history, much of the public refuses to acknowledge our blessings because, according to the logic of widely accepted America-bashing lies, we don't deserve them.

Those who embrace the idea that the USA came into being through vicious genocide against native populations, built its wealth on the unique oppression of African slaves, promoted corporate exploitation of powerless workers, and damaged countless other nations with its imperialist policies will naturally assume that we're paying the price for such sins and abuses—viewing an allegedly dark present as the inevitable product of a dark past. Bleak assumptions about our guilty ancestors allow contemporary Americans to wallow in self-pity while blaming our brutal forebears for our supposed sorry state.

In one typical aside, *New York Times* book reviewer William Grimes laments that American success "came at a price . . . for the descendents of the colonists, who have inherited a tainted legacy."

This supposedly soiled and shameful heritage, this exhaustively analyzed burden of embarrassment and apology, now pollutes our most contentious public debates. In the presidential campaign of 2008, Democratic contender Barack Obama deflected attention from the anti-American rants of his longtime pastor, Jeremiah Wright ("Not God bless America, God damn America!"), by calling for a solemn reconsideration of "this nation's original sin of slavery"—invoking the familiar notion that America bears unique guilt for its monstrous oppression of African captives. Whenever President George W. Bush spoke of spreading democracy around the globe, his critics clamored that his visionary rhetoric actually cloaked the latest chapter in a long, bitter history of reckless imperialism. In addressing economic hardships for middle-class Americans, politicians (of both parties) regularly demonize the very entrepreneurial energies and corporate organizations that deliver a level of comfort and opportunity inconceivable to prior generations. In any discussion of faith and family, the Right bemoans and the Left often applauds the same phony idea: that our society has abandoned its traditional unifying values and entered a brave new world of chaotic relativism.

While we still speak wistfully of the American dream, our popular culture prefers to peddle an assortment of American nightmares. For more than a generation we've been bombarded with these charges and warnings about our "sick society" (in the loathsome phrase of the 1960s), and the easiest way for hardworking people to respond to the scolding has been to keep quiet and mind their own business. In place of the picnics, parades, and brass bands of yesterday, we now celebrate both Memorial Day and Veterans Day with a melancholy focus on the grim elegance of the Vietnam Veterans Memorial in the nation's capital.

In fact, the Vietnam experience and the associated dislocation of the 1960s and '70s helped to dissolve the patriotic consensus that had endured for two centuries. The unprecedented U.S. failure in Indochina gave credibility, if not confirmation, to those protestors who had decried our "imperialist" foreign policy, and chose to identify their nation as "Amerika"—the Germanic spelling meant to evoke the Nazis, while the inserted *k* recalled our homegrown KKK. Once you've associated your native soil with genocidal fascists and white supremacist thugs, it's tough to return to singing the praises of the land of the free and the home of the brave—even after ultimate victory in the Cold War and the evanescent surge of unity following the terror attacks of 9/11.

By that time the tribalism and identity politics of the 1960s had become a well-established feature of our national life, with jostling interest groups largely taking the place of homogenizing notions of Americanism. African Americans, feminists, Latinos, gays, Asians, the disabled, hippies, Native Americans—each aggrieved segment of society demanded justice and redress, competing for recognition as the most victimized and gypped. Amid this clamor of suffering subgroups, the old national motto "E pluribus unum"—"Out of many, one"—sounded intolerant, disrespectful of difference and diversity, as the ideal of a melting pot gave way to a "gorgeous multicultural mosaic." The concept of an overarching, non-ironic definition of American identity looked less and less plausible.

In 1904, Broadway giant George M. Cohan jauntily identified himself as a "Yankee Doodle dandy" who had been "born on the Fourth of July." Eighty years later, Ron Kovic appropriated the latter phrase for a book and movie about his shattering experience as a paralyzed, abused, deeply disillusioned Vietnam vet. At the time of the film's release in 1989, everyone who encountered the title *Born on the Fourth of July* received it with a snicker or smirk, understanding Cohan's high-stepping glorification of flag and homeland as an embarrassing relic of ignorant and insular nationalism.

SINGULAR SHORTCOMINGS

Ironically, the very provincialism that America bashers deplore ends up helping them spread their fashionable slanders. The hardworking public knows and cares so little about all the other imperfect nations of the world that the USA's shortcomings look singular, unprecedented, and overwhelming. We tend to take our failures more seriously than do our fellow members of the international community. Other nations manage to cope with far more shameful histories of mass murder, backwardness, and barbarity without feeling the need for apologies, handwringing, or wrenching self-criticism.

For example, Oscar-winning director Ang Lee notes the overwhelming importance of unquestioning patriotism to all those who claim Chinese identity: "Chinese patriotism is not supposed to be negotiable. To us that's a black-and-white thing. You sacrifice yourself—how can you let China down?" Politicians and pundits in the People's Republic don't agonize about thousands of years of conquest and colonialism over "lesser" peoples at the edges of the Middle Kingdom.

Similarly, in France's government-run schools "the very content of education is discriminatory," according to French journalist and author Guy Sorman. "The history of colonization is taught as if it were a glorious feature of French history. In Senegal, on his first official visit to Africa, [President Nicolas] Sarkozy regretted the violence of colonization but insisted on the good intentions of the French colonizers, out there to bring civilization to the 'African man' who had 'not entered history.' "

Our French cousins celebrate Bastille Day with unapologetic pride, despite the ugly stains on the tricolor. For Mexicans and for Mexican immigrants in the United States, Cinco de Mayo doesn't provide an occasion for brooding meditation on the pain and injustice that's always characterized our turbulent neighbor to the south.

Some might explain this American penchant for harsh self-criticism as a product of our higher ideals and more lofty aspirations. Through most of its long, glittering history as a major European power, no one ever really expected Austria to serve as a "light to the nations" or a "shining city on a hill." The United States, on the other hand, has long expected to remake the world in our image, and often succeeded in that endeavor. The fact that we have attempted more shouldn't obscure the fact that we've also achieved more, and stumbled less, than other nations with significant roles in world affairs.

The bitter lies about America undermine the ongoing aspirations that alone can power the United States in its continued role as a mighty engine of human betterment.

INSTINCTIVE RESISTANCE

Most Americans feel instinctive indignation over the false charges against our country, but they lack the arguments or information to counteract them.

This book hopes to fill that void. The ten big lies exposed here constitute the most common and destructive distortions about the nation's past and present. My goal is to explode the most obvious lies and to arm Americans with the information and approaches they need to answer bitter indictments against our country.

In many corners of the continent, educators and psychologists fret over the self-esteem of our young people, hoping to protect their tender egos by encouraging them to declare "I'm a wonderful kid" or, on too many occasions, "I'm part of a wonderful—though often victimized—group." Even more important to their sense of security and confidence would be the recognition "I'm part of a wonderful country—a wonderful and unprecedented national adventure. And I can most appropriately express my gratitude for the gifts I've received by making the most of my opportunities."

The dreary alternative message of victimhood, powerlessness, guilt, and decline undermines the possibility of progress for individual and society alike.

An American Indian academic and musician named David A. Yeagley, an enrolled member of the Comanche Nation, tells a sobering story about one of his students at Oklahoma State University—Oklahoma City. A "tall and pretty" young woman he calls Rachel spoke out in a class discussion about patriotism. "Look, Dr. Yeagley," she declared, "I don't see anything about my culture to be proud of. It's all nothing. My race is just nothing. Look at your culture. Look at American Indian tradition. Now I think that's really great. You have something to be proud of. My culture is nothing."

Concerning this unforgettable interchange, Professor Yeagley observes:

> The Cheyenne people have a saying: A nation is never conquered until the hearts of its women are on the ground. . . . Who had conquered Rachel's people? What had led her to disrespect them? Why did she behave like a woman of a defeated tribe?
>
> They say that a warrior is measured by the strength of his enemies. As an Indian, I am proud of the fact that it took the mightiest nation on earth to defeat me.
>
> But I don't feel so proud when I listen to Rachel. It gives me no solace to see the white man self-destruct. If Rachel's people are "nothing," what does that say about mine?

And what does it say about each of us if we see ourselves as heirs to "nothing"—to only a tainted legacy and a birthright of shame?

A nation with no pride in its past won't feel confidence in its future. The big lies about America have transformed our heritage from a blessing into a burden, promoting impotence and paralysis. Achieving an accurate understanding of the privileged position we enjoy can replace self-pity with pride, apology with affirmation. Only this sense of shared gratitude will sustain our occasionally strained communal connections, providing elusive common ground in this freakishly favored nation in which every day brings occasion for thanksgiving.

"America Was Founded on Genocide Against Native Americans"

ORIGINAL SIN

"How can you feel so proud of a nation that's built on the genocide of innocent people?"

The caller to my radio show, breathing heavily and audibly struggling against tears, expressed her indignation at my standard opening to each hour of the daily broadcast: "And another great day in this greatest nation on God's green earth."

She took advantage of our weekly "Disagreement Day" (when listeners get the chance to challenge me on views I've previously expressed) to argue that a nation couldn't be great if it originated through a great crime.

"I walk around every day," she sighed, "and I look at the way we live and the stuff we have and the things we waste, and I try to remember that we got it all—all the money and the power and the goodies—by coming in and killing off the rightful owners of this land."

Few of our fellow citizens feel obliged to bear such a painful burden of guilt, but many, if not most, contemporary Americans have been trained to temper our instinctive patriotism with apologetic acknowledgment of long-ago misdeeds. Try talking about the nation's blessings and achievements in polite, sophisticated company and you'll provoke no end of tut-tutting qualifications, which invariably feature the "holocaust" of Native Americans. For many citizens, justice and decency demand constant consciousness of our society's original sin.

After years of freewheeling conversation on talk radio about America's past and present, I became acutely aware of this reflexive abasement and began to confront it on the air, trying to place the tortured, bloody history of white-Indian relations in a more complete and accurate context. Predictably enough, I drew condemnation as "a holocaust denier."

In September 2007 I posted a column on my blog at Townhall.com entitled "Reject the Lie of White 'Genocide' Against Native Americans." This essay drew nearly four hundred impassioned responses, sharply divided between grateful support and raging disdain. One reaction cheerfully suggested: "I'm guessing Mr. Medved was dropped on his head several times as a child to be this stupid! YES; genocide was government policy! Starvation, murder, rape, cutting babies out of the womb, mutilation of bodies. It all happened, done by your founding hero's [*sic*]. Makes me sick just to think about it. Mass murderers is what they are and is how they should be remembered! Yeah, the truth sucks, take a big bite and swallow."

Another correspondent graciously observed: "Medved is a holocaust denier . . . no different from the right wing lunatics who deny the European genocide of the Jews during WWII. . . . What happened to the American Indian is textbook genocide. Moreover, it is, in terms of numbers of those killed and the lasting legacy of cultural destruction, the worst genocide ever perpetrated."

Of course, such sentiments echo ubiquitous messages from both popular culture and public schools. In promoting its 2007 Emmy Award–

winning miniseries *Bury My Heart at Wounded Knee,* HBO publicized its television "event" with a tagline that made the charge of genocide explicit: "In the late 19th century, the U.S. government waged a systematic campaign to exterminate American Indians—and nobody seemed to care."

In recent years, Columbus Day—once a joyous commemoration of Italian American pride surrounding the epochal adventures of a brave explorer—has become a battleground between traditional celebrants and the guilt vendors. In Denver in 2007 police arrested eighty-three protestors for throwing fake blood and dismembered baby dolls on the parade route. A week earlier, a social work intern at the University of Southern Maine launched her crusade to ban the Columbus holiday, announcing that as a "Native American woman, I cannot sit quietly as this holiday is celebrated year after year. . . . I think celebrating this holiday can be compared to celebrating a day for Hitler and Fascism in Germany."

Academics in every corner of the country regularly reinforce this comparison between white settlers and Nazi butchers. David E. Stannard, a historian at the University of Hawaii, alleged that by the end of the nineteenth century, Native Americans had experienced "the worst human holocaust the world had ever witnessed, roaring across two continents non-stop for four centuries and consuming the lives of countless tens of millions of people." To Ward Churchill, former professor of ethnic studies at the University of Colorado, the fate of North American Indians amounted to a "vast genocide . . . the most sustained on record."

Rational voices seldom counteract such claims because no educated individual could deny the long history of cruelty in the collision of colonists and Indians. Even those who view Columbus as one of humanity's significant heroes will readily acknowledge nearly four hundred years of European viciousness—connected, of course, to a corresponding record of Native Americans dealing with European newcomers with regular episodes of slaughter and savagery. The historical pattern makes clear that the bloodthirsty excesses of one group provoked bloodthirsty excesses from the other in a cycle of violence that lasted for centuries with only sporadic or regional interruptions.

None of this warfare, even with abundant atrocities on both sides, amounted to genocide. Though contemporary activists freely apply the term to cover everything from the commercial slaughter of chickens to U.S. retaliation against al-Qaeda terrorists, the word *genocide* carries a precise meaning that simply does not apply to encounters between Native Americans and British settlers. It's true that genocide is always brutal and cruel, but not all cruelty and brutality qualify as genocide.

This argument goes well beyond semantics: neither the colonial governments nor, later, the U.S. government ever endorsed or practiced a policy of Indian extermination.

Even more important, the decimation of Indian populations stemmed only rarely from massacres or military actions—even those by mobs, militias, or unauthorized paramilitary groups. The historical record leaves no doubt that the overwhelming majority of Indian deaths resulted from a faceless if implacable killer: infectious diseases.

To believe the big lie about the purposeful annihilation of Native Americans, one must ignore huge sections of the historical record and accept the pernicious myth that white settlers proved uniquely and shamelessly barbaric, while embracing a romanticized, frankly preposterous image of indigenous peoples.

DEFINING GENOCIDE

Anyone who buys the claim that founders of American society perpetrated "genocide" against native populations boasts only a sloppy understanding of one of the most fearsome words in the language. *The American Heritage Dictionary* defines *genocide* as "the systematic and planned extermination of an entire national, racial, political or ethnic group." *Webster's New World Dictionary* specifically references Hitlerism, saying that the term "first applied to the attempted extermination of the Jews by Nazi Germany, the systematic killing or extermination of a whole people or nation." Other definitions in a dozen reference works all stress the words *deliberate, systematic,* or both.

More important, the long-standing legal understanding of genocide also emphasizes consciously planned slaughter. In the aftermath of the Nazi Holocaust, the United Nations General Assembly adopted a Genocide Convention that still carries the force of international law. As described in Article II, the crime of genocide involves a series of brutal acts "committed with intent to destroy, in whole or in part, a national, ethnical, racial, or religious group as such." Guenter Lewy, longtime professor of political science at the University of Massachusetts and author of the indispensable analysis "Were American Indians the Victims of Genocide?" notes the explicit emphasis on intentionality and on a conscious motive for the extirpation or reduction of a target population. He reports that a contemporary legal scholar reviewed the UN debate and remarked that evidence of such motive "will constitute an integral part of the proof of a genocidal plan, and therefore of genocidal intent."

In other words, under international law (as well as common dictionary definitions), if there's no intent, there's no genocide.

And in the tragic case of the North American Indians, it's hard to impute either intent or motive to the real mass killers of native populations—the microorganisms that convey infectious disease.

GUILTY GERMS

No one disputes that the first four centuries after European contact brought a devastating decline in the number of Native Americans. By the beginning of the twentieth century, government officials found only 250,000 Indian survivors in the territory of the United States (as opposed to 2,476,000 who identified as "American Indian or Alaska Native" a hundred years later in the census of 2000). Meanwhile, scholarly estimates of pre-Columbian North American population range from 1.2 million (in a 1928 tribe-by-tribe assessment) all the way to 20 million (a number cited by present-day activists).

Beyond all arguments about the levels of native population at its peak, historians have reached unanimity on the prime cause of its rapid decline: infectious diseases brought about between 75 and 95 percent of Indian deaths after European settlement began. In his critically acclaimed best seller *Guns, Germs, and Steel: The Fate of Human Societies*, UCLA professor Jared Diamond observes that "throughout the Americas, diseases introduced with Europeans spread from tribe to tribe far in advance of the Europeans themselves, killing an estimated 95 percent of the pre-Columbian Native American population. . . . The main killers were Old World germs to which Indians had never been exposed, and against which they therefore had neither immune nor genetic resistance. Smallpox, measles, influenza, and typhus rank top among the killers."

Diseases spread far more rapidly than European settlement and decimated even those Indian societies that had minimal contact with the newcomers. Diamond reports: "As for the most advanced native societies of North America, those of the U.S. Southeast and the Mississippi River system, their destruction was accomplished largely by germs alone, introduced by early European explorers and advancing ahead of them." These sophisticated cultures had disappeared "even before Europeans themselves made their first settlement on the Mississippi River." Contrary to the popular image, "conquistadores contributed nothing directly to the societies' destruction; Eurasian germs, spreading in advance, did everything."

Writing in *1491: New Revelations of the Americas Before Columbus*, author Charles C. Mann notes that the 1540 Hernando de Soto expedition included hundreds of pigs, his "traveling meat locker"—beasts that carried germs to which Europeans had been long exposed, but which ravaged the previously isolated native populations. In fact, genetic homogeneity, especially among remote and self-contained tribal groups, probably contributed to the vulnerability of the Indian cultures.

Many colonists marveled at their apparent good fortune when they considered the dissolution of Indian nations in advance of their arrival, as did the most celebrated British settlers of them all. As Arthur Quinn describes their thinking in *A New World:* "The Pilgrims, who were always looking for God's special providence, could find in this hideous wilderness one sign of His favor: its human emptiness. Despite all the frightening stories of Indians, the Pilgrims could scarcely find any human beings at all. During the first few months, there were only a few sightings, and one inconsequential skirmish. People had lived here before, that was certain. The Pilgrims found large caches of corn to which they helped themselves freely. Human bones were also evident. Not just the occasional skeleton, but larger collections—as if this had been a battlefield where the corpses had been left to rot."

The decimation of native populations by microbial invaders represented an enormous human tragedy, but in no sense did it constitute a crime.

"SMALLPOX BLANKETS" AND BIOLOGICAL WARFARE

But didn't British authorities, and later the Americans, show criminal intent when they deliberately infected innocent tribes with the deadliest of eighteenth-century diseases? Whenever callers to my radio show begin talking about the premeditated mass slaughter of Native Americans, it's only a matter of seconds before they invoke the diabolical history of "smallpox blankets"—the bedding and clothing cunningly provided to unsuspecting tribes in order to infect them with the variola major virus.

The desperate terror of smallpox infection—among whites and Indians alike—lasted well into the nineteenth century, when the practice of vaccination became widespread in the United States and dramatically reduced the impact of the disease. Up to that time, smallpox alone claimed far more Indian victims than all the combined episodes of pitched battle, raids, massacres, relocations, random slaughter, and persecution.

Amazingly, the notion persists that the unimaginable devastation brought about by this disease stemmed from elaborate and brilliantly executed schemes devised by mass murderers—at a time when even the most sophisticated physicians possessed no real understanding of germ theory. The endlessly recycled charges of biological warfare rest solely on controversial interpretations of two unconnected and inconclusive incidents seventy-four years apart. In both cases, agenda-driven authors cite tiny scraps of contradictory evidence to draw their dark (and dubious) inferences of an anti-Indian conspiracy. But even the most malevolent assumptions about the two isolated episodes (neither of which appears to have resulted in a significant epidemic) hardly suggest a consistent pattern of deliberate infection covering the four hundred years of white-Indian interaction.

By far the most famous example involves the ferocious 1763 war known as Pontiac's Rebellion, in which Great Lakes tribes came together to destroy British forts and settlements after the English had defeated the

Indians' allies the French in the recently concluded French and Indian War. On May 1, the Ottawa leader Pontiac told an assembled council of various tribes' warriors (according to a French chronicler): "It is important for us, my brothers, that we *exterminate* from our lands this nation which seeks only to destroy us" (italics added).

Ultimately, the natives succeeded in wiping out eight forts and murdering hundreds of troops and settlers, including women and children. Victims were variously tortured, scalped, cannibalized, dismembered, and burned at the stake.

In the midst of the wide-ranging butchery, some 550 white farmers and townspeople (including more than 200 women and children) jammed into the region's most formidable military garrison, Fort Pitt (on the site of present-day Pittsburgh). On June 22, 1763, the Indians began a siege of the fort. Desperate to prevent the enemy from overrunning his most significant outpost, the British commander, Field Marshal Lord Jeffery Amherst, ordered Colonel Henry Bouquet to organize an expedition to relieve Fort Pitt. In a brief postscript to a lengthy June 29 letter full of command details, Amherst reportedly wrote to Bouquet: "Could it not be contrived to send the Small Pox among the disaffected tribes of Indians? We must on this occasion use every stratagem in our power to reduce them."

The celebrated historian Francis Parkman reports these sentences in his 1886 book *The Conspiracy of Pontiac and the Indian War After the Conquest of Canada,* but a more recent investigation by Professor Peter d'Errico of the University of Massachusetts–Amherst failed to turn up the original letter.

Other correspondence has been readily recovered, including a July 13 letter from Bouquet to Amherst in which the incriminating words again appear in a postscript: "P.S. I will try to inoculate the Indians by means of blankets that may fall into their hands, taking care however to not get the disease myself. As it is pity to oppose good management of them, I wish we could make use of the Spaniard's method, and hunt them with English dogs, supported by rangers and some horse who would, I think effectively extirpate or remove that vermine."

In response to Bouquet, Amherst penned another lengthy missive, with yet another short postscript approving the colonel's proposed scheme. "P.S. You will do well to try to inoculate the Indians by means of blankets as well as to try every other method that can serve to extirpate this execrable race. I should be very glad your scheme for hunting down by dogs could take effect but [*unreadable*] is at too great a distance to think of that at present."

This correspondence clearly expresses the two veteran soldiers' loathing for a vicious enemy. As Professor d'Errico notes, Amherst consistently conveyed his hatred for the rebellious tribes, along with his wish for their disappearance. In a July 9 letter to another British official he said he favored "Measures to be taken as would Bring about the Total Extirpation of those Indian Nations." In a letter to still another official, dated August 7, Lord Jeffery cited the monstrous cruelty he had observed from his adversaries (scalping alive for souvenirs, branding, cutting out and occasionally devouring hearts, torture through slow skinning, piercing bodies with as many as a hundred arrows) and declared that "their Total Extirpation is scarce sufficient Attonement."

But as harsh as Amherst's language appears (intriguingly, his language of "extirpation" echoes almost precisely Pontiac's reported call for "extermination" of all British settlers), almost nothing on record indicates that he actively pursued the goal of seeing the Indians annihilated or removed (*extirpation* means "uprooting" as well as "destruction").

The eerily jaunty tone of the exchanges between Amherst and Bouquet, together with the odd presence of all such discussion only in quick postscripts following detailed letters full of command instructions, suggests that they took the blankets idea no more seriously than the notion of using dogs to hunt the savages down. If Lord Jeffery meant for a command to be taken seriously by subordinates, he surely would have given it far more prominent and authoritative placement in his correspondence. At no point did the British commander issue orders or make a policy declaration regarding extermination of the Indians.

In fact, the only evidence of personnel at Fort Pitt actually passing infected garments to Indians occurred *before* the infamous written exchanges between Amherst and Bouquet. On or around June 24, two traders at the garrison gave blankets and a single handkerchief from the fort's quarantined hospital to two visiting Delaware Indians; one of the dealers made note of the exchange in his journal, declaring, "I hope it will have the desired effect."

Whatever the intent of this interchange, there's no evidence that it led to contagion among the Indians besieging the fort: they continued to menace the stronghold in fierce good health for more than six weeks after receiving the blankets. It was Colonel Bouquet, not the smallpox virus, who finally rescued Fort Pitt, as he led five hundred troops to bloody victory at the Battle of Bushy Run on August 20. Concerning outbreaks of smallpox that afflicted local tribes both before and after Pontiac's Rebellion, historian David Dixon, author of *Never Come to Peace Again,* the definitive history of the struggle, concluded that "the Indians may well have received the dreaded disease from a number of sources, but infected blankets from Fort Pitt was not one of them."

"THOSE DOGS, THE WHITES"

Beyond the inconclusive evidence of "germ warfare" by the British military, there's one more example of allegedly deliberate infection made famous by the radical activist Ward Churchill. Before his July 2007 firing from the University of Colorado for "research misconduct" (an effort to "falsify history and fabricate history," in the words of university president Hank Brown), Churchill spoke and wrote extensively about "100,000 or more fatalities" owing to blankets distributed along the Missouri River in 1837. Guenter Lewy and other historians took Churchill to task for his "obviously absurd numbers," while UCLA anthropology professor Russell Thornton, cited by Churchill as the principal source of his conclusions, protested vehemently against the misuse of his research.

Churchill alleged that the U.S. Army distributed contaminated blankets to Mandans and other Indians near Fort Clark in current-day North Dakota. Eyewitness accounts, however, make it clear that smallpox had spread from a steamboat whose crew was infected. As Lewy recounts, the journal of Fort Clark fur trader Francis A. Chardon "manifestly does not suggest that the U.S. Army distributed infected blankets, instead blaming the epidemic on the inadvertent spread of disease by a ship's passenger." Russell Thornton similarly identifies infected passengers on the steamboat *St. Peter's* as the source.

Hiram Martin Chittenden (later famous for designing the ship canal locks in the city of Seattle) wrote a 1903 book, *The American Fur Trader of the Far West*, which is based on the diaries of Charles Larpenteur of the American Fur Company. Chittenden reveals that the crew of the *St. Peter's* made a serious effort to *prevent* a smallpox outbreak onshore. But the Indians, eager for the boat's trading goods, "could not be restrained" from approaching the vessel. Chittenden writes, "When the boat arrived at Fort Clark a Mandan chief stole the blanket of a watchman upon the boat who was dying of the disease. Mr. Chardon made every effort for the immediate return of the blanket, promised pardon for the theft, and new blankets in its place, but all to no purpose. He sent messages warning the people to keep away, and used every argument in his power, but the whole village came down to the river."

All accounts of the smallpox outbreak among the Mandan record the efforts of white traders and soldiers to reduce rather than intensify its deadly impact. For example, Charles Larpenteur relays how one of the partners in a fur-trading company called the Upper Missouri Outfit attempted to vaccinate "thirty Indian squaws and a few white men."

It made sense for the fur traders to protect, rather than annihilate, their Indian suppliers. A devastating smallpox outbreak would render the tribes unable to deliver the pelts on which the whole fur trade depended. With the natives dead, sick, or incapacitated, no one expected the beaver to obligingly deliver their own carcasses to the steamboat that called on the lonely outposts. Chittenden notes that "as the company would be the greatest sufferer from an epidemic among the Indians, they can not be accused of any selfish motives in the course they pursued."

Disregarding such realities, Ward Churchill cited as proof for his claims of genocide the deathbed curse of Mandan chief Four Bears, who blamed his smallpox on "those dogs, the whites." But Four Bears said nothing about the U.S. Army, and even Russell Thornton, whom Churchill relied on in quoting the Indian chief, scoffs at the notion of spinning this bitter denunciation as evidence of intentional infection. "My reaction to this stuff about the speech of Four Bears is it's a bunch of BS," Thornton told the *Rocky Mountain News*. "All it [the statement] says is that white men brought smallpox to Indians. Well, so what? That's nothing."

On my radio show I interviewed Elizabeth Fenn, the author of *Pox*

Americana: The Great Smallpox Epidemic of 1775–82 and the world's leading expert on the American impact of the dread disease, and I asked her directly whether her years of research had turned up any persuasive evidence that "germ warfare tactics" contributed significantly to Indian victimization. "Frankly, no," she declared.

Nevertheless, the horribly misleading charges about germ warfare have achieved a monstrous life of their own, leaving many (if not most) Americans with the impression that diseases that decimated native populations resulted from a conscious, long-standing policy of the U.S. government. No such master plan for mass murder ever existed, of course, so that all efforts to scour abundant bureaucratic records have produced only a few nasty postscripts in letters from British—not American—officials in 1763, and the largely exculpatory evidence concerning an epidemic in Mandan territory in 1837.

The Legends of "Walking Eagle"

In addition to all the controversy about Ward Churchill's historical distortions, there's the deeply embarrassing matter of his falsified Indian heritage. In 2005 he declared, "I am myself of Muscogee and Creek descent on my father's side, Cherokee on my mother's, and am an enrolled member of the United Keetoowah Band of Cherokee Indians." The Keetoowah Band promptly clarified that Churchill was never an enrolled member, and the *Rocky Mountain News* published a genealogy that found "no evidence of a single Indian ancestor." The *Denver Post* conducted a separate genealogical investigation that reached the same conclusion.

In 2006, a prominent Native American author and activist went off the record after an interview on my radio show to talk about Churchill's apparently fraudulent claims of Indian ancestry. "Of course, he's not an Indian," the writer laughed, "but we've given him an Indian name. We call him 'Walking Eagle.' You know why? Because this bird is so full of s——t he can't fly!"

CASUALTIES OF WAR

While all reliable sources agree that the vast majority of Indian deaths re-sulted from disease, those who choose to emphasize American guilt focus instead on abundant examples of brutal episodes of warfare along the moving frontier. In that context, the parade of "Indian Genocide's Great-est Hits" invariably includes the following:

- The May 1637 Mystic Massacre, a brief but bloody conflict in colonial Connecticut that has recently inspired two lurid tele-vision dramatizations, one of them an Emmy winner on PBS in 2005 and another a blood-soaked shocker on the History Channel in 2006
- The November 1864 Sand Creek Massacre, a brutal attack on a peaceful Cheyenne and Arapaho encampment in the Colorado Territory that killed almost two hundred
- Lieutenant Colonel George Armstrong Custer's November 1868 attack on a Cheyenne encampment at Washita River (in present-day Oklahoma)
- The December 1890 encounter at South Dakota's Wounded Knee Creek, the subject of Dee Brown's hugely influential 1970 best seller *Bury My Heart at Wounded Knee,* which was adapted in 2007 into an Emmy Award-winning HBO miniseries

Undeniably, each of these incidents involved violent warfare, but the "blame America" crowd has wildly misrepresented what happened dur-ing these "atrocities." In most cases the actions represented not one-sided horrors perpetrated by bloodthirsty whites against peaceful natives but rather fierce battle with casualties on both sides. Only one instance clearly involved rampaging white militia, and the U.S. government un-equivocally condemned this isolated incident. In short, none of these much-lamented episodes supports the claim that whites committed genocidal slaughter of pacifistic bystanders.

Let's take the cases one at a time.

THE MYSTIC MASSACRE

Straight from his triumph as director of the soul-stirring John Kerry bio-flick for the 2004 Democratic convention, James Moll directed the History Channel documentary about the 1637 "massacre at Mystic." The Web site for his docudrama summarized the plotline in unblushingly propagandistic terms: "White people show up, see Indians acting in ways that oppose God's will (which they know fully, being Puritans), then kill them. . . . The wholesale slaughter of the Pequots begins the long tumultuous slide that will end in European domination of the region."

The language here reflects the two dubious assumptions at the very core of most allegations of Native American genocide: that any killing was unprovoked and altogether unjustified, and that the ultimate success of the colonists ("European domination of the region") represented a decline (a "long tumultuous slide") from the primeval paradise that flourished before Puritan brutes landed in North America.

In reality, the incident at Mystic can in no way be characterized as unprovoked. The trouble began after the Pequot Indians allied themselves with Dutch fur traders to gain advantage over their ancient enemies, the Narragansetts and particularly the Mohegans, who forged alliances with the newly arrived Puritan settlers in Massachusetts and Connecticut. Fights over the fur business led Pequot warriors to murder some trappers from other tribes. A dizzying series of reciprocal raids and murders ensued: the Dutch struck back at the Pequots, who illogically retaliated by murdering a British privateer and most of his crew, while their rivals the Narragansetts gruesomely dismembered a British trader and sacked his ship while it was anchored at Block Island, Rhode Island. The English then burned the village of the Block Island Indians (who probably weren't even the guilty parties).

Eventually the Pequots besieged Fort Saybrook, a lonely English trading post at the mouth of the Connecticut River, seizing any Englishmen who ventured out. Within view of the fort, they burned one captured trader with hot embers, slowly stripped the skin from his body, and cut off his fingers and toes before he finally died. They roasted another prisoner alive. The Pequots and their allies also raided Connecticut towns, killing some thirty settlers—a serious matter for fragile communities established only two years earlier and boasting, at most, a few dozen residents each.

Viewing Pequot brutality with mounting dread, in May 1637 the tiny towns along the Connecticut River raised a fighting force of nearly a hundred men. Accompanied by more than two hundred Narragansett, Mohegan, and Niantic warriors, the militia first approached a fortified Pequot village on the coast but aborted the attack because it looked too formidable. Instead, the settlers' army launched a predawn surprise attack on a large settlement on the banks of the Misistuck (Mystic) River.

Contemporary accounts of the raid leave no doubt about the colonial militia's ferocity. Outnumbered by the Pequots, the militia set the village aflame, gathering at the exits and slaughtering all those who tried to escape the conflagration. The Indians who accompanied the colonists felt repulsed by the killing frenzy and, according to one account, shouted, "This is evil, this is evil, too furious, and too many killed." In all, at least five hundred Pequot perished, perhaps as many as seven hundred.

Though they pointedly spared women, children, and the elderly in later encounters (an indication, Guenter Lewy argues, of their lack of genocidal intent), the Puritans clearly meant to expunge all memory of their most dangerous Indian adversaries. The Treaty of Hartford that ended the struggle banned all members of the tribe from living in formerly Pequot territory, sold most survivors as slaves to their Indian enemies, and even prohibited the name Pequot as applied to any individual or group.

Nevertheless, the bitter struggle hardly amounted to a war of extermination for all local natives: the tribes who allied themselves with the English emerged strengthened and enriched.

What's more, the undeniably appalling episode of the Mystic Massacre—the bloodiest single episode in the four-hundred-year history of white-native skirmishes in North America—cannot compare to the incomprehensible mass slaughter of Europe's contemporaneous wars of religion. The Thirty Years' War (1618–49) witnessed the butchery of literally hundreds of thousands of unarmed civilians (reducing the population of the German states by an estimated one-third). To charge the

Connecticut settlers with wanton genocide is to ignore the brutal norms of warfare prevailing everywhere in the period.

THE SAND CREEK MASSACRE

Like the notorious atrocities of the Puritans against Pequots, the similarly celebrated Sand Creek Massacre occurred at a moment in history when whites were butchering one another with far more single-minded ruthlessness and efficiency than they ever applied to Indians. In the bloody Civil War year of 1864, there was rarely a day when raging warfare didn't claim hundreds of killed and wounded, and yet the two hundred Indians who died at Sand Creek became a peculiar obsession for pop culture potentates determined to remind their audiences of white oppression of Native Americans. The incident has been portrayed in both the 1970 movie melodrama *Soldier Blue* (starring Candice Bergen and Peter Strauss) and Steven Spielberg's 2005 miniseries *Into the West.* The heavy metal band Iron Maiden also commemorated the killing spree (and other mistreatment of Native Americans) with their 1982 song "Run to the Hills."

Though these pop culture treatments of Sand Creek portray the rampage as a typical expression of American society's genocidal depradations, the incident—the most clear-cut example of white slaughter—plainly represented a horrifying aberration.

The commander at Sand Creek, Colonel John Milton Chivington, had emerged as a national hero two years earlier for his role in the Battle of Glorieta Pass, known as the "Gettysburg of the West." After turning back the Confederate threat, Colonel Chivington, a former Methodist preacher and missionary, became determined to eliminate the Indian menace. Cheyenne warriors and their Arapaho allies had briefly cut off Denver from all supplies and pillaged a number of ranches outside the six-year-old mining town. In one shocking case, the natives scalped an entire family, slit the throats of two children, and sliced open a mother's body to tear her intestines over her face. Colonel Chivington vowed to kill even native children. "Nits make lice," he reportedly declared to an admiring Denver audience before leaving town in command of an irregular force of some eight hundred.

Chivington's force approached a Cheyenne camp where the chief, Black Kettle, conspicuously flew an American flag from his tepee. Officers of the U.S. Army had repeatedly assured him that Old Glory would signal his peaceful relations and keep him safe. Captain Silas Soule, commander of a company of Colorado cavalry, certainly saw the flag and refused Chivington's order to attack. While Soule's men held their fire, Chivington and his militia mercilessly shot down and bayoneted the natives, who were mostly unarmed and left defenseless because some sixty Indian braves had gone off on a hunting party. The most often repeated estimate suggests that Chivington's attackers killed 53 men—some of them elderly—and 110 women and children. The Union forces lost 15 killed and more than 50 wounded—many of them purportedly the victims of wild firing by their own frenzied and in many cases drunken comrades. Returning home, Chivington's men decorated their weapons and hats with scalps and other "trophies of war," including human fetuses, male and female genitalia, and other severed body parts.

Nevertheless, the most striking aspect of the episode involves the revulsion it inspired almost immediately. Not only did officers and soldiers at the scene feel outraged by the behavior of their colleagues, but as soon as news of the incident reached Army officials and politicians in the East, it provoked several congressional and military investigations and demands for Chivington's court-martial.

In Congress, the Joint Committee on the Conduct of the War ultimately declared: "As to Colonel Chivington, your committee can hardly find fitting terms to describe his conduct. Wearing the uniform of the United States, which should be emblem of justice and humanity, holding the important position of commander of a military district, and therefore having the honor of the government to that extent in his keeping, he deliberately planned and executed a foul and dastardly massacre which would have disgraced the verist [sic] savage among those who were victims of his cruelty." The committee called for "prompt and energetic measures" against "those who have been guilty of these brutal and cowardly acts."

In other words, far from endorsing or ordering the mass murder, the U.S. government explicitly denounced it.

That condemnation did nothing to prevent a retaliatory spasm of killing by Indian leaders. The Cheyenne and Arapaho joined forces with Sioux, Comanche, and Kiowa tribes to strike back at the settlers at the edge of the Rockies, killing more than two hundred white miners, ranchers, and merchants.

THE BATTLE OF THE WASHITA

The 1868 Battle of the Washita produced similar revulsion and indignation from the general public and governmental authorities, and tarnished the reputation of the flamboyant Civil War hero Lieutenant Colonel Custer—even though his actions never approached the horrific extremes of Colonel Chivington four years earlier.

Lieutenant Colonel Custer and his Seventh Cavalry responded to regular Indian raids into Kansas by attacking a Cheyenne encampment at Washita River on November 27. The battle began at daybreak and lasted most of the day, resulting in the death of Black Kettle, the same "peace chief" who had counted on the protection of the American flag at Sand Creek. This time, the Indians unquestionably fought back and the Americans suffered serious casualties, with 21 men killed and 13 wounded. Accounts of the Cheyenne dead varied: Custer claimed that 103 warriors fell, while captured squaws insisted that fewer than 20 died, including some women and children caught in the crossfire.

In *The Custer Reader,* historian Paul Andrew Hutton concludes: "Although the fight on the Washita was most assuredly one-sided, it was not a massacre. Black Kettle's Cheyennes were not unarmed innocents living under the impression that they were not at war. . . . The soldiers were not under orders to kill everyone, for Custer personally stopped the slaying of noncombatants, and fifty-three prisoners were taken by the troops."

Such considerations did nothing to prevent widespread condemnation of Custer. Colonel Edward W. Wynkoop, who had testified against John Chivington during the Sand Creek investigation, protested the incident by resigning his post as agent for the Cheyenne and Arapaho. The *New York Tribune,* citing Wynkoop, declared "Custer's late fight as simply a massacre" aimed at "friendly Indians." The *New York Times* published an angry letter lashing Custer's "sadistic pleasure in slaughtering Indian ponies and dogs." Far from pursuing or applauding any attempt to wipe out all the natives, the pressure from national opinion and the responsible policy makers demanded less killing, not more.

A century later the charges continued to resonate. In 1970, the acclaimed and unabashedly pro-Indian film *Little Big Man* (with Dustin Hoffman and Faye Dunaway) portrayed the episode with deliberate echoes of the vastly more bloody My Lai Massacre in Vietnam. Even the Oscar-nominated 2003 Tom Cruise movie *The Last Samurai* invokes flashbacks of Washita River as a ghastly atrocity to explain its main character's deep disillusionment with the U.S. Army and his shame at his own country.

Many of the filmmakers and popular historians who have focused on Custer's ferocity at Washita River try to connect this skirmish to the Seventh Cavalry's far bloodier engagement eight years later at Little Big Horn—emphasizing a "well-deserved" Indian desire for revenge. At the notorious battle known to history as "Custer's Last Stand," the particularly well-armed Indians outnumbered the troopers by nearly ten to one and claimed the lives of some 268 officers and men. The contrast with Washita River highlights Custer's obvious absence of genocidal intent. Unlike his later opponents Sitting Bull and Crazy Horse, "Yellow Hair" kept prisoners alive and made a point of protecting many of the women and children. At Washita River a minority of the Cheyenne actually survived, but there's no doubt that the fabled Battle of Little Big Horn qualified as a massacre: the Lakota, Northern Cheyenne, and Arapaho warriors left no survivors and no prisoners.

BURY THE TRUTH AT WOUNDED KNEE

The encounter at South Dakota's Wounded Knee Creek on December 29, 1890, has become a famous symbol of white brutality against Indians not because it was in any sense the worst of such incidents but largely because it was the last of them.

The "politically conscious" rock group Redbone (which made somewhat dubious claims of native ancestry) released a 1973 song called "We Were All Wounded at Wounded Knee" that soared to the top of the charts in several European markets. A year earlier Johnny Cash recorded "Big Foot," which described the noble agony of the Miniconjou Sioux leader who died during the incident. Twenty years later Native Canadian folksinger Buffy Sainte-Marie offered her own protest song ("Bury My Heart at Wounded Knee") to indict white society for its five hundred years of cruelty, and the Indigo Girls did a popular cover of the mournful ballad.

These songs received direct inspiration from Dee Brown's sweeping account of thirty years of suffering for various western tribes that culminated that cold day in South Dakota. His prodigiously influential best-selling book even helped to inspire an internationally celebrated "siege" in 1973 when more than a hundred radical activists from the American Indian Movement defied tribal authorities and for seventy-one days occupied the site of the 1890 tragedy.

The original confrontation at Wounded Knee Creek occurred after Big Foot's band of 120 warriors and 230 women and children gave up fleeing from the authorities who wanted to restrict them to a reservation. The Indians surrendered to the troops of the Seventh Cavalry, but when the soldiers ordered them to disarm, some of the Miniconjou tried to hide the rifles they considered essential to their survival and dignity.

Before nine in the morning on December 29, two soldiers began to struggle with an Indian named Black Coyote, who demanded that he be paid for his rifle. One of Black Coyote's fellow tribesman described him as "a crazy man, a young man of very bad influence and in fact a nobody," while two other Miniconjou suggested that he was also deaf, which might explain his behavior. As the two troopers tried to wrestle him to the ground he managed to fire a shot into the air.

In response to the single shot, a medicine man named Yellow Bird threw a handful of dirt into the air—an important symbol to his fellow members of the Ghost Dance cult, who believed that their rituals would bring dead warriors and dead buffalo back to life and rid the world of all white men. Five or six of Yellow Bird's followers then stood up, threw off their blankets in the bitter cold, produced the rifles they'd been concealing, and began firing directly toward K troop.

The melee that followed, like most other purported "massacres" of Native Americans, featured fierce fighting and losses on both sides. The battle raged for hours, with the Indians demonstrating expert handling of their well-maintained, repeating Winchester rifles and also engaging in fearless hand-to-hand combat.

By the end of the day, the overwhelming majority of Big Foot's band of 350 had been killed or wounded; at least 153 died (including at least 44 women and 18 children too young to fight). Among the U.S. soldiers, 25 died and 39 were wounded.

The statistics indicate the one-sided nature of the fight, but it *was* a fight, not an unprovoked slaughter of unarmed innocents. Neither the soldiers nor the government that commanded them had any intention of killing Indians that day, despite the mythology that's grown up around the tragedy. With true genocidal intent, the soldiers could have simply used the artillery they brought with them. On several occasions they tried to encourage the Miniconjou to surrender, but the Ghost Dance warriors chose to continue their struggle. The commanding officer himself, Major Samuel M. Whitside, lifted an Indian infant from the arms of the child's dead mother and placed him with some of the female Miniconjou survivors for protection.

Six days after the battle, President Benjamin Harrison ordered a full court of inquiry into the conduct of the troops—an amazingly rapid response in view of the remote location of the incident and the slow communications of the time. Even before the inquiry concluded its work, Major General Nelson A. Miles sharply rebuked his officers, noting the shocking toll of women and children. Despite exculpatory accounts from the three reporters on the scene, much of the press instinctively denounced the troops in similar terms. In the words of historian Robert Utley, the papers "vented outrage on a regiment that, thirsting for revenge since the Little Bighorn, had wantonly slaughtered gentle Indians and had found particular glee in butchering helpless women and children."

The court of inquiry eventually cleared the soldiers, noting Major Whitside's uncontradicted sworn testimony that "the Indians fired at least fifty shots before the troops returned the fire." In the 1963 book *The Last Days of the Sioux Nation,* Utley reached similar conclusions after painstakingly compiling a moment-by-moment account of the incident and its context.

As Utley observes, this dark episode would have been avoided "had not a few unthinking young men, incited by a fanatical medicine man, lost control of themselves and created an incident." He rightly notes the "fury" with which the U.S. soldiers responded to "what they deemed Indian treachery," but he also points out that "they did not deliberately kill women and children, although in a few instances more caution might have been exercised."

Utley concludes: "It is time that Wounded Knee be viewed for what it was—a regrettable, tragic act of war that neither side intended."

In other words, if Wounded Knee constitutes the leading illustration of what HBO called the government's "systematic campaign to exterminate American Indians," then the entire case for genocide stands exposed in all its mendacious and embarrassing flimsiness.

"THE ONLY GOOD INDIAN . . ."

The history of the most notorious "massacres" of Native Americans provides scant evidence of genocidal intent, so current-day activists who describe Indian suffering as a deliberate holocaust unfailingly trot out a single pronouncement attributed to one of the army's top officers. Even the most casual students of history have doubtless encountered the indelibly hateful comment by General Philip Henry ("Fighting Phil") Sheridan that "the only good Indian is a dead Indian."

The infamous statement originated at a conference of some fifty tribal chiefs at Fort Cobb in Indian Territory (today's Oklahoma) in January 1869. General Sheridan, the great Union cavalry hero during the War Between the States, afterward took command of military operations on the vast expanse of the Great Plains. Responsible for protecting scattered white settlements, mining camps, railroad crews, and westward-bound travelers from sudden Indian attack, he resolved to keep the natives peacefully contained on their newly established reservations. During the Fort Cobb meetings a flamboyant Comanche chief named Toch-a-way, or Turtle Dove, slapped his chest and approached General Sheridan. "Me Toch-a-way," he reportedly declared. "Me good Indian!" Sheridan then allegedly replied with a wry half smile: "The only good Indians I ever saw were dead." The other officers gathered for the occasion reportedly roared with laughter at the remark, though no one reported the reaction of the assembled chiefs.

The general later insisted that he never spoke the words attributed to him, but several eyewitnesses attested to the exchange. No one knows, however, who transmuted the remark into its tighter, punchier present form. Professor Wolfgang Mieder of the University of Vermont suggests the possibility that Sheridan only repeated an aphorism already well established on the frontier. Seven months before the general's response to Toch-a-way, the congressional delegate from the Territory of Montana, James Michael Cavanaugh, expressed similar sentiments on the floor of the House of Representatives:

> The gentleman from Massachusetts [Radical Republican Benjamin Butler] may denounce the sentiment as atrocious but I will say that I like an Indian better dead than living. I have never in my life seen a good Indian (and I have seen thousands) except when I have seen a dead Indian. . . . Gentlemen may call this very harsh language, but perhaps they would not think so if they had my experience in Minnesota and Colorado. In Minnesota the almost living babe has been torn from its mother's womb, and I have seen the child, with its young heart palpitating, nailed to the window-sill. I have seen women who were scalped, disfigured, outraged. In Denver, Colorado Territory, I have seen women and children brought in scalped. Scalped why? Simply because the Indian was 'upon the war-path' to satisfy the devilish and barbarous propensities. The Indian will make a treaty in the fall, and in the spring he is again 'upon the war-path.' The torch, the scalping knife, plunder and desolation follow wherever the Indian goes.

Such wholesale condemnation of an entire race, ignoring all the profound distinctions in history and outlook among hundreds of North American tribes, shocks our modern sensibilities. But in fact his single-minded hostility to Native Americans ran counter to the enlightened opinion of most of the Congress and the nation at large even then, at the very height of the Indian wars—a point Cavanaugh himself acknowledged

("Gentlemen may call this very harsh language"). His remarks also take note of a fairly consistent pattern during the first centuries of our history: that respect and sympathy for the Indians increased in direct proportion to the distance between the observer and the wild and open country in which most remaining natives actually lived.

Comments such as Sheridan's (or Cavanaugh's) amounted to tart observations on the untrustworthy nature of Indians, revealing repugnant racism and deep-seated hostility but constituting no official declaration of mass-murdering intent. As Guenter Lewy observes, "As for the larger society, even if some elements of the white population, mainly in the West, at times advocated extermination, no official of the U.S. government ever seriously proposed it. Genocide was never American policy, nor was it the result of policy."

TRIBE AGAINST TRIBE

In recent years nearly all pop-cultural accounts of pre-Columbian North America feature potent elements of nostalgia, stressing the supposed dignity and gentleness of native societies in order to emphasize the tragic aspects of purported genocide by white invaders. For instance, the lavish Pocahontas–Captain John Smith movie *The New World* (2005) arrived with a handsome promotional brochure explaining that the Jamestown settlers of 1607 found a "noble civilization" that "had lived in peace for hundreds of years."

For ranchers, miners, farmers, and soldiers who lived their lives in constant and legitimate fear of Indian attack, however, the indigenous cultures seemed neither noble nor peaceful; their regular description of Indians as "savages" reflected an observed pattern of terrifying brutality. Moreover, most of the white newcomers to the West understood that the bloodthirsty habits that so frightened them unquestionably predated the arrival of Europeans in North America. Even while directing their rage at white intruders, the natives continued their age-old tradition of withering intertribal warfare, contributing mightily to the failure of all efforts at resistance.

The various tribes never lived together in harmony and mutual respect, no more than the Neolithic cultures of Europe, Asia, or Africa coexisted without desperate and punishing conflict. Societies among the Indians and all other aboriginal peoples conducted devastating wars against one another that at times became struggles for domination, conquest, replacement, or even extermination.

Harvard anthropologist Steven LeBlanc spent years studying the Anasazi Indians of the American Southwest and only gradually came to reject the popular notion that North American tribes had once composed a gorgeous mosaic of diversity, living side by side in peace and dignity. In his research, he discovered pueblos built on mesas from the years 1275 to 1325—long before Europeans had arrived in the New World—that housed more than a thousand residents each, designed to be impregnable to inevitable attack. LeBlanc's book *Constant Battles: The Myth of the Peaceful, Noble Savage* shows that genocides and land raids among regional and ethnic groups had always been the norm for native peoples.

The fur-trading forts along the upper Missouri River (the same outposts Ward Churchill falsely accused of deliberately infecting nearby Indians with smallpox blankets) saw firsthand demonstrations of the genocidal bloodlust of local tribes against their competitors. A July 1860 article from the *Missouri Republican* reported in horror on Indian massacres that made it impossible for the white traders to continue their business. The journal reported:

> The various tribes of Indians along the entire upper river are reported to be engaged in a war of extermination. . . . Every day almost, war-parties were seen on the bank of the river. Bleeding scalps were seen dangling from sticks at the doors of the lodges of the chiefs and big men. . . . The probabilities are that they will allow no peace to each other till a strong military post is established at some point in their country, and the agents feel that until this is done their influence has but little force in controlling the turbulent spirits of the young and ambitious warriors.

In present-day popular culture, those "turbulent spirits" rarely appear. Kevin Costner in his Oscar-winning 1990 epic *Dances with Wolves* depicts the Lakota people (among the most feared and ferocious of all native warriors) as preposterously peace loving and tranquil—in direct contrast to the coarse, cruel, and hollow-souled federal soldiers the conflicted main character learns to despise. By contrast, Mel Gibson's anthropologically accurate *Apocalypto* in 2006 provoked furious condemnation for daring to show the Central American Mayans as practitioners of mass human sacrifice. Addressing the controversy in the *New York Times,* anthropologist Craig Childs pointed out that "parts of the archaeological record of the Americas read like a war-crimes indictment, with charred skeletons stacked like cordwood and innumerable human remains missing heads, legs and arms. In the American Southwest, which is my area of research, human tissue has been found cooked to the insides of kitchen jars and stained into a ceramic serving ladle. A grinding stone was found full of crushed human finger bones. A sample of human feces came up containing the remains of a cannibal's meal." Childs concluded: "Being told by screenwriters and archaeologists that their ancestors engaged in death cults tends to make many Native Americans uneasy. . . . Meanwhile excavators keep digging up evidence of cannibalism and ritualized violence among their ancestors."

The timeless record of intertribal and even intratribal Indian brutality in no way justifies the bloody anti-Indian excesses of European colonists or American settlers, who, after all, claimed to represent a higher and more humane civilization. The Europeans who poured into North America constituted a new and more formidable enemy, and their technological advancement allowed them to win devastating victories that previous adversaries could never achieve. But they did not introduce unprecedented cruelty or bellicosity to people who had always valued fierce warrior virtues above all others.

BLAMING THE VICTOR

The hundreds of native tribes that occupied North America warred against one another for thousands of years with inconclusive results, but within a few eventful decades the Europeans broke this eternal deadlock and swept all before them. The obvious explanation involves the fact that most Indian cultures had achieved roughly equivalent levels of development, but the white explorers represented societies so much further advanced and more technologically sophisticated that they might as well have arrived from another planet. Nevertheless, many observers today insist on ignoring this gap (which amounts to many thousands of years of social and scientific evolution) and romanticizing the "enlightened" Indians.

In a 2008 show called "The Ancient Americas" at Chicago's glorious Field Museum, the first panel proclaims: "The Ancient Americas is a story of diversity and change—not progress." Edward Rothstein notes in his *New York Times* review of the exhibition that "the text refers to a 'rich mosaic of peoples' and their 'enduring contributions to our lives today.' The varied societies surveyed are all described as 'problem solvers' trying to relate to their environment. In the show, hunter-gatherers are followed by farmers; societies with powerful individual rulers are followed by empires. But such progression, we are told, is not progress. Even old distinctions, like Stone Age and Iron Age, are discarded. Progress is an illusion."

The Field Museum's stubborn determination to avoid making value judgments on the different stages of human development produces some messages that approach self-parody. One display cheerfully informed visitors: "In many ways, hunting and gathering was a great way to live," a "lifestyle" with "more leisure time" than farmers, and with members who "respected" women and the elderly. Rothstein observes the lavish praise for the "peoples of coastal Southern California" who "created and adopted brilliant new techniques" for survival between 7000 B.C. and A.D. 1600. "But the more compelling fact," he writes, "might be that during those 9,000 years so few brilliant techniques appeared; it was a period when other societies developed writing, science and medicine. Only one major comparison to the great Western civilizations is made: that the brutality of the Incan and Aztec empires had a counterpart in the cruelty of ancient Rome."

The exhibition flatly declares at one point: "All societies are equally valid to the individuals living in them." If, then, the culture of New England Puritans offered no objective, substantive, meaningful advantages over the way of life of the nearby Pequots, then the prosperity and success of the former and disappearance of the latter must be the result of perfidy. For the cultural relativist, the invariable triumph of advanced colonial civilizations over indigenous peoples has nothing to do with the backwardness and primitive mores of the natives; rather, it must reflect the cunning and rapacity of the newcomers. According to this worldview, any society that triumphs completely and utterly over its "equally valid" neighbors falls instantly under suspicion.

If, as the Field Museum's exhibition insists, "progress is an illusion," then the startlingly easy "conquest of paradise" by white newcomers to the Western Hemisphere can't possibly reflect the superior progress of their civilization.

It's considered unfair and repugnant to "blame the victim." When it comes to European settlement of the New World, cultural relativists prefer to blame the victor.

Political Correctness Can't Trump Disease

"The exhibit points out that disease was the chief cause of suffering after European contact. Therefore, horrors that beset the Ancient Americas following 1492 would have happened if the *Nina,* the *Pinta,* and the *Santa Maria* had been manned by Jimmy Carter, the Dalai Lama, and Bono."

—P. J. O'Rourke on the Field Museum's "Ancient Americas" exhibit

---

EITHER SAD OR HORRIFYING

The "blame America" formulation in recounting the fate of Native Americans ignores or denies iron rules that always apply when members of more advanced and dynamic societies encounter aboriginal peoples who seem to belong to a much earlier era of human history.

I confronted this harsh pattern for the first time as a junior at Yale in 1968. Professor Howard Lamar, an elegant southern gentleman with a honey-coated drawl (who later served briefly as president of the university), taught a famous course on the history of the American West—a yearlong survey commonly known as "Cowboys and Indians." One day after a typically vivid and riveting lecture, one of my fellow students, with shoulder-length curly locks in the fashion of the time, confronted the professor over the grim fate of the Indians in their struggle against encroaching whites. "How could they call themselves Americans and Christians when they wiped out a whole way of life and treated their fellow human beings worse than animals?"

Professor Lamar had obviously faced similar questions (this was 1968, remember), so he quickly provided a powerful answer (which I will attempt to reconstruct based on imperfect memory). "The most important thing to keep in mind," he said, "is that the Indians were nearly all part of Stone Age cultures—*literally* Stone Age. That's why most of the arrowheads people find are made out of chipped rocks: they hadn't learned how to use metals, a skill that developed in parts of Europe and Asia more than five thousand years earlier. Think about those stories you see in the news about some headhunter in Borneo who's surviving in the jungle in a loincloth and suddenly he sees a plane overhead. He's never even seen a knife or a shoe or a wheel, for that matter, and all of a sudden he's looking at a plane. The next thing you know, his tribe is discovered and here come the doctors, the missionaries, the anthropologists. Well, the tribes can't just disappear back into the jungle. They've made contact, so whatever happens next, their old life is finished. If they fight the modern world, they lose quickly, or else they try to accommodate to it and end up swallowed by more advanced and powerful culture.

"That's what happened to the Indians. Once they got to know the white man, and saw what his machines could do and how many millions more people kept pouring into the country, they knew they couldn't win. Whites rolled over the Indians because they could. Here you have people who are making their tools out of stone, who haven't figured out the wheel, and they're facing people who are building railroads and using repeating rifles. The outcome can go only one of two ways—either sad or horrifying."

This brief explanation may not have satisfied the professor's long-haired interlocutor, but it certainly impressed me—and the force of the argument has stayed with me for some forty years.

As Americans, we instinctively see our history as unique, exceptional, and unprecedented, even when we unwittingly replicate age-old patterns.

The U.S. experience with our indigenous populations strongly resembles any and every encounter between peoples at vastly different stages of development. Even a casual student will see more similarities than differences between the fate of the Indians in North America and that of the Ainu/Utari in northern Japan, or of the Aborigines in Australia, or of other isolated, primitive groups forced to confront modernity.

Mark Twain, a fair student of human nature and world history, observed:

> There isn't a foot of land in the world which doesn't represent the ousting and re-ousting of a long line of successive "owners" who each in turn, as "patriots" with proud swelling hearts defended it against the next gang of "robbers" who came to steal it and did— and became swelling-hearted patriots in their turn. . . . Patriotism is a word which always commemorates a robbery.

WHERE DID ALL THE INDIANS GO?

Americans may feel guilty about our part in this eternal cycle of robbery, but that shame shouldn't lead to acceptance of groundless charges of genocide—especially in light of revelations provided by Indian population statistics.

The number of Native Americans identified by the Census Bureau has soared by more than 1,000 percent since 1900—a rate of increase more than three times *larger* than the robust, immigration-swelled growth of the U.S. population as a whole.

This explosion in numbers stems not from a prodigious birthrate (since family size has never been particularly large among Native Americans) but rather from a greater willingness by individuals of mixed ancestry to identify themselves as Indian. A University of Texas study found that in the past four decades, native population has "substantially exceeded growth based on statistics indicating their natural increase . . . due to persons changing their racial identification to Native American." With today's resurgent pride in native heritage, there's far less desire to avoid or erase the once-dreaded label of "half-breed"—allowing a more accurate view of the powerful process of intermarriage and assimilation that played a significant role in the precipitous decline of Indian population in the nineteenth century.

To some activists, native embrace of white culture (or white spouses for that matter) represents a form of "cultural genocide" even more insidious than mass murder. They may insist that any native who abandons his people to join the invaders is just as lost as a casualty on the battlefield, just as dead to his heritage as those who perished from disease, but it's deeply dishonest to confuse dead bodies with dead identities.

From the beginning of British settlement in North America, colonists encouraged "praying Indians"—those who adopted Christianity and often melded into settler society. The most famous of these converts, Pocahontas, married Jamestown settler John Rolfe in 1614, and their descendants took their place in the first rank of Virginia aristocracy, including a governor who proudly traced his ancestry directly to the legendary Indian princess.

"Indian women frequently married white settlers who leased Indian land, or army personnel stationed at nearby military installations," writes University of New Mexico scholar Brenda Manuelito in her article in *The Encyclopedia of North American Indians.* "The children of these mixed marriages often became important leaders because of their ability to stand between the white and Indian worlds and to act as culture brokers." Thomas Jefferson, who frequently wrote of his obsession with the unbridgeable differences between whites and blacks (despite his alleged connection with Sally Hemings), considered the distinction between Europeans and Indians to be far less significant. In fact, he urged Americans to "let our settlements and [Indians] meet and blend together, to intermix, and become one people," while his fellow Virginian Patrick Henry suggested that intermarriage be encouraged with tax incentives and cash stipends.

On the other side of the white-Indian divide, the Cherokee Nation proudly claimed descendents of mixed heritage: "Under the former laws of the Cherokee Nation anyone who could prove the smallest proportion of Cherokee blood was rated as Cherokee, including many of one-sixteenth, one thirty-second, or less Indian blood," notes the Web site Access Genealogy. "In 1905 the Cherokee Nation numbered 36,782 citizens.

Missing Indians Found

In addition to the massive numbers killed by disease, Native American tribes lost untold millions to assimilation and intermarriage. With Indian identity suddenly fashionable in American society, many families have proudly announced or discovered their partial native ancestry, suggesting that white-Indian (and black-Indian) unions have been flourishing (quietly) for centuries. Among recent celebrities who have claimed (and sometimes proved) roots in the powerful Cherokee Nation are Kevin Costner, James Garner, Elvis Presley, Rita Coolidge, Kim Basinger, Johnny Cash, Crystal Gale, Burt Reynolds, James Earl Jones, Wayne Newton, Shania Twain, Tina Turner, Cher, Chuck Norris, Dennis Weaver, Demi Moore, Carmen Electra, and Johnny Depp. Many others tout Indian ancestry, including Heather Locklear (who trumpets her Lumbee origins), Billy Bob Thornton (one-fourth Choctaw), Jessica Biel, Lou Diamond Phillips, Jessica Alba, Tommy Lee Jones, and Shannon Elizabeth.

Political leaders have also claimed partial Indian ancestry: Bill Clinton insisted that he was part Cherokee; Charles Curtis, vice president under Herbert Hoover, spent part of his boyhood on the Kaw reservation and took special pride in the fact that three of his eight great-grandparents were Indians; and Ben Nighthorse Campbell, whose mother emigrated from Portugal, represented Colorado in the Senate and serves as one of the forty-four members of the Council of Chiefs of the Northern Cheyenne Tribe, honoring his father's mixed Indian blood.

While poets and activists mourn the "vanishing American Indian," it's obvious that countless native people actually vanished (or rather assimilated) into the constantly churning melting pot of the American mainstream.

Of these, about 7,000 were adopted whites, Negroes, and Indians of other tribes, while of the rest probably not one-fourth are of even approximately pure Indian blood." The Cherokee constitution of 1839 included a clause making intermarried whites members of their nation. Sam Houston (1793–1863), onetime senator from Tennessee and the first president of the Republic of Texas, married a Cherokee woman and was adopted by the tribe.

Though some whites expressed trepidation about mixing with Indians, after the Civil War, when an air of liberation permeated the political landscape—and as Indian conflicts continued on the frontiers—interracial marriage gained proponents. "This group of reformers quickly became convinced that isolating Native Americans on reservations was not the solution to the 'Indian problem,' " says Margaret D. Jacobs in the University of Nebraska journal *Frontiers.* "Rather, they insisted, assimilation was the answer. . . . Interracial marriage between white women and Native American men offered a 'natural' way of assimilating Native Americans."

The scope and impact of assimilation and intermarriage remain almost impossible to determine. Literally tens of millions of present-day Americans claim partial Indian ancestry. Recent DNA analysis of the black community also shows a surprisingly strong admixture of Native American stock, amounting to as much as 10 percent of the ancestry of the complex community that identifies itself as African American.

Despite the prevalent charges of purposeful genocide, merger into the mainstream claimed at least as many Indian families as murder and massacre.

WHAT IF?

For most of the key turning points in the American past it's possible to imagine things turning out differently. Historians, novelists, and millions of readers love to play the "What If?" game to explore the way tiny changes could produce huge consequences: What if New York's East River hadn't experienced unseasonable fog in August 1776, shielding Washington's beaten army from likely capture by the British? What if Lee and Longstreet had launched their attack on the Union center at Gettysburg a few hours earlier and Pickett's charge had broken the federal lines? What if Franklin Roosevelt had kept Henry Wallace as his vice president in 1944, so the Soviet-sympathizing Iowan—not Harry Truman—would have become the leader of the free world when FDR died less than three months after inauguration?

The "What If?" game remains uniquely fascinating because our history boasts so many dramatic turning points at which different decisions, or altered luck, could have produced altogether unfamiliar outcomes.

But there's no way to play "What If?" when it comes to the fate of the Native Americans. No battlefield break, no changed government policy, could have produced a situation vastly different from the one that applies today.

Those who believe that a more humane or farsighted series of decisions could have preserved the tribes as truly independent, powerful, and traditionalist entities in the USA ought to explain how such a policy could have worked.

Many Native American activists cherish the idea that the Pilgrims and their successors who risked everything to travel to the New World should have recognized that other people already occupied the continent, and promptly turned around and gone home. Of course, the very idea that crown or church or guilt could have stopped the massive tides of European immigration to the New World contradicts the eternal human tendency to find and conquer new land.

Given the Europeans' huge superiority in weaponry, sophistication, communication, and economic productivity, the native warriors could barely slow their advance, with no chance at all of halting it. Even if King Philip's War or Pontiac's Rebellion had managed to wipe out three or four or ten times the number of white settlers, the attacks could have done little more than temporarily discourage the ambitious hordes who followed their dreams from the Old World.

Critics of U.S. policy also insist that the young nation betrayed its ideals by ignoring, violating, or distorting any number of treaties with Indian authorities, and it is unquestionably true that more scrupulous attention to solemn agreements and ordinary decency could have left today's reservations larger, richer in resources, and more prosperous. But the essential reality could have changed only around the edges. Tribal mores and time-honored ways could not resist modernity, no matter how much the feds appropriated to the Bureau of Indian Affairs. And the power and independence of the major Indian tribes would inevitably, if more gradually, have given way to the dominance of the many millions of people surrounding the remnant populations that survived the deadly diseases of the early colonial period.

Moreover, no component of our national population has been able to avoid the irresistible impact of assimilation, and there's no reason to believe that Indians in the long term would prove the exception. The ultimate conquest of Native American culture relied more on mass media than massacres, more on seduction than slaughter.

Recently renewed interest in authentic Indian identity represents a wholesome development that by no means requires the endless invocation of patently false charges of willfully planned mass murder. Those allegations do nothing to uplift or inspire young people of native heritage but rather serve, above all, to consign them to the ranks of the hapless and the helpless, assigning them the status of victims rather than victors.

For the society at large, lurid and unsubstantiated claims of genocide undermine the sense of pride and gratitude essential to any healthy civilization. If our nation's founding depended on deliberately dealing death to native inhabitants, then America's very existence is a crime. Distorting the record can't reduce the real suffering of previous generations but can still do serious damage to their descendants alive today. Lies about history can poison both present and future, but only the truth can do justice to the past.

"The United States Is Uniquely Guilty for the Crime of Slavery, and Based Its Wealth on Stolen African Labor"

PANHANDLING FOR JUSTICE

Frustrated by government's stubborn failure to make amends for the historic crime of slavery, a group of Oregon activists took matters into their own hands.

Led by performance artist damali ayo (no capital letters), a dozen dedicated volunteers hit the streets of Portland on October 10, 2007, to launch the first-ever "National Day of Panhandling for Reparations." They approached white passers-by demanding money for their ancestral sin of enslaving Africans, then found startled black strangers and offered them the collected cash. One recipient of this innovative largesse, Porter

Miller, fifty-eight, had been walking toward a bus stop when a smiling idealist intercepted him and handed over a few bucks to make up for the unpaid toil of his brutalized forebears. "It makes me feel better," Mr. Miller told a reporter for the Associated Press. "Makes me feel we're appreciated here."

Mr. ayo, the panhandler in chief, explained his afternoon's adventure by announcing that he was "taking the lead on a social issue. Taking it to the streets. Also to get the job done—getting those reparations paid out."

In the same spirit, but with considerably more pomp and solemnity, more than a dozen state legislatures and the U.S. Congress have considered their own formal apologies for slavery. In 2007 and 2008, resolutions expressing guilt and regret won approval in Virginia, Maryland, North Carolina, Alabama, New Jersey, and Florida.

In one typical passage, the political leaders of the Garden State resolved on November 8, 2007, that "the State of New Jersey, the Governor, and its citizens are conscious that under slavery many atrocities and gross violations of human rights were imposed upon African-Americans, and that acknowledging these facts can and will avert future tragedies, be they in the Sudan, or other parts of the world." Unfortunately, the well-intentioned resolution never explained *how* the act of politicians in Trenton "acknowledging" long-past cruelty "can and will" magically end the ongoing genocide by Arab militias in war-torn Sudan.

Meanwhile, several presidential candidates in the U.S. Senate, including Barack Obama and Hillary Clinton on the Democratic side and Sam Brownback for the GOP, cosponsored their own resolution of apology. "We've seen states step forward on this," said Tom Harkin of Iowa, another cosponsor. "I'm really shocked, just shocked," that the federal government hasn't apologized for slavery. "It's time to do so."

A few months later in July 2008, the House of Representatives took up the challenge and passed a sweeping apology resolution in a voice vote. This election-year gesture included a perplexing passage that suggested that slavery in the United States proved more degrading and dehumanizing than all other forms of bondage in all corners of the globe since the beginnings of civilization. In its second "whereas" clause, the House resolution baldly stated: "Slavery in America resembled no other form of involuntary servitude known in history, as Africans were captured and sold at auction like inanimate objects or animals." This congressional perspective of course ignored the fact that dehumanization always played a role in the process of enslavement, and for more than two thousand years institutional apologists have specifically equated slaves with beasts of burden. The overwrought resolution (written by freshman representative Steve Cohen of Tennessee) also suggested the nation could cope with its uniquely guilty past only if preening politicians struck compassionate but meaningless poses. "A genuine apology is an important first step in the process of racial reconciliation," the House proudly declared. In other words, neither abolition itself, nor extending the franchise to former slaves, nor fifty years of recent civil rights progress can count as a "first step" toward reconciliation; a hastily passed House resolution in the heat of a national campaign means so much more in bringing the races together.

Aside from its grandiose, fatuous self-importance, such rhetoric conveys the misleading impression that American society never before recognized the unimaginable suffering and profound evil involved in the kidnapping and exploitation of many generations of Africans. As a matter of fact, not only did both Bill Clinton and George W. Bush eloquently express regret for slavery during presidential visits to Africa, but in the very midst of the apocalyptic struggle that finally put an end to this monstrous institution, Abraham Lincoln placed the crime in its proper context.

In his Second Inaugural Address (March 4, 1865), President Lincoln spoke of guilt and justice to a battle-weary nation: "Fondly do we hope, fervently do we pray, that this mighty scourge of war may speedily pass away. Yet, if God wills that it continue until all the wealth piled by the bondsman's two hundred and fifty years of unrequited toil shall be sunk, and until every drop of blood drawn with the lash shall be paid by another drawn with the sword, as was said three thousand years ago, so still it must be said 'the judgments of the Lord are true and righteous altogether.' "

The current mania for apologies or reparations ignores the nation's long-ago acknowledgment that slavery represented an indefensible assault on liberty and decency, and dismisses the many fitful, imperfect efforts over several centuries to mitigate its horrendous impact. The obsessive emphasis on the "peculiar institution" perpetuates the image of African Americans as powerless victims while belittling heroic efforts for justice by Americans of all races and the remarkable progress of the black community.

Worst of all, the "slavery debate" undermines appropriate pride in this nation's role as history's most potent force for freedom and human betterment. Like the displacement and mistreatment of Native Americans, the enslavement of literally millions of Africans offers a ready-made opportunity for those who fear and resent the United States to highlight our society's allegedly racist and rapacious character. The guilt-mongers seize on slavery to spread ubiquitous lies about America—that this nation bears unique culpability for the devastation of Africa and the enslavement of its sons and daughters, and that the United States based its formidable wealth and power on stolen labor of countless slaves.

The proper response to these distortions rests on four important propositions:

1. Slavery is a timeless, universal institution, not an American innovation.
2. The slave economy played only a minor role in building American power and prosperity, and for the most part retarded economic progress more than advanced it.
3. America deserves unique credit for rapidly *ending* slavery, not distinctive blame for its establishment.
4. There's scant reason to believe that today's African Americans would be better off had their ancestors remained behind in Africa.

"THE WORST PERSON IN THE WORLD"

Unfortunately, the present tendency to exaggerate America's guilt for the horrors of slavery bears no more connection to reality than the old, discredited tendency to deny that the United States deserved any blame at all. No, it's not true that the "peculiar institution" featured kindhearted paternalistic masters and dancing, banjo-strumming field hands, any more than it's true that America displayed unparalleled barbarity, led a worldwide conspiracy, or enjoyed disproportionate benefit from the enslavement of Africans.

An effort to place America's slave-owning experience in an accurate historical and international context hardly amounts to a "defense" of slavery or an insulting effort to minimize the suffering experienced by the ancestors of today's African Americans. Nevertheless, when I posted a 2007 column on Townhall.com attempting to challenge the most popular myths about African bondage, I became the object of no end of indignant denunciation and even won the coveted title of "Worst Person in the World" on MSNBC's *Countdown with Keith Olbermann.* My critics, including Mr. Olbermann, circulated an amusing Photoshopped image of me proudly holding a bobble-head doll of Confederate hero Robert E. Lee—a kitschy effigy I'd never even seen before, let alone owned. According to outraged public opinion, I had disgraced myself as a "defender" or even "denier" of slavery and made common cause with Dixie revisionists who sought a new secession movement in which the "South would rise again."

A typical Internet comment suggested: "Slavery wasn't as bad as some liberals say it was—FOR MEDVED!!!! A lot of white racists don't think slavery was so bad. That is because of the guilt they carry for the sins of their fathers. They can't bring themselves to think that their forebears would do something so totally cruel and inhumane, so they make the oldest excuse in the world for it. Every mother has heard 'well, everybody did it.' This time Medved is the whining child, but he is defending his great grandfathers, with the 'everybody else did it' excuse."

For the record, let me note that my great-grandparents require no defense in this matter: to the very best of my knowledge, none of my ancestors on either side of the family ever owned slaves of any kind for at least the past two thousand years. My father's father became the first family member to settle in the New World (from Ukraine) in 1910; my mother and her parents didn't arrive from Germany until 1934, when they wisely elected to flee the Hitler regime. Though it's possible to argue that even these struggling immigrants benefited from the same "white privilege" that helped all nonblack Americans in the deeply racist society they found on their arrival, there's no way to impute to them "cruel and inhumane" behavior toward enslaved Africans.

In any case, a serious challenge to the prevalent distortions about slavery amounts to more than the "everybody did it" dodge. The key point is that Americans "did it" notably *less* than others—and yet many of our fellow citizens instinctively accept a special and crushing burden of guilt over our bloody past as a slave-holding nation.

If you don't believe that the present debate in this country tends to exaggerate America's responsibility for the nightmare of slavery, then ask yourself why there is no significant "reparations" movement in Brazil—despite the fact that this onetime Portuguese colony imported at least seven times as many African slaves as the future United States and abolished slavery a full quarter century *after* the Emancipation Proclamation.

And where is the present-day indignation against the 1,300-year history of ceaseless Arab slave trading—the Muslim societies that probably enslaved many more innocent Africans than did the New World, and perpetuated black slavery (in Mauritania, the Arabian Peninsula, Sudan, and elsewhere) into the twenty-first century?

These questions merely hint at the ancient, worldwide history of a horrible institution that the United States only uneasily inherited and that many of America's Founders felt conscience-bound to resist.

"EVERYWHERE IN CHAINS"

In 1762, when Jean-Jacques Rousseau declared that "man is born free, but everywhere he is in chains," his observation not only carried metaphoric weight; it accurately described the universality of slavery.

Current thinking suggests that human beings took a crucial leap toward civilization about ten thousand years ago with the submission, training, and domestication of important animal species (cows, sheep, swine, goats, chickens, and horses). Slavery, the bestialization and ownership of other human beings, developed in the same period, when skirmishing clans took prisoners and attempted to "domesticate" them for their own benefit. Pulitzer Prize winner David Brion Davis, the world's leading historian of slavery, notes that reliance on slaves "acquired a more central role when people learned to exploit the muscle power of animals, developed extensive agriculture, and built urban civilizations with complex social stratification."

Even the most primitive indigenous peoples practiced slavery in every corner of the globe. Davis writes of the Tupinamba, hunter-gatherers who populated preconquest coastal Brazil south of the Amazon. He notes that they took huge numbers of captives even though they "had no economic need for slave labor." Instead they humiliated their prisoners and fattened them up before slaughtering them in ritualized cannibalistic feasts. The more developed New World cultures of the Maya, Aztec, and Inca not only turned their slaves into brutalized and mutilated beasts of burden but also used their conquered enemies to feed a limitless lust for human sacrifice.

In a typical high school textbook, a time line of "Important Dates in the History of Slavery" begins at 4000 B.C., when "Sumerians settle in Mesopotamia with a slave labor force to do the heavy work." In *Slavery: Bondage Throughout History,* Richard Ross Watkins goes on to call Sumeria "the world's first great civilization" and notes that Sargon, its most powerful king, owned nine thousand slaves. Sargon and other rulers of the time also "used slavery as a form of punishment for any of their own people who violated the law."

Slavery became universal in the ancient world. The Egyptians began slaveholding at least as long ago as 2900 B.C. According to Robert Collins and James Burns in *A History of Sub-Saharan Africa,* "The dynastic Egyptians regularly raided for captives in the Nile Valley south of Aswan, most of whom remained enslaved in Egypt." Though many historians question the accuracy of the biblical account of Hebrew enslavement in ancient Egypt, no one doubts the Egyptian reliance on slave labor through all the millennia of their civilization.

In ancient Greece after 600 B.C., chattel slavery became cheap enough so that even people of modest means could afford to own household servants. In 330 B.C., the great philosopher Aristotle wrote approvingly, even enthusiastically, of the inevitability of a slavemaster relationship: "That some should rule and others be ruled is a thing not only necessary, but expedient; from the hour of their birth, some are marked out for subjection, others for rule. . . . Where then there is such a difference as that between soul and body, or between men and animals (as in the case of those whose business is to use their body, and who can do nothing better), the lower sort are by nature slaves, and it is better for them as for all inferiors that they should be under the rule of a master. . . . It is clear, then, that some men are by nature free, and others slaves, and that for these latter slavery is both expedient and right." Xenophon likened the teaching of slaves "to the training of wild animals," and Aristotle added that the ox was "the poor man's slave."

The Romans replicated the Greek reliance on slavery and seized so many captives from Eastern Europe that the terms *Slav* and *slave* boast the same linguistic origins. At the height of the Roman Empire, slaves represented between 25 and 40 percent of the total population. Preventing escape became a major concern for slave masters, who used branding, facial disfigurement, and permanent collars to identify their human property. This sadistic cruelty helped to provoke the famous slave rebellion of 72 B.C. led by the enslaved gladiator Spartacus (later celebrated as a favorite of Stalinist iconography and in the wonderfully kitschy Stanley Kubrick/Kirk Douglas movie of 1960). When the Roman general Crassus finally crushed the slave army, he crucified six thousand recaptured slaves along the Appian Way as a warning to others who might try to fight for their freedom.

In terms of staggering raw numbers, czarist Russia might count as the greatest slaveholding society of all time. According to an 1837 description in the *American Quarterly Register,* "The slaves belonging to the crown are not above fourteen millions, while those belonging to the nobility are estimated at more than twenty-one millions, male and female"—in other words, a clear majority of the overall Russian population of sixty million.

"THE RULING PRINCIPLE OF MY PEOPLE"

In sub-Saharan Africa, slavery also represented a timeless norm long before any intrusion by Europeans. The records of ancient intertribal conquest and capture remain cloudy because African peoples had no written language before the arrival of explorers and traders from the Islamic and Christian worlds, but when merchants showed up with desirable goods, local leaders immediately sold them captives in return.

During four hundred years of European slave trade, the white merchants were primarily the recipients rather than the collectors of the people they handled. Despite popular images of European slavers assaulting peaceful tribes with guns blazing, chaining and dragging away their victims, in fact the Portuguese and other merchants procured their cargo from willing indigenous African vendors along the coast. The esteemed African American historian Nathan Huggins pointed out that "virtually all of the enslavement of Africans was carried out by other Africans." Most of these African traders "saw themselves as selling people other than their own," since the concept of a single African "race" was the dubious invention of Western colonists.

The kings of Dahomey (today called Benin) attacked neighboring villages on a regular basis to seize slaves for commerce. In 1840 King Gezo told English visitors he would do anything the British wanted him to do "except to give up the slave trade." He proudly declared: "The slave trade is the ruling principle of my people. It is the source and glory of their wealth. . . . [T]he mother lulls the child to sleep with notes of triumph over an enemy reduced to slavery."

ISLAMIC GUILT, GREED, AND CRUELTY

In the tormented history of sub-Saharan African, the Arab slave trade lasted longer, covered far greater geography, and most likely enslaved more human beings than the European traders who came later and concentrated on the west side of the continent. "Slave trading had gone on for centuries," writes Marcus Rediker, an unforgettable guest on my radio show and author of *The Slave Ship: A Human History.* "From the seventh century to the nineteenth, more than nine million souls were carried northward in the trans-Saharan trade organized by Arab merchants in North Africa and their Islamic allies. These slaves were traded in highly developed commercial markets. In many areas, when European slave traders arrived on the coast, they simply entered preexisting circuits of exchange and did not immediately alter them."

Actually, Rediker's estimate of nine million helpless Africans seized and sold by Muslim traders falls at the low end of the spectrum. Other scholars suggest that Arabs and their Islamic allies enslaved as many as twenty million human beings over the span of more than a thousand years, compared to approximately eleven million (according to the most common current estimate) traded by European Christians in four hundred years.

The Islamic slave trade involved barbarity and greed that resembled and sometimes exceeded the monstrous cruelty for which European slave merchants stand rightly condemned. Ronald Segal, author of *Islam's Black Slaves: The Other Black Diaspora,* said in an interview that in the Muslim world "the casualties involved in enslavement wars were absolutely unspeakable." Moreover, slave ownership was more widespread in Islamic societies, so much so that "even small shopkeepers owned slaves." The wealthy collected concubines as status symbols "the way people in the West collect motorcars"; one ruler had fourteen thousand. To protect these harems, Muslims preferred eunuchs; since ordinary castration was technically against Islamic law, young black males underwent an even more savage procedure that mutilated their bodies to the "level of the abdomen."

Slavery continued openly in the Islamic world for nearly a century after its elimination in the West. Muslim slavers filled the vacuum left by the British abandonment of the slave trade in royal possessions in 1822. In *Britain and Slavery in East Africa,* Moses Nwulia asks, "What earthly comfort did the slave derive from being told that henceforth he was beyond the reach of the grasping hands of the white Europeans but good game for the supposedly benign whites from Asia? What spiritual enlightenment did he derive from being told that the same God who created the Christians and Muslims frowned upon Christian slave trade but sanctioned Muslim slavery?"

That same "divine sanction" continued for the Islamic world well into the twentieth century: Saudi Arabia outlawed slave owning only in 1962. The Islamic Republic of Mauritania finally moved toward abolition in 1981, but the practice continued unabated, even after a 2003 law that made slave ownership punishable with jail or a fine. As recently as December 2004, the BBC cited Boubakar Messaoud of Mauritania's SOS Slaves organization: "A Mauritanian slave, whose parents and grandparents before him were slaves, doesn't need chains. He has been brought up as a domesticated animal."

The organization Christian Solidarity International continues to purchase Sudanese slaves in order to free them, recently paying $100 (or two cows) for an adult captive. A press release revealed that in March 2007 alone the group bought ninety-six male slaves, who had been seized as part of the Muslim northern government's "jihad" on the nation's Christian and animist south. Six of the young men had been raped by their Islamic masters, and 99 percent had received frequent and sadistic beatings.

The long, savage history of Muslim slavers and their depredations in every corner of Africa makes a mockery of the trendy sentimental attachment of many African Americans to an alien Islamic culture that not only abused their ancestors but still afflicts their cousins. The fascination with Arab names (Jamal or Ayesha, not to mention Muhammad Ali or Kareem Abdul-Jabbar), even among non-Muslims in the black community, and the glamorization of Arab civilization as somehow authentically African grow in spite of incontrovertible evidence of more than a millennium of brutal Islamic enslavement.

Activists and agitators who obsess over America's dark history with slavery make scant mention of the undeniable record of Islamic exploitation and viciousness, even though by the most conservative estimate the Muslim world transported and enslaved at least *twenty times* as many Africans as ever made their way to the British settlements that later became the United States.

AT MOST, 3 PERCENT

Even when historians isolate the transatlantic slave trade from the greater crime of Muslim enslavement, the English colonies in North America accounted for only a tiny fraction of the hideous traffic in human beings. David Brion Davis, in his magisterial 2006 history *Inhuman Bondage: The Rise and Fall of Slavery in the New World,* concludes that colonial North America "surprisingly received only 5 to 6 percent of the African slaves shipped across the Atlantic." Hugh Thomas in *The Slave Trade* calculates the percentage as slightly lower, at 4.4 percent.

This means that the British North American colonies received at most 3 percent of all human beings taken from Africa for lives in bondage (and this figure counts the lowest estimates for the centuries of Islamic en-slavement).

In other words, the overwhelming majority of the transatlantic slave trade—at least 94 percent—went to Central and South America or the West Indies. For instance, slave ships transported a total of 480,000 Africans to all of America north of Mexico but carried 3.6 million to Brazil alone. Another 4 million went to the islands of the West Indies, with the relatively small island of Cuba receiving double the number of slaves imported to all of North America throughout the history of British settle-ment. The Portuguese, and later the Spaniards, established and monopo-lized the transatlantic slave trade nearly two hundred years before the English even established their first settlements in the Western Hemisphere.

Americans have been widely and perpetually criticized for our provin-cialism—for our limited knowledge of languages, cultures, and histories other than our own. This limited focus has led to a prodigiously exagger-ated sense of U.S. guilt—and gain—from the epic crime of slavery.

"A FOUNDING POPULATION"

Those who emphasize U.S. guilt for the crime of slavery would argue that it hardly matters that the United States played only a minuscule role in the overall European (and Islamic) rape of Africa; what counts is the much larger role captive Africans played in the establishment and pros-perity of the United States. They insist that even if the vast majority of enslaved Africans went elsewhere, enough of them (nearly half a million) arrived in North America and made a huge difference in struggling set-tlements suffering from chronic labor shortages.

Secretary of State Condoleezza Rice told the *Washington Times* in March 2008, "Black Americans were a founding population. Africans and Europeans came here and founded this country together—Europeans by choice and Africans in chains. That's not a very pretty reality of our founding." Her comments echo the attitude of pioneering African Amer-ican historian Lerone Bennett Jr., who in a 1961 book pointedly noted that the Dutch man-of-war that brought the first twenty African slaves to North America docked at Jamestown in 1619, "a year before the arrival of the celebrated *Mayflower,* 113 years before the birth of George Washington, and 244 years before the Emancipation Proclamation."

These first African arrivals, Angolan Bantus, took their place in a Virginia colony already heavily dependent on indentured servants—mostly poor Englishmen who voluntarily pledged to work under contract for a specified period of time, usually four to seven years, in exchange for their passage to the New World and sustenance during their servitude. The initial group of Africans labored on a basis similar to that of white indentured servants, and within a decade most of them had worked their way to freedom. Even by 1660, Africans constituted only 3.5 percent of the rapidly growing Virginia population of twenty-seven thousand—giving the lie to the claim that even this southern, slaveholding colony built its prosperity, infrastructure, or institutions on the backs of slaves.

For generations, the British settlements did little to codify or clarify the status of Africans, many of whom continued to toil like white indentured servants. (In *The Origins of American Slavery,* Betty Wood notes that for most of the seventeenth century "Europeans and West Africans labored side by side in the tobacco fields" on many Virginia plantations.) Only in 1705—a century after the foundation of Jamestown, eighty-six years after the arrival of the Angolans—did Virginia finally establish laws identifying West African slaves as the property of their masters.

At the same time, the insatiable need for agricultural labor (to grow tobacco in Virginia, rice and indigo in the Carolinas), combined with the emerging trade with the slave-saturated Caribbean, rapidly intensified the importation of enslaved Africans. Between 1660 and 1715, the overall population of Virginia tripled, but the number of slaves increased more than tenfold. The invention of the cotton gin in 1794 gave renewed life to the institution of slavery, creating a booming new economy in states west of the mountains (Alabama, Mississippi, Louisiana) to replace tobacco plantations with their depleted soil and the limited profits of rice and indigo.

PROMOTING POVERTY, NOT PROSPERITY

No one can deny the significant role that slave labor played in the colonial economies and in the development of the newly independent Republic; as today's press repeatedly emphasizes, skilled slave workers even helped to construct the U.S. Capitol and the White House in the freshly established federal city of Washington, D.C. At the time of the Revolution, Africans and their descendants lived nearly everywhere in the new nation and, according to common estimates, constituted up to 10 percent of George Washington's Continental Army. The first national census under the Constitution (in 1790) marked a high point for the slave population as a percentage of the U.S. total—18 percent (694,000 of 3,894,000), compared to less than 13 percent who identify as African American in the census today.

Even at this peak, more than 82 percent of Americans counted as "free"—meaning that the claim that the Republic built its overall prosperity on African bondage would depend on the dubious (indeed, ridiculous) assumption that the small slave minority represented an immensely more productive segment of the economy.

In fact, all indications suggest the opposite: that the persistence of slavery in southern states limited the pace of economic development, while abolition in the commercial states of the North led to quickening growth in population, wealth, and productivity.

Pennsylvania passed an emancipation law in 1780; Connecticut and Rhode Island followed four years later; New York approved emancipation in 1799. These states (with dynamic banking centers in Philadelphia and Manhattan) quickly emerged as robust sources of commerce and manufacturing, greatly enriching themselves, while the slave-based economies in the South languished by comparison. The Northwest Ordinance (unanimously adopted in 1787, before the drafting of the Constitution) banned slavery in the vast territory of the upper Midwest, facilitating explosive growth in the states of Ohio, Indiana, Illinois, Wisconsin, and Michigan. At the time of the Revolution, Virginia stood as the most populous and wealthiest state in the confederation, but by the onset of the War Between the States, the Old Dominion had fallen far behind a half dozen northern states that had outlawed slavery two generations earlier.

Anticipating the "irrepressible conflict" with the North, the editor of the Lynchburg *Virginian* understood his region's painful vulnerability. "Dependent upon Europe and the North for almost every yard of cloth, and every coat and boot and hat that we wear, for our axes, scythes, tubs and buckets, in short, for everything except our bread and meat, it must occur to the South that if our relations with the North are ever severed," he wrote, "we should . . . be reduced to a state more abject than we are willing to look at even prospectively." By the census of 1860, the percentage of the population that was enslaved had slumped to 12.5 percent (due to robust immigration to the free North) and citizens of the Union states outnumbered white Confederates by a ratio of more than three to one.

The prewar statistics comparing the booming, bustling North to the underdeveloped, agrarian South hardly show a national economy dependent on slavery. Even if we leave out the four "border states" (Maryland, Delaware, Missouri, and Kentucky) that ultimately stayed in the Union, the North enjoyed every advantage for a protracted struggle. In northern states, railroad mileage (covering a similar geographic area) beat the South by a three-to-one ratio, and southern commercial shipping proved virtually nonexistent. In terms of bank capital, the North topped the South by more than four to one, while the value of the North's manufactured goods exceeded southern production by a staggering ten to one. In short, by every measure the slave-based economies developed far less prosperous and powerful societies than their northern, industrialized counterparts—an economic gap that dictated the ultimate outcome of the nation's most devastating conflict.

Of course, antebellum America operated a national economy with undeniable interdependence among the various regions, so few northern companies and communities could claim to remain altogether untouched by slavery. (Some of today's most famous reparations lawsuits involve New England banks or insurance companies and midwestern railroads that did business with southern slaveholders.) Nevertheless, the overwhelming economic dominance of the northern states that had banned slavery for more than half a century indicated that involuntary servitude played a relatively minor role in America's mid-nineteenth-century emergence as an economic powerhouse.

Even in Dixie itself, only a small minority of white citizens owned slaves. Census records from 1860 show just a fourth of the total free population owning any slaves at all, and a mere 0.7 percent held title to big plantations with fifty slaves or more. "What do these statistics mean?"

asks Clint Johnson in *The Politically Incorrect Guide to the South.* "They mean that the typical Southern slaveholder was more likely to be working in the field beside his slaves than sitting on the verandah sipping a mint julep."

The numbers also indicate that for all of the magnolia-scented nostalgia attached to the antebellum South, for all the pop culture images of belles and cavaliers cavorting in baronial estates recalling Scarlett O'Hara's Tara, the infamous slave system produced great wealth for only the tiniest minority in a struggling, hardscrabble region that remained predominantly and persistently poor.

George Washington, Liberator?

Every American knows that America's first president owned slaves, but few realize the growing hatred of the institution that characterized the last twenty years of Washington's life. During his second term as president he told an English visitor: "I clearly foresee that nothing but the rooting out of slavery can perpetuate the existence of our union by consolidating it on a common bond of principle."

Washington ended up freeing all his own slaves, making careful arrangements in his will for their liberation. In December 1800, a year after his death, Abigail Adams visited Martha Washington at Mount Vernon. She wrote to her sister: "One hundred and fifty of [Mrs. Washington's slaves] are now to be liberated, men with wives and young children who have never seen an acre beyond the farm are now about to quit it, and to go adrift into the world without horse, home or friend. Mrs. Washington is distressed for them. At her expense she has cloaked them all, and very many of them are already miserable at the thought of their lot. The aged she retains at their request; but she is distressed for the fate of others. She feels a parent and a wife." Nevertheless, within a month she had set them all free.

CREDIT FOR ABOLITION

Present-day anguish over the historic shame of slavery plays an increasingly prominent role in even the most glowing accounts of the nation's origins. No Fourth of July celebration would be complete without pointed reminders that many of the Founders—including the redheaded Virginian who penned the words "all men are created equal"—themselves owned slaves. Contemporary sensibilities indict the patriot generation for its failure, in the midst of launching its unprecedented experiment in self-government, to uproot instantaneously an ancient institution passed on to them by their fathers and grandfathers.

Nevertheless, the debate over the slave trade at the Constitutional Convention showed that even Founding Fathers from southern states had developed profound discomfort with the continued seizure and enslavement of Africans. George Mason of Virginia condemned the "infernal traffic" and Luther Martin of Maryland viewed any protection of the slave trade as "inconsistent with the principles of the Revolution and dishonorable to the American character." Gouverneur Morris of Pennsylvania, who crafted the language for large sections of the final draft of the Constitution, thundered against slavery itself, denouncing it as a "nefarious institution" and "the curse of heaven."

The opponents of the slave trade succeeded in securing a constitutional provision for ultimate elimination of the importation of human cargo. Later, in urging ratification of the Constitution, slaveholder James Madison argued in *Federalist* No. 42 that this provision constituted "a great point gained in favor of humanity, that a period of twenty years may terminate for ever within these states" what he termed "an unnatural traffic" that amounted to "the barbarism of modern policy."

Within a mere hundred years of these founding arguments, the successors and allies of these men of principle and practicality had succeeded in abolishing slavery not just in their fledgling Republic but in all the nations of the West. During three eventful generations, one of the most ancient, ubiquitous, and unquestioned of all human institutions (considered utterly indispensable by the "enlightened" philosophers of classical Greece and Rome) became universally discredited and finally illegal—with Brazil at last liberating its enslaved hordes in 1888. This worldwide mass movement (spearheaded in Britain, the United States, and elsewhere by fervent evangelical Christians) brought about the most rapid and fundamental transformation in all human history.

While the United States (and the English colonies that preceded our independence) played no role in creating the institution of slavery or even the trade in African captives (pioneered by Arab, Portuguese, Spanish, Dutch, and other merchants long before the establishment of British North America), Americans did contribute mightily to the spectacularly successful antislavery agitation.

As early as 1646, the Puritan founders of New England expressed their revulsion at the enslavement of their fellow children of God. When magistrates in Massachusetts discovered that some of their citizens had raided an African village and seized two natives to bring them across the Atlantic for sale in the New World, the General Court condemned "this haynos and crying sinn of man-stealing." The officials promptly ordered the two blacks returned to their native land. Two years later, Rhode Island passed legislation denouncing the practice of enslaving Africans for life and ordered that "any slaves brought within the liberties of this Colonie" be set free after ten years "as the manner is with the English servants."

A hundred and thirty years later John Adams and Benjamin Franklin both committed themselves to the abolitionist cause, and Thomas Jefferson included a bitter condemnation of slavery in his original draft of the Declaration of Independence. This remarkable passage saw African bondage as a "cruel war against human nature itself, violating its most sacred rights of life & liberty," and declared that "a market where MEN should be bought and sold" constituted "piratical warfare" and "execrable commerce." Unfortunately, the Continental Congress removed this prescient, powerful denunciation in order to win approval from Jefferson's fellow slave owners—and in part because the attempt to blame the crimes of slavery entirely on King George seemed too transparently manipulative even for patriots in the midst of a bitter war. Nevertheless, the Declaration and the American Revolution became a powerful inspiration to the international antislavery cause and the new worldwide emphasis on human rights.

Nowhere did idealists pay a higher price for liberation than they did in the United States. Confederate forces (very few of whom ever owned slaves) may not have fought consciously to defend the "peculiar institution," but Union soldiers and sailors (particularly at the end of the war) proudly risked their lives for the emancipation cause. Julia Ward Howe's powerful and popular "Battle Hymn of the Republic" explicitly called on federal troops to follow Christ's example of sacrifice: "As He died to make men holy, let us die to make men free."

And many of them *did* die, some 364,000 in four years of combat—or the stunning equivalent of five million deaths as a percentage of today's U.S. population.

Meanwhile, the economic cost of liberation remained almost unimaginable. In most other nations, the government paid some form of compensation to slave owners at the time of emancipation, but southern masters received no reimbursement of any kind when they lost an estimated $3.5 billion in 1860 dollars (about $70 billion in today's currency) of what David Brion Davis describes as a "hitherto legally accepted form of property."

The most notable aspect of America's long and corrupting entanglement with slavery involves not its tortured, bloody existence but the unprecedented speed and determination with which the forces of freedom and decency roused the national conscience and ended this age-old evil.

BETTER OFF IN AFRICA?

The word *reparations* comes from the same Latin root *(reparare)* as the word *repair*, and implies a correction or adjustment for past harm. One of the goals of today's reparationists, aside from securing belated payment for centuries of unremunerated slave labor, involves a desire to make victims whole—to compensate contemporary African Americans for the foul crime perpetrated against their ancestors.

Unfortunately, any effort to erase slavery's impact and to match the status of American blacks descended from bondsmen with that of their African cousins whose families had never been enslaved would mean a drastic *reduction* in the U.S. residents' living standards. Keith B. Richburg, a Pulitzer Prize finalist and former *Washington Post* Africa bureau chief, describes the popular nostalgia for "Africa—Mother Africa," which "is often held up as a black Valhalla, where the descendants of slaves would be welcomed back and where black men and women can walk in true dignity."

Richburg himself felt a deep pull to his ancestral homeland, where he believed he might find "a little bit of that missing piece of myself." But his personal experience in Africa revealed that the romantic image of the "black Valhalla" bore no connection to reality.

"Sorry, but I've been there," he declares flatly.

Richburg's indispensable book, *Out of America: A Black Man Confronts Africa,* provides an unforgettable and heartbreaking description of his disillusion—and at times horror—at the chaos, corruption, and violence that characterize contemporary life in African nations. After casting off preconceptions and spending three years, "most of my time on the road, . . . exploring, discovering Africa," Richburg saw a bitter history, a terrifying present, and a frightening future:

> What future has a place where the best and brightest minds languish in dank prison cells? Where a ruthless warlord aims mortar shells into a crowded marketplace, and where teenagers strip down cars and fit them with antiaircraft guns to roam through the streets terrorizing and looting? Where a dictator begs the international community for food aid to avert mass hunger even as he erects a new international airport in his dirt-poor hometown? What future is there in a place where the poets are hanged by the soldiers, and where the soldiers riot and kill when they are unpaid? Where entire villages are left so ravaged by disease that only the very old and very young still linger?
>
> I've looked in my crystal ball and tried to see some slivers of light. I've really tried. But all I can see is more darkness.

In view of this dark reality, of the terrible situation that has long prevailed in places such as Nigeria and Ivory Coast and Sierra Leone and Zimbabwe, could any African American say with confidence that he or she would have fared better had some distant ancestor not been enslaved and brought to the United States? Slavery undeniably represents a moral abomination, just as surely as America has a long record of racism and injustice. But it's also obvious that Americans of African descent enjoy much greater prosperity and human rights than citizens whose families lived for millennia in the copious bosom of the "mother continent."

Keith Richburg's years in Africa led him to conclude:

> Malcolm X said we black people in America are more African than American—"You're nothing but Africans"—but I don't feel it. I feel more lonely here in Africa than I have ever felt in America. In America, I may feel like an alien, but in Africa, I *am* an alien. . . . There is more, something far deeper, something that I am ashamed to admit: I am terrified of Africa. I don't want to be from this place. In my darkest heart here on this pitch-black African night, I am quietly celebrating the passage of my ancestor who made it out.

"In short," Richburg writes, "thank God that I am an American."

NEW, WILLING IMMIGRANTS

In recent years, more and more Africans have embraced the promise and generosity of the United States—arriving in this country (to apply the distinction cited by Condoleezza Rice) "not in chains, but by choice."

The Census Bureau reports that by 2005, the population of foreign-born blacks totaled 2,815,000, with the majority arriving just since 1990. Two-thirds of these black immigrants hail from the Caribbean and Latin American; the remaining third arrive directly from Africa.

This stunning figure means that the number of black people alive today who journeyed to this country willingly is more than five times *greater* than the number of slaves brought here against their will over the course of centuries of brutal slave shipments to North America.

Even if fanatical "Afrocentrists" fantasize about their glorious destiny had their kidnapped ancestors never crossed the ocean, real-life natives of the "mother continent" (and other representatives of the worldwide

African diaspora) readily understand that they're better off here. Best-selling author (and Indian immigrant) Dinesh D'Souza suggests that while new arrivals compare American life with the reality of their home countries, "African-American leaders, by contrast, use a utopian standard in judging the United States. Their argument is not that the United States is a worse place for them to live than Haiti or Ethiopia, but that the United States falls short in comparison to the Garden of Eden."

Africa, unfortunately, falls even shorter of the ideal than America. The suffering and slaughter that Richburg identified tell the story in visceral and personal terms, while statistical data further reveal the crushing realities of daily life in "the motherland."

The major slave-collecting regions lag far behind black communities in the United States in indicators of living standards and health. Take, for instance, the part of West Africa known during the eighteenth century as "the Bight of Benin," also designated "the Slave Coast," since it exported almost 1.4 million slaves during the eighteenth century, according to Marcus Rediker. That area, between the Volta and Benin rivers, now includes Togo, Benin, and southwest Nigeria. In 2006, Nigeria's population of 144.7 million had a life expectancy of 46.6 years, an infant mortality rate of 100 per 1,000 live births, and a yearly per capita income of $640 in U.S. dollars.

By comparison, the National Center for Health Statistics reports that as of 2004, the life expectancy at birth for African Americans was 73.1 years and the infant mortality rate 13.6 per 1,000 live births, and Census Bureau figures from 2006 put average per-capita income for black Americans at $31,969.

These are basic statistics, and do not measure many of the other factors that help make life worth living—such as rule of law, safety from random violence, freedom of expression, cultural richness, social mobility, and political free choice. Even in terms of raw numbers (which provide even starker contrasts when analyzing other onetime slave regions such as Sierra Leone, Congo, and Angola), the contrast with the United States suggests that long-ago journeys to America, no matter how cruel or unwelcome at the time, resulted ultimately in longer lives, fewer dead babies, more educational opportunities, vastly greater income, and more political freedom.

Of course, some activists would blame Africa's lack of progress on the devastating impact of Western colonialism, but the United States played virtually no role in the colonization of the continent. The British, French, Italians, Portuguese, Germans, and others all established brutal colonial rule in Africa; tiny Belgium became a particularly oppressive and bloodthirsty occupying power in the Congo. The United States, on the other

At the Height of Slavery, Blacks Choose America over Africa

Even at a time when the vast majority of American blacks endured the unspeakable brutality of slavery, liberated slaves strongly preferred a future in the United States to any prospective return to Africa.

Beginning in 1816, the American Colonization Society made determined efforts to persuade "free negroes" to establish a refuge in West Africa based on American ideals. Over the course of several decades a dazzling array of powerful white leaders supported the colonization project—including Presidents Thomas Jefferson, James Madison, James Monroe, and Abraham Lincoln, Speaker of the House Henry Clay, Senators Daniel Webster, Stephen Douglas, and William Henry Seward, poet Francis Scott Key, General Winfield Scott, and Chief Justices John Marshall and Roger B. Taney.

The resulting settlement became the independent nation of Liberia in 1847. But in the course of a generation Liberia drew no more than thirteen thousand colonists from the United States—at most 5 percent of America's free people of color. Why? Because free black communities passionately objected to the idea of leaving the nation that had once enslaved them. According to historian John Hope Franklin, opposition rose "to a fever pitch" with mass meetings in Baltimore, Boston, New York, Hartford, New Haven, Pittsburgh, Philadelphia, and many other cities. The great bulk of free blacks condemned any talk of returning to Africa as a distraction from the crucial work of slavery abolition—and winning equal rights and full citizenship in the United States after achieving liberation.

hand, sponsored only one long-term venture on the African continent: the colony of Liberia, an independent nation set up as a haven for liberated American slaves who wanted to go "home." The fact that so few availed themselves of the opportunity (see sidebar, page 68) or heeded the back-to-Africa exhortations of the turn-of-the-century black nationalist Marcus Garvey indicates that descendants of slaves understood they were better off remaining in the United States, for all its faults.

˙ A DEBT TO AMERICA

The ongoing agitation for apologies and reparations wrongly encourages grudges rather than gratitude, condemnation above confidence, since the focus on the long, tragic history of enslavement exaggerates both U.S. guilt and African American powerlessness. The corresponding bitterness brings benefit to neither the black community nor the nation at large.

If the millennia of enslavement require some formal (and formulaic) apology, let the United Nations express its regrets in the name of all humanity rather than making demands for specific redress from the U.S. Congress or, ludicrously enough, the legislature of New Jersey. At least the General Assembly could presume to speak for those European powers (Portugal, Belgium, Netherlands, France, Spain, Britain) and Islamic states that played a much greater role than the United States of America in seizing slaves and imposing colonialism in Africa. In terms of benefiting from slavery, the Caribbean and Latin American nations that received literally 95 percent of the transatlantic captives surely owe more "payback" for unrequited toil than the United States—where postslavery waves of immigration (including black immigration) produced a labor force many times larger than that generated by the slaves and their descendants.

These incontrovertible facts remain too rarely noted to derail the tireless international efforts to impose on the United States an ugly, distinctive, and hugely disproportionate burden of guilt. Nearly 150 years after emancipation, slavery has emerged once again as an inexplicably hot topic—as if the evil institution becomes more and more relevant and influential the further it recedes into the past. Ironically, the present generation of distant slave descendants seems more haunted, more obsessed, more wounded by the bondage experience than their own grandparents and great-grandparents who struggled to overcome the impact of far more immediate oppression.

In this context, any effort to consign discussion of slavery to American history classes rather than legislatures, political campaigns, or campus demonstrations meets with furious and indignant resistance.

In 2001 my friend David Horowitz, an activist and author, drafted a provocative ad for university newspapers offering ten arguments against reparations to blacks. He attempted to buy space (through his L.A.-based Center for the Study of Popular Culture) to place the manifesto in seventy-one campus publications, but forty-three of these august institutions of higher learning turned down his money because they deemed the ad too disturbing for students supposedly accustomed to the freewheeling exchange of ideas. Meanwhile, fifteen of the college papers that actually ran David's declaration apologized for it after the fact, though without offering specific reparations to all the offended students.

To many observers, the most explosive element of the disputed ad came with point nine, under the heading "What About the Debt Blacks Owe to America?"

The text crisply noted:

If not for the anti-slavery attitudes and military power of white Englishmen and Americans, the slave trade would not have been brought to an end. If not for the sacrifices of white soldiers and a white American president who gave his life to sign the Emancipation Proclamation, blacks in America would still be slaves. If not for the dedication of Americans of all ethnicities and colors to a society based on the principle that all men are created equal, blacks in America would not enjoy the highest standard of living of blacks anywhere in the world, and indeed one of the highest standards of living of any people in the world. They would not enjoy the greatest freedoms and the most thoroughly protected individual rights anywhere. Where is the gratitude of black America and its leaders for those gifts?

The outrage that greeted this deliberate provocation centered on the notion that Horowitz was somehow suggesting that slavery itself represented one of America's "gifts," or denying the authentic suffering of many generations of bondage, bigotry, and discrimination.

Recognizing that painful legacy doesn't require accepting its central importance for confronting the problems of the present; ritualized expressions of shame over sins of the past do nothing to ensure a more productive future. In the incongruous context of presidential politics, leaders promise to inspire the public with endless and emotional conversations about race, while ordinary Americans await that process with the dread and embarrassed fascination associated with the prospect of picking at scabs in public.

But even the most predictable and tedious discussions about slavery and its aftermath can benefit from an effort to clear away the most prevalent lies about slavery—the accusation that this nation bears special blame for a wretched institution that flourished for ten thousand years, or built illicit continental prosperity on the labor of a small, enslaved minority.

Such unthinking indictments by poseurs, provocateurs, and even panhandlers lack any sense of depth, perspective, or context and obscure the fact that honest examination of the record of past generations provides the basis for pride as well as guilt.

"The Founders Intended a Secular, Not Christian, Nation"

THE PERILS OF IMMINENT THEOCRACY

Following the 2004 reelection of George W. Bush, a frenzied flurry of books and articles warned unsuspecting Americans of the imminent takeover of their cherished Republic by an all-powerful, implacable theocratic conspiracy.

In *American Fascists: The Christian Right and the War on America*, former *New York Times* correspondent Chris Hedges breathlessly reported:

> All it will take is one more national crisis on the order of September 11 for the Christian Right to make a concerted drive to destroy

American democracy. . . . This movement will not stop until we are ruled by Biblical Law, an authoritarian church intrudes in every aspect of our life, women stay at home and rear children, gays agree to be cured, abortion is considered murder, the press and the schools promote 'positive' Christian values, the federal government is gutted, war becomes our primary form of communication with the rest of the world and recalcitrant non-believers see their flesh eviscerated at the sound of the Messiah's voice.

According to Hedges (a recent—and surprisingly genial—guest on my radio show), it makes no sense to try to reason with the "Christian Fascists" he fears. "All debates with the Christian Right are useless," he writes, because they "hate the liberal, enlightened world formed by the Constitution."

Scores of other releases from major publishers sought to arouse the nation's slumbering conscience to confront the perils of "the American Taliban." These titles include the blockbuster best seller *American Theocracy* plus additional cheery volumes such as *Jesus Is Not a Republican: The Religious Right's War on America*; *The Baptizing of America: The Religious Right's Plans for the Rest of Us*; *Why the Christian Right Is Wrong*; *Liars for Jesus*; *The Theocons: Secular America Under Siege*; *The Hijacking of Jesus*; and many, many more.

Some worried observers expected Christian conservatives to remake America along the lines of Iran or Nazi Germany, while others suggested that they would follow the genocidal path of Communist China. In reviewing the Oscar-nominated documentary *Jesus Camp*, Stephen Holden of the *New York Times* solemnly declared: "It wasn't so long ago that another puritanical youth army, Mao Zedong's Red Guards, turned the world's most populous country inside out. Nowadays, the possibility of a right-wing Christian American version of what happened in China no longer seems entirely far-fetched."

Paul Krugman (yet another acclaimed commentator for the *New York Times*) argued that the theocrats would seize power through quiet subversion: "The infiltration of the federal government by large numbers of people seeking to impose a religious agenda—which is very different from simply being people of faith—is one of the most important stories of the last six years. It's also a story that tends to go unreported, perhaps because journalists are afraid of sounding like conspiracy theorists. But this conspiracy is no theory."

Krugman then provided a series of purportedly chilling examples, even asking his no doubt nervous readers: "Did you know that Rachel Paulose, the U.S. Attorney in Minnesota—three of whose deputies recently stepped down, reportedly in protest over her management style—is, according to a local news report, in the habit of quoting Bible verses in the office?"

Of course, another midwestern attorney, Abraham Lincoln, famously indulged the same habit in every office he ever occupied (very much including the White House). He prominently featured scriptural citations ("A house divided against itself cannot stand") in many of his most celebrated public utterances.

Though Lincoln's contemporaries found plenty of reasons to criticize or dismiss the cagey politico from Illinois, none of them attacked him for inappropriately inserting religious sentiments into public discourse. Americans of the 1860s understood and accepted the Christian values and vision that had shaped the Republic in the "four score and seven years" of its initial existence.

Contemporary hysterics who try to terrify the public about the Religious Right's "war against America" base their scare stories on the widely touted lie that our Founders meant to establish a secular nation, not a Christian one.

If nothing else, the alarmists must judge our constitutional Framers as miserable failures, since the nation they launched remains by far the most Christian—and least secular—society in the developed world. Recent polling shows that 73 percent of Americans believe in the existence of hell, 70 percent prefer presidential candidates who are "strongly religious," and clear majorities refuse to support an atheist for the highest office. Some 80 percent of our fellow citizens currently identify themselves as Christians of one sort or another, so the public rightly sees America a "Christian nation"—in the same sense that India is a Hindu nation and Mexico is a Catholic nation, even though those two countries (like the USA) don't provide governmental endorsement for a single "official" faith.

In keeping with widely embraced notions about the religious essence of the United States, a September 2007 poll by the nonpartisan First Amendment Center showed that fully 55 percent of respondents agreed with the statement that "the Constitution establishes a Christian nation." When asked about that survey in an interview with Beliefnet, presidential contender John McCain responded, "I would probably have to say yes, that the Constitution established the United States of America as a Christian nation. But I say that in the broadest sense. The lady that holds her lamp beside the golden door doesn't say, 'I only welcome Christians.' We welcome the poor, the tired, the huddled masses. But when they come here they know that they are in a nation founded on Christian principles."

Despite the cautious and qualified tone of McCain's remarks, enraged partisans leaped at the chance to attack the candidate. The executive director of the National Jewish Democratic Council, an advocacy group for the Democratic Party, called the senator's statements "repugnant," while the general counsel of the mainstream American Jewish Committee declared that "to argue that America is a Christian nation . . . puts the very character of the country at stake."

Charles Haynes, senior scholar at the Freedom Forum's First Amendment Center, made the most sweeping and profoundly misleading comments. Regarding the poll that provoked the McCain dustup in the first place, Haynes noted that its results "suggest that a great many people have deeply misunderstood the Constitution. The framers clearly wanted to establish a secular nation."

This contention isn't just confused and unfocused; it is appallingly, demonstrably, and inarguably wrong.

Militant separationists of the past fifty years embrace the fanciful notion that they alone can discern the true intentions of the Founding generation—intentions that remained miraculously hidden to all scholars, jurists, and politicians in the first century and a half of our nation's history, and not least to the Founders themselves.

The whole chain of twisted reasoning regarding our allegedly "secular" heritage depends on a series of ludicrous myths and distortions that must give way to a few fundamental but (to religion haters) uncomfortable truths:

- The earliest settlers came to establish, not to escape, devoutly Christian societies.
- The Founders worried about government's interference with religion far more than they did about religious influence on government; in fact, they viewed fervent faith as an indispensable component of a healthy society.
- Separationist extremists, not Christian conservatives, seek the radical transformation of the nation and its institutions, overturning the long-established constitutional balance in the process.

SEEKING PURITY, NOT TOLERANCE

The myth of America as a secular haven from the faith-based fanaticism of Europe rests on the widespread and erroneous assumption that the first colonists fled to the New World to escape "religious persecution." Schoolchildren who celebrate the traditional Thanksgiving holiday learn that the Pilgrims boarded the *Mayflower* in pursuit of the "freedom to practice their faith"—a pretty and politically correct spin that obscures some of the essential elements of the crucial story of the Plymouth Colony. The Pilgrims escaped from England in 1608 and then found complete freedom in Holland, twelve years before they set sail for their destiny in Massachusetts. They left the Netherlands not because that nation imposed too many religious restrictions but because the Dutch honored too few. The pluralism and tolerance they found in Amsterdam and Leyden horrified the Pilgrims, separatists who preferred an isolated situation in the wilderness that facilitated the building of a unified, disciplined, strictly devout religious utopia, not some wide-open haven for believers of every stripe. The Pilgrims earn our admiration (and even our love) for their courage and idealism, but their religious outlook hardly qualifies as broad-minded. Like the other stalwart believers who followed, they came to the new world seeking purity, not freedom.

A decade after Plymouth's founding, the Puritans pursued similar purposes in establishing the Massachusetts Bay Colony. Succeeding generations (famously including President Ronald Reagan) have cherished the shipboard sermon of the leader of that settlement, John Winthrop, who exhorted the settlers in biblical terms: "For we must consider that we shall be as a city upon a hill. The eyes of all people are upon us." In addition to the warmer, fuzzier passages of this immortal exhortation ("For this end we must be knit together in this work as one man. We must entertain each other in brotherly affection"), Winthrop included words to indicate the unabashedly theocratic plans for the new colony: "When God gives a special commission he looks to have it strictly observed in every article." In no sense did the New England pioneers intend to establish communities for each individual to follow the dictates of his own conscience or the private promptings of the Holy Spirit. Winthrop explained: "The end is to improve our lives, to do more service to the Lord, the comfort and increase of the body of Christ, whereof we are members, that ourselves and posterity may be better preserved from the common corruptions of this evil world, to serve the Lord and work out our salvation under the power and purity of his holy ordinances."

All of the other New England colonies except Rhode Island carved homes out of the wilderness on the same basis. They aimed to establish model religious communities that would be more rigorous and restrictive, not more open and accepting, than the corrupt and politicized Church of England. Massachusetts, Connecticut, New Hampshire, and later Vermont and Maine strictly enforced Sabbath rules, mandated attendance at worship services, and used tax money to support religious seminaries (prominently including Harvard and Yale)—all befitting "Christian Commonwealths."

If anything, the New England colonists distrusted and defied the Church of England for its backsliding and compromises rather than its vigorous imposition of religious standards. They built remarkably successful self-governing settlements, but no one could describe their colonies as living laboratories of religious freedom. Between 1658 and 1660, in fact, Massachusetts authorities hanged four Quaker missionaries (including a woman, Mary Dyer) who defied repeated arrests and banishments to try to spread their heretical ideas in a society that considered them unacceptably sinful.

Of the original thirteen colonies, ten mentioned religious purposes in their founding documents. Even Virginia, where most of the early settlers seemed to care more about finding gold than finding God, received an initial charter from King James that described a mandate for the "propagating of Christian Religion to such People as yet live in Darkness." Delaware's charter explicitly commands "further propagation of the Holy Gospel."

Other denominations (Quakers in Pennsylvania, Catholics in Maryland) founded their colonies not to create secular or diverse environments but to provide denominational havens for their coreligionists. Even in the Dutch settlement of New Amsterdam (which became New York in 1665), director-general Peter Stuyvesant, the son of a minister, attempted to impose the dictates of his Calvinist faith, ruthlessly driving out Quakers and only reluctantly accepting a boatload of Jews. Among the original colonies, only Roger Williams's quirky Rhode Island made a consistent priority of religious tolerance and openness to dissenters.

FIGHTING FOR SANCTITY, NOT "SEPARATION"

Those who maintain that our Founding Fathers fought their Revolution in part to ensure "separation of church and state" must somehow explain the favorite marching song of the Continental Army. The much better-known "Yankee Doodle" became widely popular after the war, but in the midst of the fighting George Washington's men more commonly sang "Chester," an unforgettably stirring 1770 hymn by Boston composer William Billings. The lyrics (apparently written by Billings himself) placed the bloody conflict in a frankly religious perspective:

> *Let tyrants shake their iron rod,*
> *And Slav'ry clank her galling chains*
> *We fear them not, we trust in God*
> *New England's God forever reigns. . . .*

The song goes on to note that "God inspir'd us for the fight" against the redcoats' "infernal league," before concluding with this verse:

What grateful Off'ring shall we bring?
What shall we render to the Lord?
Loud Hallelujahs let us Sing,
And praise his name on ev'ry Chord.

HBO's superb 2008 miniseries *John Adams* appropriately shows John and Abigail (Paul Giamatti and Laura Linney) singing part of this hymn in church in the early days of the struggle.

John's cousin Samuel Adams also embraced the sentiments of the song as one of the most radical and, simultaneously, one of the most ardently religious of all the Revolutionary leaders. His colleague in the Continental Congress, Dr. Benjamin Rush, wrote of Sam Adams: "He considered national happiness and the public patronage of religion as inseparably connected; and so great was his regard for public worship, as the means of promoting religion, that he constantly attended divine service in the German church in York town while the Congress sat there . . . although he was ignorant of the German language."

This same combination of fierce religiosity and fearless commitment to the independence cause occurred again and again among the American patriots: to a great extent, they represented the controversial and impassioned "Religious Right" of their time. Those who held more moderate, tolerant, relaxed religious views, or embraced the conventional, "mainstream" Church of England, more likely took their place among the Tories who supported the crown, or else joined that one-third of colonists (according to the famous estimate of John Adams) who remained neutral or undecided in the great struggle.

The independence fighters had been disproportionately touched by the fervor of the Great Awakening, that explosion of Christian enthusiasm and revival inspired in the previous generation by visiting British evangelists such as George Whitefield and the Wesley brothers. During the Revolutionary War fighting pastors became so numerous that the British derided them (with reference to their dark robes) as the "Black Regiment."

In *The Light and the Glory,* Peter Marshall and David Manuel tell the story of Peter Muhlenberg, the thirty-year-old pastor of a German American Lutheran church in Virginia's picturesque Shenandoah Valley. On a

Sunday morning after the fighting had begun in Massachusetts in 1775, Reverend Muhlenberg took as the text for his sermon the celebrated line from Ecclesiastes 3:1: "For everything there is a season and a time for every matter under heaven." He concluded his presentation with a solemn prayer, then raised his voice and continued to speak: "In the language of the Holy Writ, there is a time for all things. There is a time to preach and a time to fight." He paused for maximum impact, then shocked the congregation by throwing off his pulpit robe to reveal the freshly made uniform of a colonel in the Continental Army. "And now is the time to fight!" he roared. "Roll the drums for recruits!" That same afternoon Pastor Muhlenberg marched off toward Boston at the head of a column of three hundred men. This regiment became the celebrated Eighth Virginia, with the pastor himself reaching general's rank as commander of Washington's first light infantry brigade.

The American Revolutionaries saw their battlefield and political opponents not only as enemies of liberty but as enemies of God Himself, and they emphasized religious revival as an essential component of potential victory. Dr. John Witherspoon, esteemed religious scholar and president of the College of New Jersey (later Princeton University), wrote a widely distributed 1776 pamphlet declaring that "he is the best friend to American liberty who is most sincere and active in promoting true and undefiled religion, and who sets himself with the greatest firmness to bear down on profanity and immorality of every kind. Whoever is an avowed enemy of God, I scruple not to call him an enemy of his country."

George Washington similarly viewed Christian commitment as an indispensable means for rallying the troops and securing "the blessings of Providence." The day after he took command of the Continental Army outside of Boston in 1775 he issued a general order proclaiming that "the General most earnestly . . . requires and expects of all officers and soldiers not engaged in actual duty, a punctual attendance of divine services, to implore the blessing of Heaven for the means used for our safety and defense." Throughout the war, he seemed virtually obsessed with organizing his men in prayer and suppressing "profane cursing, swearing and drunkenness," in part by ordering regular days of fasting or thanksgiving. In 1778, a typical general order announced: "The commander in chief directs that Divine service be performed every Sunday at 11 o'clock in each brigade which has a Chaplain. . . . While we are duly performing the duty of good soldiers, we certainly ought not to be inattentive to the higher duties of religion. To the distinguished character of a patriot, it should be our highest glory to add the more distinguished character of a Christian."

DEFENDING UNITY, NOT SECULARISM

None of the religious proclamations or commands by Washington or by the Continental Congress proved in the least bit controversial—no eighteenth-century equivalent of the ACLU popped up at Valley Forge to threaten the commander in chief with a nasty lawsuit unless he dropped his habit of ordering his beleaguered troops to fast and pray. Military and political leaders of the Revolutionary conflict never expressed a desire to disentangle government or the military from religious associations; if anything, they sought a more fervently, sincerely Christian society—a nation of "undefiled religion," in Witherspoon's phrase—in contrast to the corrupt ways of the mother country.

Why, then, the strict avoidance of religious references in the Constitution? The Declaration of Independence included a half-dozen mentions of "Providence" or "the Creator," but our "charter of liberty" some eleven years later contains only the briefest, innocuous identification of the signing date as "the Year of our Lord one thousand seven hundred and Eighty seven."

Today's secularists predictably point to this absence of explicitly Christian content as the surest sign that the Founders never meant to establish a religious nation. The Freedom from Religion Foundation offers a brochure entitled "Is America a Christian Nation?" that declares: "The U.S. Constitution is a secular document. It begins 'We the people' and contains no mention of 'God' or 'Christianity.' Its only references to religion are exclusionary, such as 'no religious test shall ever be required as a qualification to any office or public trust' (Article VI) and 'Congress shall make no law respecting an establishment of religion, or prohibiting the free exercise thereof' (First Amendment)."

In advancing such arguments, secular activists fail to recognize (or at least acknowledge) that the Framers, with their constitutional approach, meant to protect unity, not secularism. The Founders certainly encouraged biblical faith in the broadest sense, but they understood the need to discourage squabbling or discrimination among the various religious denominations to be found within the new nation.

The states took pains to continue the cooperation that had prevailed in the Revolution. During the war, Connecticut Congregationalists, Virginia Anglicans, New Jersey Presbyterians, and North Carolina Methodists had all managed to fight side by side and to participate jointly in the "Divine service" ordered by General Washington. Soldiers from New York and Massachusetts had even served uncomplainingly under a Quaker from Rhode Island—the courageous and gifted General Nathanael Greene—despite the fact that their ancestors had ruthlessly persecuted (and even executed) unwanted Quaker interlopers. On the battlefield, Americans of every denomination (including a disproportionate number of soldiers in the Continental Army from the tiny Jewish minority) managed to follow the exhortation of Benjamin Franklin's famous "Join or Die" cartoon, depicting a snake chopped into several regional slices.

After the war, then, the states tried to avoid battles over doctrine and practice, but they sustained their determination to encourage Christianity in the more general sense. Weeks before the Constitutional Convention convened in 1787, Congress adopted the Northwest Ordinance, which stated: "Religion, morality, and knowledge being necessary to good government and the happiness of mankind, schools and the means of education shall forever be encouraged." These words (reenacted by the First Congress under the Constitution) made clear that to the Founders, the propagation of "religion" and "morality" represented the prime (and necessary) purpose of schooling.

In other words, with the Revolution concluded, the leaders of the struggling new nation didn't suddenly jettison the Christian fervor with which they had won the war. Contrary to claims by today's separationists, they didn't instantly transform themselves into skeptical nonbelievers who hoped to drive organized faith out of the public square.

A proper understanding of the First Amendment reflects the importance of religion to the new republic. The Freedom from Religion Foundation characterizes the First Amendment's Establishment Clause as "exclusionary," but the clause actually protected established churches in the states. At the time of the Constitution, the governments of six of the thirteen states (New Hampshire, Massachusetts, Connecticut, Maryland, South Carolina, and Georgia) endorsed specific denominations and provided public money for church construction and maintenance. With its entry into the union in 1791, Vermont joined them with yet another established church. "In most of the other states," veteran journalist M. Stanton Evans noted of "unabashedly Christian" America at the time of its founding, "there remained a network of religious requirements for public office, reflecting the pervasive, taken-for-granted Christian nature of the people being represented. These requirements usually mandated that a candidate for office had to be a Christian, in some instances quite specifically a Trinitarian, and in numerous cases a Protestant in the bargain."

Congressional leaders who debated the First Amendment expressed no intention of interfering with the states that openly promoted and funded religious institutions; in fact, they struggled to find language that would prohibit "Congress from legislating either to establish a national religion or to disestablish state religion," according to Louisiana State University law professor John Baker in the indispensable *Heritage Guide to the Constitution*. Even Harvard's Laurence Tribe, the most esteemed liberal legal scholar of his generation, has acknowledged: "A growing body of evidence suggests that the Framers principally intended the Establishment of Religion Clause to perform two functions: to protect state religious establishments from national displacement, and to prevent the national government from aiding some, but not all, religions."

In fact, less than twenty-four hours after Congress approved the First Amendment, they clearly indicated the way they understood its language by passing the following resolution: "Resolved, that a joint committee of both Houses be directed to wait upon the President of the United States, to request that he would recommend to the people of the United States a day of public thanksgiving and prayer, to be observed by acknowledging, with grateful hearts, the many signal favors of Almighty God, especially by affording them an opportunity peaceably to establish a Constitution for their safety and happiness." In the proclamation duly announcing the "day of public thanksgiving and prayer" that Congress had requested, President Washington declared November 26 "to be devoted by the

People of these States to the service of that great and glorious Being, who is the beneficent Author of all the good that was, that is, or that will be."

It never occurred to this First Congress that their call for public prayer would conflict with the amendment they had adopted a day earlier prohibiting "an establishment of religion."

JEFFERSON'S "FAITH-BASED INITIATIVES"

Even Thomas Jefferson, author of the phrase "a wall of separation between church and state," felt generally comfortable with a governmental role in encouraging a faith-based perspective. His fateful 1802 letter to the Danbury Baptist Association that first suggested the "wall of separation" idea concluded with a distinctly religious phrase: "I reciprocate your kind prayers for the protection & blessing of the common father and creator of man." The presidential letter expressed earnest agreement with Jefferson's Connecticut correspondents that "no man ought to suffer in name, person, or effects on account [of] his religious opinions."

The Supreme Court's 1947 ruling in *Everson v. Board of Education* appropriated the language of Jefferson's letter to justify an unprecedented restrictive view of governmental entanglement with religion. The Court did so despite the fact that the presidential missive, a ceremonial document with no official standing, followed adoption of the First Amendment by some thirteen years and emphasized Jefferson's concern with potential government harassment of minority faiths rather than worries over the state's ongoing promotion of religious principles and institutions. In fact, in 1803, the year after his famous letter, Jefferson recommended to Congress the approval of a treaty that provided government funds to support a Catholic priest in ministering to the Kaskaskia Indians. Three times he signed extensions of another measure described as "an Act regulating the grants of land appropriated for Military services and for the Society of the United Brethren for propagating the Gospel among the Heathen."

In other words, George W. Bush hardly counted as the first president to promote the use of governmental resources for "faith-based initiatives."

Jefferson also paved the way for his successors in his ostentatious participation in church services. As president, he participated weekly in Christian worship in the Capitol building; until 1866, in fact, the Capitol hosted worship every Sunday and intermittently conducted a Sunday school. No one challenged these seventy-one years of Christian prayer at the very seat of federal power—least of all the many living participants in the congressional sessions who had drafted the First Amendment itself.

Nor did these firsthand witnesses to "original intent" challenge the seven states with established churches. In *Ten Tortured Words,* an invaluable book on the Establishment Clause, Stephen Mansfield writes: "For all of that generation, the understanding was certain that the states were permitted to establish religion or support religion as aggressively as the people allowed." President Jefferson explicitly shared that viewpoint, expressed in a public address of March 1805: "In matters of religion, I have considered that its free exercise is placed by the constitution independent of the powers of the general [federal] government. I have therefore undertaken, on no occasion, to prescribe the religious exercises suited to it, but have left them, as the constitution found them, under the direction and discipline of State or Church authorities acknowledged by the several religious societies."

PRO-FAITH JUDGES

In that spirit, established "official" churches survived in several states well into the nineteenth century. Connecticut disestablished its favored Congregational denomination only in 1818, New Hampshire in 1819, and Massachusetts in 1833—some forty-five years after the adoption of the First Amendment. The changes reflected the religious "quickening" of the time (viewed by some as a second Great Awakening), with new sects and philosophies clamoring for recognition and fresh adherents. In any event, public opinion and legislative decisions, not judicial dictate, brought disestablishment.

The leading judges of the early Republic outspokenly endorsed governmental support for religious institutions. John Marshall, the father of American jurisprudence and for thirty-four epochal years (1801–35) the chief justice of the United States, wrote a revealing letter to Jasper Adams on May 9, 1833, declaring: "The American population is entirely Christian, and with us Christianity and Religion are identified. It would be strange indeed, if with such a people, our institutions did not presuppose Christianity, and did not often refer to it, and exhibit relations with it."

His colleague on the Court (1796–1811), Justice Samuel Chase, wrote a 1799 opinion *(Runkel v. Winemill)* that held: "Religion is of general and public concern, and on its support depend, in great measure, the pace and good order of government, the safety and happiness of the people. By our form of government, the Christian religion is the established religion, and all sects and denominations of Christians are placed upon the same equal footing, and are equally entitled to protection in their religious liberty."

The most authoritative explanation of the First Amendment came from Joseph Story, a Supreme Court justice from 1811 to 1845 (appointed by President Madison, the father of the Constitution) and, as a longtime Harvard professor, the leading early commentator on the Constitution. He observed:

> The general if not universal sentiment in America was that Christianity ought to receive encouragement from the State so far as was not incompatible with the private rights of conscience and the freedom of religious worship. An attempt to level all religions, and to make it a matter of state policy to hold all in utter indifference, would have created universal disapprobation, if not universal indignation. The real object of the First Amendment . . . was to exclude all rivalry among Christian sects, and to prevent any national ecclesiastical establishment which should give to a hierarchy the exclusive patronage of the national government.

None of today's Christian conservative organizations seek to institute the "national ecclesiastical establishment" clearly prohibited by the Establishment Clause. The leading organizations on the Religious Right— Focus on the Family, the Christian Coalition, the American Family Association, the Traditional Values Coalition, and so forth—all represent interdenominational coalitions, drawing Catholics and Mormons, Episcopalians and evangelicals of every sort. Meanwhile, those who worry over Christian conservative influence clearly favor the folly described by

Justice Story: a "state policy" to hold all religions "in utter indifference." This effort to sever ties between faith and state—including the absurd efforts to remove the words "under God" from the Pledge of Allegiance or the motto "In God we trust" from our coinage—produces precisely the sort of "universal indignation" Justice Story predicted nearly two hundred years ago.

"In God We Trust"

During the darkest years of the War Between the States, Christians appealed to the Treasury Department to place the word *God* on our coins. In one typical letter, the Reverend M. L. Watkinson of Ridley Township, Pennsylvania, worried that "antiquaries of succeeding generations" would sort through the relics of 1860s America and assume that its citizens lived in a godless society. If, however, the nation invoked the Almighty on its coinage, it "would relieve us from the ignominy of heathenism." The director of the Mint suggested the words "Our God, our country" or "God, our trust," but it was treasury secretary (and later chief justice) Salmon P. Chase who came up with the alternative "In God We Trust." This choice echoed the concluding verse of "The Star-Spangled Banner": "And this be our motto: 'In God is our trust.'"

Coins continued to carry these words despite strong disapproval from President Theodore Roosevelt, a devout Christian who in 1907 wrote, "It seems to me eminently unwise to cheapen such a motto by use on coins, just as it would be to cheapen it by use on postage stamps, or in advertisements." Despite such objections, the words remained a cherished tradition on coins (and later paper money) and became the official national motto by act of Congress on July 30, 1956. In the same era, the legislators added the phrase "under God" to the Pledge of Allegiance, hoping to overcome "imperialistic and materialistic Communism" and "to remind all of us of this self-evident truth" that "as long as this country trusts in God, it will prevail."

STRUGGLING FOR FAITH,
NOT CELEBRATING DOUBT

Advocates of strict separation find so little support from the Founders in state papers or legal opinions that they often turn to intimate examinations of the personal faith (or lack of faith) of the extraordinary individuals who launched the Republic. Jefferson and Franklin in particular never embraced the conventional Christian faith of their day and spent their long lives probing and arguing over the nature of God and the meaning of the Bible. Their well-known explorations have led to false assumptions and misleading statements about the Founders in general, such as the widely repeated lie that they counted as "deists, not Christians."

Deists, according to the standard definition *(Webster's New World Dictionary)*, believe "that God exists and created the world but thereafter assumed no control of it or the lives of people." But the Founders—very much including Jefferson and Franklin—almost obsessively cited God's unceasing control of the world and of the great events in which they participated. The Revolutionary generation regularly searched for a supernatural hand in their affairs and made every effort to discern the Divine will. In a letter to his friend Thomas Jefferson on July 20, 1776, patriot John Page observed: "We know the Race is not to the swift nor the Battle to the Strong. Do you not think an Angel rides in the Whirlwind and directs this Storm?"

Far more prominently, in his First Inaugural Address, George Washington declared as his "first official act" his "fervent supplications to that Almighty Being who rules over the universe" that He might bless the new government. Washington went on to reflect that "no people can be bound to acknowledge and adore the invisible hand which conducts the affairs of men more than those of the United States." In other words, the first president, in his first official act, explicitly rejected the deist idea that God plays no constant or present role in our affairs.

Newsweek editor Jon Meacham, author of *American Gospel: God, the Founding Fathers, and the Making of a Nation*, notes that even the most religiously adventurous of the Framers resorted to scriptural imagery when suggesting a national seal to the Continental Congress on the fateful day of July 4, 1776. "Franklin's vision was biblical, as was Jefferson's," he writes. "Franklin wanted an image along these lines: 'Moses standing on the shore and extending his Hand over the Sea, thereby causing the same to overwhelm Pharaoh who is sitting in an open Chariot, a Crown on his Head and a Sword in His Hand. Rays from the Pillar of Fire in the Clouds reaching to Moses, to express that he acts by Command of the Deity. Motto, Rebellion to Tyrants is Obedience to God.' "

In his portraits, Meacham makes clear the God-haunted nature of the men who made a Revolution. They all "delved and dabbled in religion; while Jefferson edited the Gospels, Benjamin Franklin rephrased and re-arranged the Book of Common Prayer . . . John Adams considered the ministry but chose law instead; for the rest of his life he was a Unitarian who privately confessed a weakness for the beauty of Episcopal liturgy. . . . Samuel Adams, a fierce advocate of independence, was a Puritan who looked askance at other faiths, but knew that faith and political warfare were a deadly combination."

Even the most radical of the Founders, pamphleteer Thomas Paine, would fit more comfortably with today's religious conservatives than with the secular militants who claim him as one of their own. At the time, the restless revolutionary's attack on traditional Christian doctrine in *The Age of Reason* alienated virtually all of his American comrades. Nevertheless, in a 1797 speech to a learned French society, he maintained that schools must concentrate on the study of God, presenting his argu-ments with an eloquent insistence on recognizing the Almighty that would delight James Dobson of Focus on the Family but mortally offend the secular purists of the ACLU:

> It has been the error of the schools to teach astronomy, and all the other sciences and subjects of natural philosophy, as accomplish-ments only; whereas they should be taught theologically, or with reference to the Being who is the author of them: for all the princi-ples of science are of Divine origin. Man cannot make, or invent, or contrive principles. He can only discover them; and he ought to look through the discovery to the Author. . . . When we study the el-ements of geometry, we think of Euclid. When we speak of gravita-tion, we think of Newton. How then is it, that when we study the

works of God in the creation, we stop short, and do not think of God? It is from the error of the schools in having taught those subjects as accomplishments only, and thereby separated the study of them from the Being who is the author of them.

RELIGION'S BENEFITS AS IMPORTANT AS ITS TRUTHS

Despite Tom Paine's reverence for the "Author" of nature, his former American colleagues still denounced him for his rejection of Christianity. In a diary notation of July 26, 1776, John Adams asserted: "The Christian religion is above all the religions that ever prevailed or existed in ancient or modern times, the religion of wisdom, virtue, equity, and humanity, let the blackguard Paine say what he will, it is resignation to God, it is goodness itself to man."

Like Adams, the other Founders looked beyond Christianity's truths (even when they generally accepted them) and passionately affirmed its benefits. They unanimously agreed on the importance of fervent faith in protecting and nourishing the Republic they had launched. Washington's Farewell Address provided the most famous formulation of this belief: "Of all the dispositions and habits which lead to political prosperity, religion and morality are indispensable supports. In vain would that man claim the tribute of patriotism who should labor to subvert these great pillars of human happiness, these firmest props of the duties of men and citizens. The mere politician, equally with the pious man, ought to respect and to cherish them."

Adams, his successor in the White House, wrote to his cousin Zabdiel Adams in 1776: "Statesmen, my dear Sir, may plan and speculate for liberty, but it is Religion and Morality alone, which can establish the principles upon which Freedom can securely stand."

Whatever their theological disagreements or doubts, those who created this new nation in the eighteenth century shared a unanimous faith in the positive impact of vital religious institutions. For more than 150 years, the national leaders who followed them echoed their confidence in the importance of religiosity to the health of society and the stability of government.

In sharpest contrast to today's secular militants who fear the increased influence of religious faith, the Founders worried over the potential impact of its diminished status. While separationists today sound the alarm over "theocracy," the Revolutionary generation felt dread and horror (particularly after the French Revolution) at the rule of "unbelief."

By the time Tocqueville visited the flourishing Republic in the early 1830s, he noted the universal conviction that Christian enthusiasm played a powerful role in the nation's success. "In the United States," he wrote, "Christian sects are infinitely diversified and perpetually modified but Christianity itself is an established and irresistible fact which no one undertakes either to attack or defend."

REJECTING THE NATIONAL HYMNAL

The blending of faith and nationalism became an additional "irresistible fact" more than two centuries ago, reinforcing the American idea that religion serves the cause of the nation just as the nation, ultimately, serves the cause of religion. In the emotional days after the September 11 attacks, secular activists objected to performances of "God Bless America" or "God Bless the USA" in public schools, but their inability to suggest faith-free alternatives highlighted their alienation from the American mainstream. All our most revered nationalist songs emphasize the Republic's special connection to the Almighty.

Our national anthem indicates that the idea of this relationship preceded today's Religious Right by at least two hundred years. "The Star-Spangled Banner" includes Francis Scott Key's incontrovertibly religious sentiments in its final verse:

> *Blest with vict'ry and peace, may the heaven-rescued land*
> *Praise the Power that hath made and preserved us a nation*
> *Then conquer we must when our cause it is just*
> *And this be our motto: "In God is our trust."*

The nation's other most beloved patriotic hymn, "America the Beautiful," features a chorus with the cherished line, "America! America! God shed His grace on thee." Katharine Lee Bates began writing the words after reaching the top of Pike's Peak in Colorado in 1893 and entering a state of near-religious ecstasy upon contemplation of the Great Plains to the east. She included verses that repeatedly ask assistance from the Almighty ("America! America! God mend thine every flaw / Confirm thy soul in self control / Thy liberty in law").

Meanwhile, "The Battle Hymn of the Republic," the stirring marching song of the War Between the States, isn't merely religious (with its chorus invoking the biblical word *hallelujah*) but is also specifically Christian. The final, moving verse—most often sung in a reverent hush—poetically declares:

> *In the beauty of the lilies Christ was born across the sea*
> *With a glory in his bosom that transfigures you and me*
> *As He died to make men holy, let us die to make men free,*
> *While God is marching on.*

Finally, "America" (also known as "My Country, 'Tis of Thee") provides no safe haven for those who yearn to disentangle religious and patriotic messages, not with its inescapably churchy concluding verse:

> *Our fathers' God to Thee*
> *Author of liberty*
> *To Thee we sing*
> *Long may our land be bright*
> *With freedom's holy light*
> *Protect us by Thy might*
> *Great God, our King.*

The most recent of the popular patriotic melodies first appeared on the eve of World War II as a love letter to the nation from an immigrant boy who became the leading Broadway composer. Irving Berlin donated all proceeds from "God Bless America" to the Boy Scouts (another politically incorrect institution) and implored the Almighty to "stand beside her and guide her / Through the night with the light from above."

Some contemporary Americans clearly feel uncomfortable with our long history of weaving together a sense of national identity with claims of divine mission, our consistent assumption that the Almighty has selected this nation for His purposes. These alarmed opponents of "theocracy" have every right to argue that we will enjoy a brighter, better future by severing the old association between faith and nationalism, but they shouldn't mischaracterize the past—or suggest a return to an era of absolute church-state separation that never existed.

DEMANDING RADICAL TRANSFORMATION

A candid review of the nation's religious heritage demonstrates that it is today's aggressive secularists, not religious conservatives, who seek radical change in the social contract. From the first settlers through the end of World War II, virtually all elements of society accepted and even celebrated the deeply Christian nature of our government and culture.

Christian conservatives seek to restore America far more than they hope to change America. Their most controversial goals—banning abortion, limiting marriage to male-female unions, returning prayer to schools, educating kids for self-control rather than condoms, displaying religious symbols on public property, restricting obscenity on the public airwaves—hardly count as daring innovations or revolutionary transformations.

As recently as the years of my own childhood, the United States cheerfully, even proudly embraced all the rules and norms now considered radical and theocratic by critics of the Christian Right. In Pennsylvania, the state of my birth, the old law required that "at least ten verses from the Holy Bible [be] read, without comment, at the opening of each public school on each school day." Four other states enforced similar legislation requiring mandatory Bible readings every morning before class, and twenty-five more states had laws on the books explicitly authorizing "optional" Bible readings, before the Supreme Court struck down all such statutes in the *Abington* decision of 1963.

Does that mean Eisenhower's America constituted some dictatorial theocracy? Did we only throw off the crushing yoke of religious tyranny with the sweeping church-state Supreme Court decisions of the 1960s?

Recent skirmishes over religious displays on public property high-light the fact that it's secular militants who want to remake America in a style unrecognizable to citizens of an earlier era. Only on rare occasions do people of faith attempt to insert Christian symbols in new venues— as did the controversial judge Roy Moore with his (ultimately banished) Ten Commandments monument in Alabama. For the most part, the symbolic disputes involve memorial crosses, Ten Commandments, displays, or nativity scenes that appeared without challenge for fifty or a hundred years until the ACLU brought suit to cleanse the landscape of such "unconstitutional" pollution.

In the past fifty years the separationists have enjoyed remarkable success in stripping away signs of religious influence, but it's at best arguable that they have shaped a better country in the process. The majority resists the march forward to some religion-free utopia and yearns rather for a more relaxed, more balanced relationship between faith and state, and for the spirit of the beloved old songs.

If it's true that the Founders actually intended to create a secular society rather than a Christian one, then it's obvious that they failed miserably. And to most citizens, America doesn't feel like a failure.

Even the most avid religious activists intend no theocratic coup, but pray rather for further blessings from the Creator:

> *America! America!*
> *May God thy gold refine*
> *Till all success*
> *be nobleness*
> *And ev'ry gain divine.*

"America Has Always Been a Multicultural Society, Strengthened by Diversity"

"OUT OF ONE, MANY"

Those who argue that we would all benefit from a more diverse and multicultural United States must search in vain for inspiring international examples to support their approach.

Consider, for instance, the baleful experience of our Canadian neighbors. Despite prodigious natural resources and one of the highest living standards in the world, the nation has teetered for more than forty years on the verge of dissolution, implacably split between its French-speaking and English-speaking communities. Fortunately for beleaguered nationalists, the hordes of newly arrived immigrants from Asia and elsewhere display a strong preference for English and for federal power—playing a crucial role in blocking Quebec's Francophone majority from prevailing in its secessionist agenda.

On the other side of the Atlantic, the picturesque country of Belgium offers a more pointed and poignant illustration of the high cost of multiculturalism. After 177 years of national existence, after building and losing a vast (and brutal) African empire, after serving as a blood-soaked battlefield in two world wars, Belgium in the twenty-first century faces the impending collapse of its privileged polity. A parliamentary crisis paralyzed the nation through most of 2007 and the first months of 2008, preventing the installation of a functioning government. The Flemish majority and its parties sought greater autonomy and separation from the less prosperous, French-speaking Walloons, with neither side affirming a Belgian identity. Most experts expected an inevitable separation in the style of 1993's "Velvet Divorce" that saw the former Czechoslovakia divided into the Czech Republic and Slovakia. In any event, Brussels sophisticates joked that inhabitants of Flanders and of Wallonia shared only a common pride in their distinctively flavorful Belgian beer and famously decadent chocolate—hardly a sufficient basis for durable national identity.

Like most other experiments in multiculturalism, the Belgian experience of distinct, stubbornly unassimilated nationalities trying to share the same state exposes the folly behind the current mania for promoting diversity as a blessing and a boon. Despite abundant diversity disasters from around the world—including the unspeakably bloody breakup of Yugoslavia in the last years of the twentieth century—the fervent fans of multiculturalism insist on an odd and extreme sort of American exceptionalism. They characterize the United States as the one nation in history that's strengthened, rather than threatened, by simultaneously sustaining disconnected tribal identities within its borders. According to the politically correct orthodoxy, we've always been a diverse collection of numerous nationalities with no single, unifying American culture.

This notion denies the authentic American record, which demonstrates the value of assimilation, not separateness, and it implicitly rejects our national motto, "E pluribus unum"—"Out of many, one." In 1998, Vice President Al Gore provoked derisive merriment when he bumblingly mistranslated this maxim while praising diversity in off-the-cuff Milwaukee remarks. No, "E pluribus unum" doesn't mean "Out of one, many," but many admirers of Mr. Gore and his enlightened agenda seem to wish that it did.

To them, the famous melting pot never functioned as advertised, and even in those limited instances where it did they feel no pride in its assimilationist achievements. The Web site of the Association for the Study of African American Life and Culture, listing itself as "the Founders of Black History Month," noted in April 2008: "From its inception, America has been a landscape peopled by diverse ethnic and racial groups and today virtually all peoples are represented. If America has always been racially and ethnically diverse, the nation's self-image has not always recognized its multicultural history. Until the last decades of the twentieth century, America has seen itself largely as the flowering of the Anglo-Saxon culture and prided itself on allowing immigrants to adopt the American way."

Activists and educators sought to move past this outdated ideal, particularly at our elite universities. In 1987, Jesse Jackson led celebrated protests at Stanford against the tyranny of the "dead white guys" curriculum with the catchy chant of "Hey, hey, ho, ho, Western Civ has got to go!" By that time, most campuses already featured separate programs for black studies, women's studies, Chicano studies, Asian studies, Native American studies, gay (or "queer") studies, and many other areas of special-interest emphasis. Despite these lavishly costly efforts, multicultural mandarins remained unsatisfied.

On March 31, 2008, 345 of the 1,350 students at self-consciously "progressive" Hampshire College in Amherst, Massachusetts, staged an angry walkout to insist on more aggressive support for campus diversity. The youthful idealists demanded the immediate hiring of new staff to correct the college's "Eurocentric" focus, including a "dean of multicultural affairs" to augment the existing presidential assistant for diversity, four new full-time faculty to teach ethnic and queer studies, permanent staffing at the Cultural Center, Women's Center, and Queer Community Alliance, plus new "multi-culti" specialists at the college's health services and "a position in Institutional Advancement geared toward raising funds that specifically address issues of diversity on campus." The students also demanded "mandatory anti-oppression trainings for faculty, staff, Public Safety, and Residential Life staff and interns"; a "queer-identified" residential hall and another dorm specifically for students of color; cutting "financial ties with countries that occupy and practice racial apartheid"; and "closing of the college on Columbus Day and Martin Luther King, Jr. Day to hold a campus-wide teach-in on racism and imperialism." Addressing the "rainbow rights" of Hampshire College's forward-looking student body constitutes serious—and painfully expensive—business.

The crusaders for multiculturalism show scant concern for the unprecedented nature of their utopian project, and sneer at the old ideal of unifying Americanism. In place of the cherished vision of immigrants from everywhere blending their disparate backgrounds into something new, united, and definably American, they now trumpet the novel goal of distinct races, nationalities, and interest groups intensifying their differences and glorying in their separateness. The diversity devotees love to talk of America's future as a gorgeous, complex mosaic featuring thousands of tiles with colors far more intense than dull and out-of-style patriotic pageants shaded only in red, white, and blue. Unfortunately, the randomly assembled components the tribalists describe offer only eye-popping abstractions as their design elements, rather than a recognizable national portrait.

In fact, the new vision of a diverse, divided America arises from misleading assumptions about our past and present—distortions that require clarification and correction.

INCONVENIENTLY UNICULTURAL ORIGINS

For starters, the multiculturalists overlook the nation's inconveniently unicultural origins. The Founders didn't just see themselves as members of a mostly homogeneous Anglo-Protestant society; they affirmed their common language, heritage, and core religious values as a point of pride.

In their fine book *Decision in Philadelphia*, Christopher and James Lincoln Collier provide a vivid portrait of America at the time of the Constitutional Convention. "The United States in 1787 was by no means as diverse as the bewildering ethnic crazy quilt it is today. Over 75 percent of the white population was of British and Irish stock. Among the whites, 85 percent spoke English as a first language, and although there were some Catholics and a handful of Jews, the country was overwhelmingly Protestant." The only significant white ethnic group beyond the British, the Protestant Irish, and the Scots-Irish was the Germans—representing up to 30 percent of the population in Pennsylvania, but eagerly and quickly assimilating into the new American identity. The Jewish population at the time of the Revolution amounted to a paltry three thousand—or one-tenth of one percent of the overall population—though a disproportionate number of those sons of Israel fought in Washington's army (including my wife's ancestors—she is a proud Daughter of the American Revolution).

Distinctive ethnic pockets persisted in remote villages and frontier settlements. Future president Martin Van Buren grew up in the village of Kinderhook, New York, speaking the Dutch language of his ancestors (who had come to the New World 150 years earlier). This ethnic identity mattered little, however, either to Van Buren's supporters or to his critics; by the time of his major campaigns in the 1830s and '40s, the nation had widely embraced the idea that an identity as an American, this fresh nationality on the world stage, easily should trump any distinctive ancestry.

The first influential expression of this ideal came from Michel Guillaume Jean de Crèvecoeur (better known as J. Hector St. John de Crèvecoeur), whose origins obviously weren't British. In his best-selling pamphlet "Letters from an American Farmer," published at the conclusion of the Revolutionary War, he asked a question that generally puzzled Europeans:

> What then is the American, this new man? He is neither an European, nor the descendant of an European. . . . *He* is an American, who leaving behind him all his ancient prejudices and manners, receives new ones from the new mode of life he has embraced, the new government he obeys, and the new rank he holds.
>
> He becomes an American by being received in the broad lap of our great *Alma Mater*. Here individuals of all nations are melted into a new race of men, whose labours and posterity will one day

cause great changes in the world. . . . The American ought therefore to love this country much better than that wherein either he or his forefathers were born. Here the rewards of his industry follow with equal steps the progress of his labour; his labour is founded on the basis of nature, *self-interest;* can it want a stronger allurement?

Even in 1782, the "new man" identified as an American displayed unique initiative and drive, secure in the conviction that "the rewards of his industry follow with equal steps the progress of his labour." This is the characteristic of the self-selected population that chose to take the enormous risks associated with abandoning a familiar life and setting off with aspirations for a fresh start.

Albert Gallatin, a French-Swiss orphan who immigrated to Pennsylvania at age eighteen in the midst of the Revolution, embodied this ideal. After coming to this continent, Gallatin involved himself in politics and went on to win election as U.S. senator (though his opponents fought to eject him because they challenged whether he'd waited long enough for his status as a naturalized citizen). He later became House majority leader and the longest-tenured secretary of the treasury in U.S. history, serving under both Presidents Thomas Jefferson and James Madison, who never questioned his notable accent or obviously foreign origins.

The emphasis on dissolving and even erasing old identities and the insistence on embracing the prevailing culture of the United States actually contributed to two of the most significant military defeats in our early history. The Continental Army's ill-fated expedition to conquer Quebec in 1775–76 expected to draw strong support from French Canadians, who resented their English neighbors. To the surprise of the American generals, however, the French rallied strongly to defend their homes against the invasion, precisely because they believed the Yankees would prove far less tolerant of their different language and Catholic religion than were the relatively easygoing Brits. The same calculation played a significant role in the failed U.S. efforts to seize Canada in the War of 1812.

In other words, far from representing a paragon of diversity and multiculturalism, the new United States looked markedly less multicultural than the British Empire—especially in view of the United Kingdom's official recognition of separate Scottish, Welsh, and Irish nationalities. The young USA offered no comparable gestures to acknowledge the citizens of diverse origins who lived within its borders.

The only significant group in early America that remained excluded from the prevailing Anglo-Protestant culture was the black population—nearly 20 percent of the total, and most of them slaves. Under the cruel terms of slavery these African Americans found themselves reduced to the status of property rather than neighbors or citizens. Despite their substantial presence (particularly in the southern states) they hardly contributed to a multicultural community because their heritage, traditions, and languages received no recognition whatever—and, in fact, faced ruthless extirpation.

Free blacks, however, also represented a significant segment of early America—amounting to more than fifty thousand citizens at the time of the Revolution, including the famous Crispus Attucks, the first casualty of 1770's Boston Massacre. The so-called free negroes actually demonstrated the singular, dominant role of the prevailing American culture, since they embraced the identity, values, traditions (including slave owning, for many of them), faiths, language, and politics of their white Anglo contemporaries, making no attempt whatever to honor a distinctive African or ex-slave identity.

These free black citizens constituted as much as 10 percent of the Continental Army, and foreign officers with thick accents also gave that fighting force a deceptively cosmopolitan atmosphere. Such Revolutionary heroes as the Frenchman Lafayette, the German Von Steuben, and the Poles Pulaski and Kosciuszko were adventurers from abroad drawn to the struggle through idealistic commitment, not the American products of separate ethnic communities.

"KNOW-NOTHINGS" AND THE REJECTION OF DIVERSITY

The citizens of the early Republic never embraced the joys of diversity and reacted with suspicion and even murderous hostility to the first major wave of dramatically distinctive immigrants.

In the 1840s, millions of Irish and Germans arrived in the United

States with a crucial difference from prior Irish and German citizens: these newcomers were overwhelmingly Catholic (the Germans mostly from Bavaria) and thus exacerbated the suspicions of a populace deeply distrustful of anything touching the Vatican. In July 1844, a series of brutal anti-Catholic riots destroyed whole neighborhoods in Philadelphia, with churches, schools, and firehouses burned to the ground; the mobilization of five thousand heavily armed militia was required to restore order. The riots began because a local bishop, Francis Kenrick, had outraged local opinion by daring to request permission for Catholic students in the public schools to use the Catholic version of Scriptures for their required daily Bible readings.

The nativist movement represented by the rioters soon swept the country under the auspices of the Order of the Star-Spangled Banner and the American Party, better known as the "Know-Nothings." Between 1854 and 1858, the rabidly anti-immigrant Know-Nothings elected mayors in Philadelphia, Chicago, Washington, D.C., and San Francisco, and elected governors in California and Massachusetts—also seizing majorities in the Massachusetts legislature.

In 1856, former president Millard Fillmore ran for the White House as the Know-Nothing candidate. His platform called for severe restrictions on future immigration, a ban on all foreign-born citizens in public office, increasing the waiting period for naturalized citizenship from five to twenty-one years, requiring public schools to hire only Protestant teachers, and mandating all schools to use only the Protestant Bible for daily Bible readings. Fillmore drew an impressive 21.6 percent of the popular vote and claimed the eight electoral votes of Maryland, finishing third behind the victorious Democrat (James Buchanan) and the first presidential candidate of the new Republican Party (John C. Frémont).

After the War Between the States, the Know-Nothing Party completely disappeared, and the nativist movement in general became an insignificant factor in American life for the next fifty years. In part, the reduction in anti-Catholic and antiforeigner sentiment stemmed from the heroic participation by immigrants in the War for the Union. Germans in particular played a stunningly disproportionate role, with their strong opposition to slavery and their impassioned support for the federal cause: 516,000 German-born soldiers participated in the war, constituting an astonishing 23.4 percent of all Union troops.

In short, the nativists didn't give up their insistent opposition to a multicultural America, but they did come to recognize that even Catholic immigrants represented no long-term threat to the old ideas of the prevailing Anglo-Protestant culture. Germans, Irish, and other newcomers proved themselves good neighbors who enthusiastically embraced an American identity without trying to impose their alien traditions on others. Know-Nothing fears about an organized conspiracy by the pope to impose his rule on the United States (the subject of innumerable tracts, speeches, and editorials for more than twenty years) proved just as groundless as the current paranoia about a secret plan for "North American Union" or "Reconquista" of the American Southwest.

"NO SUCH THING AS A HYPHENATED AMERICAN"

While the most dire Know-Nothing fears receded in the face of assimilationist immigrant attitudes, even mainstream leaders echoed nativist warnings that separate communities and identities based on national origin represented a real threat to the Republic.

In a famous 1915 address to an Irish Catholic audience, former president Theodore Roosevelt made an unforgettable and passionate plea for the ideal of one nation, indivisible:

> There is no room in this country for hyphenated Americanism. When I refer to hyphenated Americans, I do not refer to naturalized Americans. Some of the very best Americans I have ever known were naturalized Americans. Americans born abroad. But a hyphenated American is not an American at all. . . . The one absolutely certain way of bringing this nation to ruin, of preventing all possibility of its continuing to be a nation at all, would be to permit it to become a tangle of squabbling nationalities, an intricate knot of German-Americans, Irish-Americans, English-Americans, French-Americans, Scandinavian-Americans or Italian-Americans, each preserving its separate nationality, each at heart feeling more sympathy

with Europeans of that nationality, than with the other citizens of the American Republic. There is no such thing as a hyphenated American who is a good American. The only man who is a good American is the man who is an American and nothing else.

President Woodrow Wilson, TR's archrival, emphatically agreed with Roosevelt on this essential point. "Any man who carries a hyphen about with him carries a dagger that he is ready to plunge into the vitals of this Republic whenever he gets ready."

These sentiments hardly represented a new idea; throughout the period of the nation's heaviest immigration (as a percentage of the overall population) the public and our leaders expressed near-unanimous agreement on the importance of affirming American, rather than ethnic or ancestral, identification. In December 1888, Henry Cabot Lodge (later chairman of the Senate Foreign Relations Committee), gave a Forefathers' Day address in Boston, declaring:

> Let every man honor and love the land of his birth and the race from which he springs and keep their memory green. It is a pious and honorable duty. But let us have done with British-Americans and Irish-Americans and German-Americans and so on, and all be Americans. . . . If a man is going to be an American at all let him be so without any qualifying adjectives; and if he is going to be something else, let him drop the word American from his personal description.

The largest of all immigrant groups quickly embraced the assimilation and unqualified Americanism that Lodge demanded, aided by the anti-German sentiments that swept the country during World War I (when we renamed sauerkraut "liberty cabbage") and World War II. Demographers identify those of German ancestry as the largest single component of the current U.S. population, representing nearly fifty-one million individuals, or 17 percent of the total—a higher percentage than that of blacks, Latinos, Irish, or any other group. Yet few Americans of German descent (certainly not President Eisenhower) emphasize their ethnic identity or insist that they represent a separate, distinct culture within the Republic.

"INTO THE CRUCIBLE WITH YOU ALL!"

In 1908, a melodramatic update of the Romeo and Juliet story became a major stage hit and introduced a new term into the national vocabulary. The play *The Melting Pot,* by poet and novelist Israel Zangwill, told the tale of two lovers of bitterly divergent backgrounds who manage to make a new life together in New York City. The romantic hero, a composer named David who is at work on "An American Symphony," tells his lover: "Understand that America is God's Crucible, the great Melting Pot where all the races of Europe are melting and reforming! A fig for your feuds and vendettas! Germans and Frenchmen, Irishmen and Englishmen, Jews and Russians—into the Crucible with you all! God is making the American!"

Later, as the star-crossed romantics stand before the setting sun and look out at the Statue of Liberty, David waxes poetic about the red-and-orange sunset: "It's the Fires of God round His Crucible! There she lies, the great Melting Pot—Listen! Can't you hear the roaring and the bubbling? There gapes her mouth, the harbor where a thousand mammoth feeders come from the ends of the world to pour in their human freight. Here shall they all unite to build the Republic of Man and the Kingdom of God!"

This exuberant vision touched a deep chord in the nation in 1908 and still has the power to inspire a hundred years later. The ideal of the melting pot doesn't make immigrant heritage irrelevant or extinct; it incorporates those traditions into the ever-emerging identity of "the American, this new man." When asked to name classic American foods, many citizens would cite selections such as hot dogs (from frankfurters, a German import) or pizza (an obvious Italian import), if not tacos or chop suey. St. Patrick's Day now counts as an American celebration as much as an Irish one; millions of people with no drop of Hibernian blood love to participate in the yearly revelry.

In academic circles, the "mixing bowl" or "cultural mosaic" theory challenged the melting pot ideal in the 1950s and '60s. According to this theory, ethnic identity never really melted away but rather combined with other elements like the flavorful ingredients of a salad.

Refusing to Melt

Ironically, the influential writer who popularized the vision of the United States as "the Great Melting Pot" proved stubbornly unmeltable himself and never chose to make his home in the nation he most ardently admired. Born in London to Eastern European Jewish immigrants, Israel Zangwill (1864–1926) lived his life as a British subject while embracing a succession of radical and visionary causes, including pacifism, feminism, and Zionism. He broke from the mainstream Zionist movement in 1905 and led efforts to create a Jewish homeland in various territories that might prove more convenient than today's Israel—including tracts in Canada, Australia, Mexico, Uganda, and, even less promisingly, Libya and Iraq. His novel *Children of the Ghetto* won literary acclaim and achieved best-seller status, but his theatrical melodrama *The Melting Pot* became his most conspicuous success, playing to packed houses in major U.S. cities. At the premiere in Washington, D.C., on October 5, 1909, President Theodore Roosevelt leaned over the edge of his box and shouted, "That's a great play, Mr. Zangwill, that's a great play!"

In 1972, Michael Novak's influential book *The Rise of the Unmeltable Ethnics* looked at blue-collar Americans who, contrary to many expectations, stubbornly retained their Polish or Italian or Greek identity. But thirty-five years after the ethnics looked so unmeltable, Novak himself conceded that their distinctive connections with old-country norms and traditions had substantially dissolved. Intermarriage remains the most powerful engine of this process, which, as in Zangwill's play, continues its inexorable "roaring and bubbling." Among all American ethnicities (with the singular exception of African Americans) outmarriage has become a norm, not an exception—even within the Asian community (composed significantly of recent immigrants). According to 2006 statistics from the U.S. Census Bureau, a stunning 41 percent of U.S.-raised, married Asian

women had a white spouse, and demographers expect the rates of intermarriage to rise even higher.

Hispanic immigrants (illegal as well as legal) display a similar pattern
to a surprising extent. According to demographer Reynolds Farley in a
study for the Russell Sage Foundation, among native-born, married Hispanics in the age group twenty-five to thirty-four, 32 percent of both
men and women married white "Anglo" spouses. These figures call into
serious question the future of the Hispanic classification as a separate
ethnic, let alone racial, identity.

After two or at most three generations of life in the United States, all
immigrant groups (very much including Mexican Americans) largely as-
similate—learning English, participating in communal life, and clearly
identifying more with their American fellow citizens rather than the people of the old country.

The ongoing integration of extraordinarily diverse immigrant groups
continues to operate reliably, undeterred by the recent rise in the overall
percentage (to more than 13 percent) of the population that's foreign-
born. A front-page headline in *USA Today* on August 15, 2007, proclaimed
a reassuring reality: "Along a Brooklyn Avenue, a Melting Pot—and Peace."
The story featured a haunting photo of a man sitting in the window of a
barbershop, which reflected an American flag flying across the street. A
large sign in Urdu, promoting its barbers, hung in the window; a smaller
sign above it noted, "We speak English/Russian/Yiddish & Urdu."

The article's subhead read, "Enemies in other parts of the world live
in harmony here. What's their secret?" The residents of Coney Island Avenue, a "five-mile commercial strip, which is populated at various stops
by pockets of West Indians, Latinos, Pakistanis, Indians, Orthodox Jews,
Chinese, Russians, Israelis and Ukrainians," have their own theories. A
professor who rides the bus daily along the corridor credits the need to
cooperate in order to survive and get ahead. A Pakistani grocer says instead that it's because they see culturally different people sharing similar
goals. An Orthodox rabbi says community leaders labor to find cohesion;
a day care center operator says a focus on business to the exclusion of
other issues keeps neighbors cordial. The barber says there's no reason
not to be nice—for him, "hair is hair."

A consensus, in other words, seems to credit the profit motive—Crèvecoeur's historic American confidence that "here the rewards of his industry follow with equal steps the progress of his labor." A promotional slogan for Atlanta once described the Georgia metropolis as "the city too busy to hate." In the same sense, successive waves of new arrivals have proven themselves too busy to hate, too preoccupied with the absorbing and exhausting business of economic advancement to allow ethnic assertion or ancient rivalries to stand in their way. By their very choice in journeying to the United States, newcomers from anywhere seize as their own one of the most fundamental American values: the drive to advance and to climb the ladder, providing more opportunity for their children than they enjoyed themselves. A freewheeling economy that's always rewarded entrepreneurial energy allows natives and newcomers to unite (and compete) in their shared desire to make money and create wealth, the very essence of our common culture.

ENGLISH *ÜBER ALLES*

As noted, more Americans today boast German heritage than British, and yet no one could argue that the culture of the United States contains more Teutonic elements than English ones.

Despite the inane insistence of multiculturalists that no one nationality deserves primacy in terms of contemporary American identity, it's obvious that the earliest settlers from the British Isles played a wildly disproportionate role in shaping the nation. We speak English, embrace British traditions of jurisprudence and politics, even model our great universities on the medieval buildings at Oxford and Cambridge. America's British heritage isn't merely "first among equals" but the obvious standard to which all newcomers have managed to adjust.

A simple thought experiment can prove the point: Imagine (or recall) traveling to one of the English-heritage nations (Canada, Australia, or the United Kingdom) and consider your level of comfort and familiarity during your visit (even if you do have to learn to drive on the wrong side of the road). Then imagine a similar trip to Germany or China or Mexico or any nation of Africa, requiring a far more complicated adjustment for any American tourist of any ethnicity.

American society owes an incomparable debt to British culture. As David Hackett Fischer makes clear in his invaluable book *Albion's Seed,* even our sometimes mystifying and profound regional differences mirror the regional differences in England that distinguished and divided the early settlers. Astonishingly enough, scholars have recently traced baseball itself, perhaps the most sacred of all American cultural icons, to English roots—or to the "city game," played in London streets even before the first settlement at Jamestown.

In a controversial 1995 *Atlantic Monthly* article called "The Diversity Myth," Benjamin Schwartz appropriately cites our Anglo foundations:

> Although in 1790 only about 60 percent of the white U.S. population was of English origin, America was culturally quite homogeneous; most of the non-English people had lost much of their cultural distinctiveness to the unsparing dominance of the English language, customs, and institutions, and had lost much of their original genetic character to English numerical superiority. The American "nationality" was not a blending of all the peoples that populated the United States, or even an amalgam of the white Europeans inhabiting the country. An "American" was a modified Englishman. To become an American was to subject oneself to a hegemony so powerful that many Americans ignored or denied existing diversities.

In this context, today's movement for "English only" represents not some mean-spirited backlash against immigrant strivers but rather an altogether predictable reassertion of American norms. Despite efforts by politicians and business interests in banking, media, and the education establishment to appeal to the massive Spanish-speaking market, overwhelming evidence suggests that today's Latino immigrants (like all their predecessors) develop English proficiency by the third generation (at latest). Newcomers want to learn the language and folkways of America every bit as much as their native-born neighbors want them to do so.

Yes, various ethnicities eventually melt down in the "crucible" of American life, but the resulting molten metal has been poured into forms and molds shaped long ago in the British Isles.

OVERSTATING DIVERSITY

Here's another simple truth: most contemporary accounts grotesquely exaggerate the "diversity" of American life—a distortion that seems to serve the purposes of both champions of multiculturalism and its fiercest opponents. For years, we've been subjected to outrageously misleading stories about "minorities" now constituting an American "majority" and about the implacable decline of the nation's traditional white, Christian identity. These trends have led three-time presidential candidate Pat Buchanan to proclaim "the death of the West" (in the title of a best-selling book). In a more recent end-is-nigh cry of desperation (*Day of Reckoning,* 2007) Buchanan considered the shifting population figures and announced: "It is the belief of the author and premise of this book that America is indeed coming apart, decomposing, and that the likelihood of her survival as one nation through mid-century is improbable—and impossible if America continues on her current course. For we are on a path to national suicide."

When we debated these issues on my radio show, I tried to talk Pat down off the ledge, since, to paraphrase Mark Twain, reports of the demise of America's old values have been greatly exaggerated. Unfortunately, the end-of-America contingent on the hard Right (who apply race-based assumptions to classify Asian and Hispanic immigrants as largely incapable of assimilation) reinforces the multicultural mullahs of the far Left (who claim the new diversity in population figures demands the abandonment of old "Eurocentric" standards and norms).

Obviously, those on all sides who pontificate most hysterically over drastic shifts in American demographics only rarely bother to check the actual census data.

The most recent figures on U.S. racial percentages suggest that 80.1 percent of us (2006) identify ourselves as "white"; 12.8 percent say "black

American," 4.4 percent "Asian American," and (for 2005) 7.9 percent "some other race" or "two or more races."

The confusion associated with these numbers (which total, obviously, more than 100 percent) stems from the Census Bureau's laughably cautious efforts to acknowledge any and every racial combination. "For Census 2000," says the bureau's Web site, "63 possible combinations of the six basic racial categories existed, including six categories for those who report exactly one race, and 57 categories for those who report two or more races." A 2001 *Miami Herald* article counted up 126 possibilities when Hispanic/non-Hispanic options were included. "The problem . . . is that when tallying race, people can be counted up to six times, so the total of the percentages exceeds 100," the article notes. "For example, Tiger Woods would be counted four times, assuming he filled out his Census form the way he describes himself in interviews"—as "a mixture of Caucasian, black, Native American and Asian."

Since Hispanics are (rightly) not identified as a single "race" (after all, blond Cuban American movie star Cameron Diaz and Afro-Dominican baseball slugger David Ortiz hardly look like they share a racial identity), the U.S. Census allows respondents (as of the year 2000) to check as many boxes as apply. For the befuddled, its Web site painstakingly explains, "People of Hispanic origin may be of any race and should answer the question on race by marking one or more race categories shown on the questionnaire, including White, Black or African American, American Indian or Alaska Native, Asian, Native Hawaiian or Other Pacific Islander, and Some Other Race. Hispanics are asked to indicate their origin in the question on Hispanic origin, not in the question on race, because in the federal statistical system ethnic origin is considered to be a separate concept from race." Instead, the government seems to classify by language (but only if that language happens to be Spanish), lumping together people from the Caribbean, South America, Central America, Spain, Mexico, and parts of Asia, vastly different as they may be. Of the population's 14.5 percent (41.9 million) who do register as Hispanic, 48 percent of them say they are "white"—largely explaining the surprisingly high total of the overall population identifying as white.

Even with all the added choices, the notion that the United States has lost its traditional "white" majority is arrant nonsense. At the time of the Constitution, the population was 80 percent white; as of 2006, the nation self-identified as 80.1 percent "white."

By the same token, the nation remains overwhelmingly Christian (and Protestant, for that matter), despite the claims of a "post-Christian America": 79.8 percent of census respondents in 2001 identified themselves with one or another Christian denomination. Only 5.2 percent claimed membership in a non-Christian faith, with Jews (1.4 percent) the leaders in that group. Only 0.6 percent of Americans are Muslim, 0.5 percent Buddhist, and 0.4 percent Hindu.

Obviously, Third World immigration and divergent birthrates have produced a more varied and exotic population base in countless cities and suburbs: one need only consider the proliferation of foreign-language media and the explosion of ethnic restaurants even in small towns. (During my boyhood, "foreign food" meant Italian and Chinese only—who knew from Thai, Indian, Ethiopian, Mexican, and so forth?) Clearly, the immigrant influx (including more than twelve million who arrived illegally) creates major challenges for schools, workplaces, and neighborhoods. Ron Wakabayashi, executive director of the Los Angeles County Commission on Human Relations, told the *Washington Post:* "Politicians like to say that diversity is our greatest strength. That is b.s. Diversity simply is. The core question is how do we extract its assets while minimizing its liabilities."

The Great American Game may provide the Great American Answer to that question. On opening day 2008, among the 855 players on major league rosters, some 28 percent were foreign-born—or more than double the percentage in the overall population. Nevertheless, the participation of gifted athletes from Japan and Korea, Venezuela and Aruba doesn't detract from the success of a ball club or from its popularity with hometown fans. Linguistic challenges may rattle managers and coaches, but the overriding factors of common purpose (playing to win) and clearly defined rules (enforced by umpires) take precedence over any differences in culture or values. When major league ballplayers (or ordinary citizens) learn to function as part of the same team, cooperating for shared goals, then diversity of background becomes altogether irrelevant.

THE AFRICAN AMERICAN EXCEPTION

The black community remains the only important subgroup with a long-standing and current claim to a meaningfully separate cultural identity. The circumstances of African Americans have been irreducibly different from the very beginning—as the only segment of the population that didn't choose to come here, they bore stigmatization as property and less than human, and survived centuries of mistreatment through vile and violent bigotry. Not surprisingly, blacks developed a distinctive culture because of their enforced separation for hundreds of years. Nevertheless, African Americans managed to make prodigious contributions to the "melting pot" process: what we consider characteristically American music evolved largely out of ragtime, blues, and jazz, which in turn derived from ancient African traditions. In other words, for all their separate and segregated status over the centuries, blacks have played a huge if often unacknowledged role in the development of the dominant culture.

Moreover, for all the differences between the European American and African American experience, the members of both huge groups remain much closer to one another than to compatriots in former homelands across vast oceans. There's no question that I'd find far more in common with the black family up the block (or even in a faraway urban ghetto) than I would with a resident of the dreary Ukrainian village my grandfather left in 1910. Likewise, African Americans who travel in the "mother continent" (like *Washington Post* reporter Keith Richburg, author of *Out of America*) come home feeling far more American than African.

The general lack of vibrant, substantive cultural connections between American blacks and Africa may in part reflect the cruel efforts by slaveholders and other oppressors to erase the cultural legacy of the motherland, but after four hundred years on this continent no one could seriously question the American identity of our thirty-five million citizens of African ancestry. In fact, the spectacular economic and educational progress of so many African Americans over the past fifty years involves precisely those individuals who've most enthusiastically embraced that U.S. identity (in the tradition of the unabashedly American Dr. King) rather than affirming separatist notions of Afrocentrism. In noting that "diversity and immigration are not identical," Harvard's Robert Putnam remarks, "The ancestors of most African-Americans have been in the U.S. longer than the ancestors of most white Americans."

In any event, even among African Americans—our most distinctive and enduring subculture—there's never been mass support for the idea of carving out an ethnic homeland (the exclusive province of lunatics such as Louis Farrakhan) or repatriation to Mother Africa (only handfuls followed Marcus Garvey's "back to Africa" craze or supported ill-starred white efforts to forge a haven for ex-slaves in Liberia).

This means that despite the disinformation of political correctness and the regular exaggeration of U.S. diversity, our nation stands little chance of experiencing calls for dismemberment in the tradition of Czechoslovakia, Yugoslavia, Canada/Quebec, Belgium, or even England/Scotland. When America went through a wrenching, supremely bloody struggle to preserve the Union, that battle arose out of regional and political differences rather than ethnic ones. Irish and Jewish Americans, for instance, fought prominently on both sides of the War Between the States—as did African Americans, amazingly enough. While 180,000 black troops (including former slaves) fought nobly for the Union cause (see the excellent 1989 film *Glory*), an estimated 50,000 black Confederates (almost entirely "free negroes" of the time) went to battle to defend Dixie.

AMERICAN DNA

Beyond the links of culture, values, and pursuit of profit forged in the still-bubbling melting pot, new research suggests that all immigrants and descendants of immigrants may share elements of distinctively American DNA.

"A 'nation of immigrants' represents a highly skewed and unusual 'self-selected' population," writes John D. Gartner, a psychologist at Johns Hopkins University Medical School, in the 2005 book *The Hypomanic Edge: The Link Between (A Little) Craziness and (A Lot of) Success*. "Do men and women who risk everything to leap into a new world differ temperamentally from those who stay home? It would be surprising if they didn't."

Gartner applies a clinical designation—"hypomanic"—to describe those with adventurous initiative to seek a new life and a new homeland. "Hypomanics are ideally suited by temperament to become immigrants," he explains. "If you are an impulsive, optimistic, high-energy risk taker, you are more likely to undertake a project that requires a lot of energy, entails a lot of risk, and might seem daunting if you thought about it too much. . . . America has drawn hypomanics like a magnet. This wide-open land with seemingly infinite horizons has been a giant Rorschach on which they could project their oversized fantasies of success, an irresistible attraction for restless, ambitious people feeling hemmed in by native lands with comparatively fewer opportunities." Gartner uses biographies of prominent Americans (Alexander Hamilton, Andrew Carnegie, Hollywood's Selznicks and Mayers) to show how this genetically hardwired psychological proclivity—*not* a disorder, he emphasizes—propels Americans to a range of common behaviors.

But there's a second explanation for an inbred immigrant urge. "We don't know enough about the genetics of hypomania to say that it's what drives the American temperament," says Peter C. Whybrow, a psychiatrist at UCLA's Semel Institute and author of *American Mania: When More Is Not Enough* (published almost simultaneously with Gartner's *Hypomanic Edge*). "But we do know that in the American population you find a much higher prevalence of the D4-7 allele, which is the risk-taking gene. I think the factor that distinguishes the inhabitants of the United States is much more likely to be a novelty-seeking gene than some form of manic-depressive illness."

In short, increasing numbers of analysts take seriously the notion of a uniquely American DNA, demonstrating that even in our very genes, and not just our shared culture and heritage, our populace may be bound together by common traits and temperaments not present in comparable measure anywhere else on earth.

At first glance, these inherited propensities might seem to exclude African Americans, since the capture and forced transport of hundreds of thousands of their slave ancestors in no way reflected a self-selecting, risk-taking population. But a hundred years of massive immigration from the Caribbean, and more recently from every nation of Africa, scrambles the picture for blacks. A full 8 percent of today's African

Americans count as foreign-born—and more than 20 percent of the black population in Florida, New York, and New Jersey. Those who chose to migrate here from Nigeria or Eritrea, along with the grandchildren of West Indian immigrants who elected to make the journey in the early twentieth century, could well display inherited characteristics associated with whites, Asians, and Latinos who also came here through conscious and often courageous choice.

Whether it's genetically predetermined or a socially conditioned personality trait, risk taking and perseverance seem to define our national character. Americans of every origin appreciate our freedom to take the initiative, to seize control of our own situations. A nation founded upon

From Punjabi to "Good Ol' Boy"

Louisiana Republicans have never been celebrated for their enthusiastic embrace of diversity; as recently as 1991, KKK leader and former Nazi David Duke drew enough votes to become the GOP candidate in the general election (though the official party disowned him). How, then, did the "Bubba" voters of the Bayou State come to embrace the dark-skinned child of Punjabi immigrants with a given first name (Piyush) they wouldn't even try to pronounce?

Louisiana governor "Bobby" Jindal won in a landslide in 2007, and became a leading prospect for a future spot on a national ticket, by embracing down-home Americanism, not some multicultural version of his Indian American heritage. As a small boy he took the name Bobby (inspired by the character Bobby Brady on *The Brady Bunch* TV show), and in high school he converted from Hinduism to Catholicism. He visits Pentecostal and fundamentalist churches to give testimony about the role of faith in his life and touts the virtues of American—and Louisianan—values. Citizens of his state seem less interested in the fact that he's their first-ever Asian American governor than in his success as the first leader in many years to cut state spending and taxes while enacting meaningful ethics reform.

self-determination and self-government, tempered with the humility and ethics of religion, attracts people with a common energy who more easily come to share a common worldview.

THE WEAKNESS OF TOP-DOWN IDENTITIES

The thrust of our nation's history and perhaps even the genes of our bodies push us in the opposite direction from Al Gore's muddled dream of multiple American identities—"out of one, many." With political correctness bearing down on educational institutions and corporations struggling to seize any sort of competitive advantage, we must endure the current tendency to classify individuals as members of one or another group in our "beautiful mosaic"—those of mixed race, transgendered individuals, people of size, Asian–Pacific Islanders, the physically challenged, the neopagans, and countless others. Few of these current categories emerged organically or spontaneously, with significant segments of the population claiming some proud new identities and building communities accordingly. The term "white community," for instance, represents a laughable absurdity. No one says to himself, "I'm proud of my white heritage" or "I love my white brothers and sisters" (aside from a few neo-Nazis in barbed-wire compounds). The designations "Hispanic" and "Asian" amount to similarly artificial constructions: in terms of linguistic heritage, religious culture, or even physical appearance, immigrants from Pakistan and Korea may both win classification as "Asian" but will have as much in common with their Euro-American neighbors as with one another.

Ultimately the "diversity deans," multicultural consultants, and obsessive-compulsive bean counters trying to impose divisions from the top down can't stand up to the unifying force of our shared goals and character. Americans instinctively transcend all the artificially constructed cultural divides, managing to work together, live side by side, and, in increasingly significant numbers, marry one another.

With relief and confidence, we can savor even fractious intergroup disputes in these United States without serious fear of imminent fragmentation or collapse. Meanwhile, we follow disturbing developments over the many (and often armed) separatist movements in Europe, Asia, the Middle East, and Latin America, where true multiculturalism continues to bear its invariably bitter fruit. We can even watch with a touch of rue the unfolding fate of quarreling Flemings and Walloons in ill-arranged little Belgium, where the beer is stronger than any unifying nationalism and the chocolate's sweeter than the future.

"The Power of Big Business Hurts the Country and Oppresses the People"

THE ROAD TO DIVIDENDS.

"MORE MONEY THAN THE WORLD HAS EVER SEEN"

Like most other Americans of the past hundred years, I learned as a young child all about big business and its evil, destructive agenda.

To honor my sixth-grade graduation, my parents presented me with a hefty, handsome volume called *The American Past*, which instantly became my favorite history book. Along with more than a thousand stunningly evocative photos, paintings, and political cartoons, the lively text by Roger Butterfield captured my youthful imagination with its righteous denunciation of the greedy "robber barons" who wrecked the country in the shameful Gilded Age.

Under the menacing heading "The Big Business Republicans," Butterfield described this dark chapter in our history:

> The men who ran the United States from 1865 to 1900 made more
> money than the world has ever seen. They had little respect for gov-
> ernment or public opinion, which they bought and sold as they
> pleased. . . . Most Americans of the 1870s accepted the rule of big
> business as a natural and desirable thing. The Civil War and its af-
> termath had exhausted the nation's emotions and considerably tar-
> nished its ideals. . . . At the very top of the big business heap sat men
> who believed that everything they did was justified by God and the
> new Darwinian theory of evolution. . . . All Americans whose wel-
> fare did not coincide with the profits of large corporations were ful-
> filling a valuable function as victims of progress.

Of course, countless other authoritative accounts emphasized similar
frightening themes, including Howard Zinn's celebrated 1980 best seller
A People's History of the United States—widely used even today as a textbook in both high schools and colleges. Zinn begins Chapter 11 ("Robber Barons and Rebels") on an unmistakably ominous note:

> In the year 1877, the signals were given for the rest of the century:
> the black would be put back; the strikes of white workers would not
> be tolerated; the industrial and political elites of North and South
> would take hold of the country and organize the greatest march of
> economic growth in human history. They would do it with the aid
> of, and at the expense of black labor, white labor, Chinese labor, Eu-
> ropean immigrant labor, female labor, rewarding them differently
> by race, sex, national origin, and social class, in such a way as to cre-
> ate separate levels of oppression—a skillful terracing to stabilize the
> pyramid of wealth.

If anything, the general public views contemporary corporate
leaders as even more dangerous, degenerate, and scheming than the
nineteenth-century captains of industry. Ironically, the big corporations that dominate Hollywood entertainment lead the way in promul-

gating the image of businessmen as immoral, sadistic exploiters and even killers.

At the 2008 Academy Awards ceremony, major acting honors went to accomplished and terrifying performances in two anticorporate diatribes. Tilda Swinton won as Best Supporting Actress for playing an icy-veined control freak who murderously dispatches a whistle-blower threatening her cancer-causing company in *Michael Clayton,* and Daniel Day-Lewis captured the coveted Best Actor Oscar for his performance in *There Will Be Blood* as a monstrous early 1900s oilman who betrays his deaf son, abuses religious faith, kills two associates for the crime of annoying him, and lives in angry isolation amidst his stolen wealth.

Many more recent films drew equally ecstatic reviews for comparably hostile views of corporate corruption. *The Constant Gardener* (2005), for which Rachel Weisz won the Best Supporting Actress Oscar, depicted drug companies testing their products on poor Africans with deadly re-sults. "We're not killing people who wouldn't be dead otherwise," says one fictional pharmaceutical honcho with a shrug. George Clooney won Best Supporting Actor for his role in *Syriana* (also 2005), an "exposé" of Middle East violence that showed far more sympathy to suicidal jihadists than to U.S. oil companies or the CIA. In a deliberate attempt to echo the famous Gordon Gekko "greed is good" monologue from Oliver Stone's *Wall Street,* the tendentious script features a cynical energy executive singing the praises of corruption. "Corruption is our protection," says character Danny Dalton, played by Tim Blake Nelson. "Corruption keeps us safe and warm. Corruption is why you and I are prancing around in here instead of fighting over scraps of meat out in the streets. Corruption is why we win!"

According to a 2006 analysis by the Business and Media Institute of the Media Research Center ("Bad Company II: Oscar-Nominated Movies Bash Business, but Hollywood Claims That's Entertainment"), "Businessmen were depicted as criminal or simply unethical four times as often . . . as they were portrayed in a positive light." The report notes that "the list of their crimes was staggering, including drug use, drug smuggling, prostitution, corruption, assault, attempted murder, murder and genocide."

Few films (or books), for that matter, went further in indicting big business than the acclaimed 2004 documentary *The Corporation,* featuring interviews with some of the most influential intellectuals of our time, including Noam Chomsky, Michael Moore, and Kathie Lee Gifford. Reviewer Mick LaSalle of the *San Francisco Chronicle* praised the picture for "illustrating the tendencies of the modern corporation—the placing of money ahead of human health and safety, the ruthless pursuit of profit, the disregard for the community, the environment and animal life, etc. . . . Viewers come away with the uneasy sense that the defeat of communism may very well have cleared the way for another form of heartless, godless totalitarianism to threaten freedom—governments of the corporations, by the corporations and for the corporations."

No wonder *corporation* has become a dirty word to so many Americans. A Pew Research Center poll reported in 2005 that "favorable opinions of business corporations are at their lowest point in two decades." By 2008, Gallup reported corrosive hostility to big business in general, with only 20 percent of the public expressing "a great deal" or "quite a lot" of confidence in major corporations. Of sixteen American institutions, only HMOs and Congress scored worse.

Contempt and distrust toward major business organizations spread and intensify every year—despite the undeniable fact that these companies make possible our productivity, pleasures, and private opportunities. Big corporations provide virtually all the commodities and comforts we consume—including the slick, business-bashing movies unleashed by major Hollywood conglomerates on a regular basis.

Just look at the variety of technologies that enable me to write—and you to read—these words. Leave aside the stunningly complex computer hardware and software that allow me to transfer my thoughts to a word processor and send them across a continent to my publisher when I'm through. I'm also relying on a light fixture and bulb above my desk to illuminate it and electricity to drive the light and the computer; on the books stacked on the filing cabinet behind me, printed and distributed across the country; on the paper and the pens that allowed the scribbled notes; and, very significantly, on the ceramic mug filled with steaming coffee, made with beans brought from far corners of the globe, then roasted and packaged and finally brewed in the wonderfully efficient coffeemaker stored beneath our kitchen sink.

The most eloquent explanation of benevolent corporate power came from the late economist Milton Friedman in his invaluable PBS series *Free to Choose*. Holding up an ordinary pencil and speaking directly to the camera, the Nobel Prize winner ruminated over its origins:

> There's not a single person in the world who can make this pencil. Remarkable statement? Not at all. The wood from which it's made, for all I know, came from a tree that was cut down in the state of Washington. To cut down that tree, it took a saw. To make a saw, it took steel. To make the steel, it took iron ore. This black center— we call it lead, but it's really graphite, compressed graphite—I'm not sure where it comes from, but I think it comes from some mines in South America. This red top up here, the eraser, bit of rubber, probably comes from a land where the rubber tree isn't even native, and is imported from South America by some businessmen with the help of the British government. This brass barrel? I haven't the slightest idea where it came from, or the yellow paint, or the paint that made the black lines, or the glue that holds it together. Literally thousands of people cooperated to make this pencil—people who don't speak the same language, who practice different religions, who might *hate* one another if they ever met. . . . What brought them together and induced them to cooperate to make this pencil? There was no commissar sending out orders from some central office. It was the magic of the price system, the impersonal operation of prices that brought them together and got them to cooperate to make this pencil so you could have it for a trifling sum. That is why the operation of the free market is so essential—not only to promote productive efficiency, but even more to foster harmony and peace among the peoples of the world.

The "trifling sum" Dr. Friedman described has remained surprisingly stable at about ten cents—barely a minute of labor for a typical American worker. Corporations—some of them spanning the globe with their operations—make possible this miracle of cooperation that places the marvelously functional writing implement into your hand.

And yet we take for granted the stunning ingenuity behind these achievements and commonly curse the productive big businesses that enrich our lives with untold options and efficiencies. Prominent commentators, politicians, academics, activists, and malcontents of both Left and Right never tire of deriding for-profit companies as some parasitic alien life-form that devours honest toil, crushes creativity, pollutes the environment, and steals power from ordinary Americans.

A few irresistible truths about corporate power in the United States can liberate everyday citizens (if not the most "enlightened" intellectuals) from such sour and ungrateful folly.

CORPORATIONS SETTLED THE CONTINENT

Though many of today's young idealists recoil at the very mention of the term *corporation*, it was precisely such business organizations—for-profit ventures that raised investment money by selling shares—that planned and established the early settlements that eventually became the United States.

As early as 1606, King James I chartered the Virginia Company, which consisted of a pair of corporations, for the express purpose of "planting" the Jamestown and Plymouth colonies. Those famous settlements, as well as the later Massachusetts Bay Colony (and Walter Raleigh's celebrated but doomed outpost at Roanoke), all depended on British investors who put up the considerable capital to fund the expensive business of sending "venturers" across the ocean. Of course, some of the sponsors shared religious ideals with the settlers they recruited, but they all cherished the (often frustrated) hope of earning handsome returns on their risky investments.

As the colonies flourished between 1700 and 1776, British authorities granted just seven new corporate charters; most new enterprises required only modest capital and relied on a few wealthy merchants as bankers and insurers. But then American independence brought explosive growth in internal development and entrepreneurial activity. In *The Rise of the American Business Corporation* (2001), Richard Tedlow reports that during the period between the end of the Revolutionary War in 1783 and the inauguration of Jefferson in 1801, "nearly 350 enterprises were incorporated." Pulitzer Prize winner Walter McDougall comments in *Freedom Just Around the Corner* (2005), "Even the rich few could not have raised the capital needed to develop the continent if deprived of the right to sell stocks and bonds to the many."

After 1815, Tedlow points out, $118 million was poured into creating canals, which allowed water travel where natural rivers did not exist. But the improvement in transportation made possible by trains was exponential—as was the need for cash to pay it. In this feverish climate during the 1840s and '50s, more than $1 *billion* in investments powered private railroad corporations, and backers seeking involvement in the thrilling new ventures led to the flowering of Wall Street as the center of buying and selling.

THE FOUNDERS ATTACKED GOVERNMENT, NOT BUSINESS

Today's anticorporate activists love to invoke the Boston Tea Party as inspiration for their various boycotts and demonstrations against the high price of oil, gas-guzzling SUVs, unhealthful fast foods, or sweatshop-produced clothing.

Colonial patriots, however, saw themselves as pro-business but antigovernment. The Sons of Liberty and others who organized the Stamp Act Protests, the Boston Tea Party, and other colonial challenges to British authority aimed their wrath (and occasional property destruction) not at traders or merchants but at British officials who insisted on telling the colonists what they could buy and how much they must pay.

In the Declaration of Independence, Thomas Jefferson specifically condemned King George III for "imposing taxes on us without our consent" and for sending his tax collectors to interfere with commerce: "He has erected a multitude of New Offices, and sent hither swarms of Officers to harass our People, and eat out their substance." Any contemporary American who has faced an IRS audit can relate to Jefferson's complaint. The Declaration also attacked the king for his protectionist export-import policy and "for cutting off our Trade with all parts of the world."

The Founding Fathers never embraced antibusiness attitudes because most of them were themselves entrepreneurs. George Washington and John Hancock may have been the two richest men in the colonies. Washington, who loved speculating on frontier real estate, became one of America's largest landholders. After retiring from the presidency, he turned one of his five farms into a distillery and became, according to John H. Fund in the *Wall Street Journal*, "probably the No. 1 whiskey producer" in all of America. Fund quotes Jim Rees, executive director of the Mount Vernon estate: "He was a true disciple of the free enterprise system, and he sensed that our new system of government would encourage people to think creatively, take chances and invest."

Hancock, the president of the Continental Congress who placed his flamboyantly oversized signature at the top of the Declaration of Independence, owned America's most formidable fleet of merchant ships. He had learned how to run a big business from his uncle, successful tea and mercantile importer-exporter Thomas Hancock, who adopted him upon the death of his clergyman father. At age twenty-seven, upon his uncle's death, he inherited the family business, and quickly earned a reputation for fairness and business acumen. His resistance to King George's increasingly outrageous taxes led to the seizure of his ship *Liberty;* in reaction he started smuggling in necessities such as tea, lead, paper, and glass, encouraging Boston colonists to rally against the crown and ultimately rebel.

The Founders' desire to establish a stable, prosperous business climate led to their dissatisfaction with the ineffective government under the Articles of Confederation and animated their intention to write a strong, new federal Constitution in 1787. Not surprisingly, the resulting document emphasized their commercial concerns: when laying out the powers of the new Congress, they addressed all of the first eight provisions of Article 1, section 8 to the economic system ("power to lay and collect taxes," "to establish . . . uniform laws on the subject of bankruptcies," "to coin money," and so forth) before finally covering such matters as setting up courts and raising an army.

THE WORST OF THE "ROBBER BARONS" ·
ABUSED POLITICS, NOT MARKETS

Popular historians such as Roger Butterfield and Howard Zinn love to vilify America's "robber barons," the notoriously greedy, predatory capitalists who dominated the late nineteenth century while allegedly corrupting our government and exploiting the public. The term "robber barons" first appeared in an angry Kansas tract of 1880 denouncing the high fees that local railroads imposed on struggling farmers. The title deliberately recalled the arrogant, medieval German warlords who extorted high fees from ships passing through sections of the Rhine under their feudal control. In 1934, radical New York journalist Matthew Josephson—an open sympathizer with the Communist Party—revived and popularized the phrase as the title of his disdainful but wonderfully readable account of the titans of nineteenth-century commerce. At the height of the Great Depression, with FDR himself denouncing the "economic royalists" who resisted his governmental expansion, New Dealers seized upon the epithet "robber barons" to attack most major industrial and banking figures, thereby implying that they accumulated their vast fortunes through illicit and extortionist tactics.

In fact, many of the allegedly evil "robber barons" succeeded because they brought valuable services and goods—and low prices—to American consumers, not because they oppressed the masses. In his indispensable book *The Myth of the Robber Barons,* Burton W. Folsom of the University of Pittsburgh makes the important distinction between "political entrepreneurs" and "market entrepreneurs," who played very different roles in the development of the new nation and its economy. The political entrepreneurs manipulated their insider influence in Washington and in state capitals, relying on sweetheart deals, special concessions, and government-granted monopoly power rather than their own efficiency and competitive advantages. In contrast, market entrepreneurs—including so-called robber barons such as steamship pioneer Cornelius Vanderbilt and railroad builder James J. Hill—refused to entangle themselves with the political process and built their much more successful and durable corporations without favoritism from bureaucrats or officeholders.

As Folsom writes of the emerging and crucial steamship industry: "Political entrepreneurship often led to price-fixing, technological stagnation, and the bribing of competitors and politicians. The market entrepreneurs were the innovators and rate-cutters. They had to be to survive against subsidized opponents." Vanderbilt's efficiency allowed him to undercut fares charged by government-backed lines, which not only gave consumers a better deal but also "marked the end of political entrepreneurship in the American steamship business."

Significantly, all of the most important economic reform movements, from the Jeffersonians at the turn of the nineteenth century up through the early Progressives at the turn of the twentieth, sought to disentangle government from the free market, not to impose new bureaucratic controls. As the great historian Forrest McDonald wrote: "The Jacksonian Democrats engaged in a great deal of anti-business rhetoric, but the results of their policies were to remove or reduce governmental interference into private economic activity, and thus to free market entrepreneurs to go about their creative work. The entire nation grew wealthy as a consequence."

CORPORATE POWER BROUGHT PROGRESS, NOT OPPRESSION

Ubiquitous lies about "robber barons" reflect larger distortions about the Gilded Age, in which they reshaped the country. While leftist historians have always derided the era following the War Between the States as a time of corruption and complacency, no single generation in human history raised living standards more rapidly, absorbed and assimilated comparable waves of immigration, settled more vast and remote frontiers, built as many new states and glittering cities, or brought a nation so quickly to the top rank of world power.

In the introduction to their book *The Confident Years,* about U.S. life from 1865 to 1914, the editors of *American Heritage* magazine enthused: "It was a period of exuberant growth, in population, industry and world prestige. As the twentieth century opened, American political pundits were convinced that the nation was on an ascending spiral of progress that could end only in something approaching perfection. Even those who saw the inequity between the bright world of privilege and the gray fact of poverty were quite sure that a time was very near when no one would go cold or hungry or ill clothed. These were indeed the Confident Years." In other words, an era of rampant capitalist power that saw the emergence of giant corporations that touched the lives of every American corresponded with the most dynamic and dazzling achievements in our history.

Of course, the period also witnessed a surge in radicalism (among both agrarian populists and urban unionists) and a good deal of labor unrest. But Harvard historian Crane Brinton *(The Anatomy of Revolution)* pointed out that revolutionary sentiments generally develop in periods of long-term economic progress, not abject deprivation. When business produces a sharp increase in living standards, the "revolution of rising expectations" leaves workers and farmers impatient for more rapid advancement.

The working class, in fact, benefited mightily from the explosive growth of the Gilded Age. As Gary Walton and Hugh Rockoff document in their *History of the American Economy,* between 1860 and 1890 real wages (adjusted for inflation) increased by a staggering 50 percent in America. Meanwhile, the average workweek shortened, meaning that the real earnings of the average American worker increased by something more like 60 percent in just thirty years.

Moreover, many other eras associated with big business have brought extraordinary prosperity to the nation at large and the great majority of its citizens—such as the 1920s, when President Calvin Coolidge produced snickers from cognoscenti by saying, "The chief business of the American people is business," and the 1950s, when Defense Secretary (and former General Motors CEO) Charles ("Engine Charlie") Wilson purportedly declared, "What's good for General Motors is good for America." His actual statement, "For years I thought what was good for the country was good for General Motors and vice versa," sounds far more reasonable, but either way the equation makes sense. How could a positive development for one of the nation's most significant corporate employers, producing affordable cars for the masses, possibly fail to benefit the nation at large?

Our current situation unfortunately illustrates the opposite formulation: what's bad for General Motors has unequivocally proven bad for America, as any recent trip to Detroit, the onetime "Motor City," will instantly reveal.

CORPORATE GROWTH BRINGS CHEAPER GOODS, WITH BETTER JOBS

Thomas J. DiLorenzo, economics professor at Loyola College in Maryland, highlights the deeper impact of corporate expansion. "Capitalism improves the quality of life for the working class not just because it leads to improved wages but also because it produces new, better, and cheaper goods," he writes in his 2005 book *How Capitalism Saved America.* "When Henry Ford first started selling automobiles only the relatively wealthy could afford them, but soon enough working-class families were buying his cars."

The efficiency and productivity made possible by corporate organization gave typical Americans a range of choices and an economic power unimaginable for prior generations. Federal Reserve Board economists W. Michael Cox and Richard Alm make this clear in their book *Myths of Rich and Poor:*

> A nineteenth-century millionaire couldn't grab a cold drink from the refrigerator. He couldn't hop into a smooth-riding automobile for a 70-mile-an-hour trip down an interstate highway to the mountains or seashore. He couldn't call up news, movies, music and sporting events by simply touching the remote control's buttons. He couldn't jet north to Toronto, south to Cancun, east to Boston or west to San Francisco in just a few hours. . . . He couldn't run over to the mall to buy auto-focus cameras, computer games,

mountain bikes, or movies on videotape. He couldn't escape the summer heat in air conditioned comfort. He couldn't check into a hospital for a coronary bypass to cure a failing heart, get a shot of penicillin to ward off infection, or even take aspirin to relieve a headache.

Jeremiads about the "horrifying" gap between rich and poor miss this point—that poor people in America's twenty-first century enjoy options and privileges that even the wealthiest couldn't claim a hundred years ago. Far from oppressing the working class, the corporate system has vastly improved the purchasing power of all Americans. Cox and Alm note that a worker in 1900 labored two hours and forty minutes to earn the cost of a three-pound chicken; in 1999, a mere twenty-four minutes of toil could buy him the bird. If anything, the growth in rewards for working have only accelerated in the past fifty years. In 1950, typical workers put in more than two hours to afford 100 kilowatts of electricity; by 1999, the cost had dropped to fourteen minutes.

As business success made consumer goods steadily more affordable, the corporate heads who directed that process made cultural resources steadily more accessible. Writing of the mighty industrialists of the last century, John Steele Gordon notes in *An Empire of Wealth* that "the people who were building great fortunes began to found or endow museums, concert halls, orchestras, colleges, hospitals, and libraries in astonishing numbers in every major city. [Andrew] Carnegie had written that 'a man who dies rich, dies disgraced,' and gave away nearly his entire fortune, building more than five thousand town libraries among numerous other beneficiaries." These institutions continue to serve Americans today, enhancing the lives of rich and poor, who can still view the magnificent art collections of Henry Clay Frick, J. P. Morgan, and J. Paul Getty. In his ninety-seven years of prodigiously eventful living, John D. Rockefeller not only endowed the Rockefeller Foundation and international campaigns against numerous diseases but also built the University of Chicago, Rockefeller University, Acadia National Park in Maine, Colonial Williamsburg in Virginia, Rockefeller Center, the Museum of Modern Art, and the Cloisters of the Metropolitan Museum of Art, among many public resources.

"What He Had Done to Get That Money"

Andrew Carnegie (1835–1919) earned universal praise with his prodigious philanthropy—building more than three thousand public libraries in forty-seven states (and other nations around the world), founding the Carnegie Institute of Technology (now part of Carnegie Mellon University), and establishing Carnegie Hall in New York, the Carnegie Endowment for International Peace, and much more. Antibusiness bias, however, leads many observers to speculate that he turned to charity in order to assuage his guilt over his success as a captain of industry. For a 1999 PBS *American Experience* program about the impoverished Scottish immigrant who became "the richest man in the world," biographer Joseph Frazier Wall suggested: "Maybe with the giving away of his money, he would justify what he had done to get that money."

And what had he done, exactly?

When Carnegie retired at age sixty-six (and sold his business to J. P. Morgan and associates to create the vast new company U.S. Steel), he employed 31,162 full-time workers at three major mills. His organizational genius helped create the steel business that played a crucial role in American industrialization and prosperity. However laudable his charitable endeavors (he managed to give away nearly all his money before he died at eighty-three), the creation of jobs and wealth in his business career benefited his countrymen even more.

THE FALSE CHOICE OF "PEOPLE VS. PROFITS"

Adam Smith defined capitalism more than two hundred years ago in *The Wealth of Nations*, describing the essence of the system as a series of mutually beneficial agreements: "Give me that which I want, and you shall have this which you want." This captures the essential fairness and decency of the free-market system, which relies on voluntary associations that enrich both parties.

Concerning the process of industrialization, which saw millions of workers powering the engines of major corporations, the great economist Ludwig von Mises trenchantly observed:

The factory owners did not have the power to compel anybody to take a factory job. They could only hire people who were ready to work for the wages offered to them. Low as these wage rates were, they were nonetheless much more than these paupers could earn in any other field open to them. It is a distortion of facts to say that the factories carried off the housewives from the nurseries and the kitchens and the children from their play. These women had nothing to cook with and to feed their children. These children were destitute and starving. Their only refuge was the factory. It saved them, in the strict sense of the term, from death by starvation.

The same process applies to newly opened factories throughout the developing world today, despite the efforts by antiglobalist and anticorporate activists in the United States to obliterate the only jobs that keep suffering millions from a return to misery and destitution. But corporations have also begun responding to consumers' increasing calls for goods labeled "fair trade," which, according to the International Fair Trade Association, indicates that the items come from organizations that display "concern for the social, economic and environmental well-being of marginalized small producers and don't maximise profit at their expense." In October 2007 the *New York Times* reported that Sam's Club, Dunkin' Donuts, McDonald's, and Starbucks already sell some fair trade coffee, and that "dozens of other products, including tea, pineapples, wine and flowers, are certified by organizations that visit farmers to verify that they are meeting the many criteria that bar, among other things, the use of child labor and harmful chemicals." Corporations' response to market-driven demand for goods produced under equitable circumstances illustrates their ability to improve the lives of both suppliers and consumers, thereby "doing well by doing good."

At the end of the day, corporations exist not in order to provide welfare for workers or cheap products for consumers but rather to earn profits for investors and operators. If they succeed in earning such profits, they can provide more jobs at higher pay, and better products at lower cost. If a company fails at bringing in those profits, it will shed jobs and provide fewer products—ultimately going out of business altogether.

The idea that laborers or customers somehow benefit if a corporation feels squeezed or faces shrinking profits remains one of the profoundly illogical legacies of discredited Marxism. If governmental regulators crack down on a given company, they most often harm, rather than help, the interests of its workers (and shareholders, obviously). In the free-market system, the boss, Peter, can't benefit in the long term at the expense of his employee Paul. They either prosper together or fail together. Increased profitability brings increases in capital that allow increases in productivity—directly and simultaneously rewarding management and labor (not to mention the public at large). Political demagogues who rail against "immoral" or "obscene" profits need courses in remedial economics. For a corporation, only a lack of profitability counts as immoral, and going out of business represents the ultimate obscenity.

Nevertheless, politicians and activists continue to call for the government to regulate the business world in order to spur efficiency and innovation, or even to replace the private sector altogether. A notable example involves the demands for government to force development of new technologies for energy independence, even though there's no historical precedent to support the idea that bureaucratic dictates will work better than the profit motive in bringing industrial breakthroughs. Senator Jay Rockefeller, Democrat of West Virginia, commented in April 2008 that he wanted the feds to control all energy innovations because he believed "the public" should own all resulting patents. If his great-grandfather John D. Rockefeller had followed the same logic, he couldn't have developed the remarkable system of petroleum refinement and delivery that Senator Jay now seeks to replace.

IS BIG BUSINESS REALLY WORSE THAN SMALL BUSINESS?

An August 2007 *Wall Street Journal*/NBC News poll showed that the public felt much more confidence in "small businesses" (54 percent) than "large corporations" (11 percent). Politicians invariably echo and pander to these preferences, describing the small-business owner as plucky, heroic, and a blessing to his community, while speaking of big business as some sort of enemy to the public interest.

This makes little sense, since every big business started out as a small operation before success brought growth, and virtually every small business dreams of getting bigger one day. Not far from my home stands the original Starbucks coffee shop (still operating) at Seattle's Pike Place Market: a cramped and unprepossessing shop that couldn't accommodate more than twenty customers at a time. Did that quaint operation, launched in 1971, do a better job providing brewed beverages to its patrons than today's multibillion-dollar, globe-straddling colossus with fifteen thousand stores in forty-four countries? Any coffee connoisseur regards the now universal availability of strong, fragrant gourmet java as one of the major improvements in American life over the past twenty years.

Could any sane observer honestly believe that a small business could do a better job than big international companies in providing us with the automobiles and computers and cell phones and medical supplies that do so much to enrich our lives?

And what of the huge corporations that brought the upgrade in lifestyle that occurred in the early twentieth century? Henry Ford's innovations and ceaseless expansion enabled America to shift within a single generation from horse-drawn transportation to automobiles built on assembly lines. "Declining production costs allowed Ford to cut automobile prices—six times between 1921 and 1925," notes Digital History, a consortium of university and governmental databases. "The cost of a new Ford was reduced to just $290. This amount was less than three months' wages for an average American worker; it made cars affordable for the average family." Amazingly enough, the cost of a no-frills, entry-level car remains shockingly stable nearly a century later—still costing about three months' wages (roughly $12,000) for the typical worker.

Ford's growth also led to innovations that benefited his workforce. Digital History reports that he "introduced a minimum wage of $5 in 1914—twice what most workers earned—and shortened the workday from nine hours to eight hours. Twelve years later, Ford reduced his work week from six days to five days." None of this would have been possible had the Ford company remained a small business. As Digital History writes, "Ford demonstrated the dynamic logic of mass production: that expanded production allows manufacturers to reduce costs, and therefore, increases the number of products sold; and that higher wages allow workers to buy more products." This in turn enabled the nation's westward expansion and the creation of suburbs. Car-owning families enjoyed vastly enhanced options in their choice of vacations and began the American obsession with camping in national parks and other places of scenic beauty. The trucking industry allowed Americans far from the source of products to partake of a wide variety of items never before available.

A massive company with national aspirations proved essential to the rapid proliferation of another technology that dramatically changed life for ordinary Americans: the telephone. Gardiner Hubbard founded the Bell Telephone Company in 1877 and moved quickly to connect users— setting up the first manual switchboard by 1878, establishing telephone service between Boston and Providence by 1881 and between New York and Chicago by 1892, and stringing overhead wires across the nation, coast to coast, by 1915. In 1880, just 47,900 telephones were in use; by 1920, nearly 3.9 million were in use, meaning that "one individual in every eight in the United States has a telephone," as the *Washington Post* reported that year; by 1930, half of American households had phones. What had begun as a small business inevitably and appropriately gave way to consolidated enterprises that could connect the nation.

CORRUPTION PLAGUES BIG GOVERNMENT MORE THAN BIG BUSINESS

In recent years a series of tawdry and destructive corporate scandals (Enron, Tyco, WorldCom, and many more) has led the commentariat to conclude that we need to turn to government to redeem and purify a hopelessly corrupt and compromised business world. This assumption ignores the long history of hideous corruption in every endeavor of flawed humanity—including religion, education, charities, and, most spectacularly, government itself. Giving public officials, elected or appointed, the power to decide winners and losers in the business world—by offering tax breaks and subsidies on one hand and regulatory citations and fines on the other—makes the temptations for bribery and favoritism become more acute, not less so. This means that efforts to "clean up" the business world with increases in regulation, supervision, or investigation often lead to more mess and less efficiency as business leaders try to balance the sometimes contradictory demands of meddling bureaucrats and market forces.

The idea that every government official counts as all-wise and incorruptible makes no more sense than the assumption that each corporate honcho displays flawless judgment and stainless ethics. But the market system allows the public greater and swifter recourse against an abusive or inefficient corporation than it does against an abusive or inefficient government. The customer can always decline to patronize a business, a product, or a service he dislikes, but with a dysfunctional government you're stuck till the next election—or long after that, in this era of entrenched and immovable bureaucratic power. A determined individual can escape the reach of even the most ubiquitous business, but the only way to choose a different national government is to flee the country. Yes, corporate power can corrupt government, and government power even more frequently corrupts and warps corporations, but the best way to avoid this mutually destructive influence is to bring about less bureaucratic involvement in the free market, not to insist on more.

ESCAPING "URINETOWN"

Contemptuous hostility to big business has become so reflexive, so ubiquitous, that it's infected even the poshest precincts of Broadway, where prized theater tickets cost so much (more than a hundred bucks a pop) that those who can afford them most probably draw wealth from major corporations as employees or investors.

For several years elite audiences flocked to an edgy, Tony Award–winning musical aptly described by the *Seattle Times* as "a keen satire that targets corporate greed." In *Urinetown,* a twenty-year drought and a desperate water shortage lead an all-powerful corporation (Urine Good Company, or UGC) to ban private toilets and to charge exorbitant fees for the public facilities they control. Anyone daring to seek unauthorized relief faces exile to the dreaded penal colony (no pun intended) Urinetown, from which no prisoner ever returns. Naturally, the oppressed citizens revolt, hoping to relieve themselves of corporate domination and create a brave new world where each man and woman is free to pee.

Audiences and critics loved this dark, raucous morality play, hailing its daring messages against "capitalist control" and its "Brechtian style" (invoking the memory of Bertolt Brecht, onetime East German Communist apparatchik and author of *The Rise and Fall of the City of Mahagonny*). *Urinetown* earned a startling ten Tony nominations and won for Best Original Musical Score and Best Book of a Musical.

The happy crowds that left the show humming "Follow Your Heart" or "It's a Privilege to Pee" might not have thought too deeply about its messages, but if they had, they might have considered that corporations in the real world made their money building bathroom fixtures and usable toilets, not controlling private urinary behavior. The Kohler Company and others produced great fortunes crafting precisely the sort of comfortable private facilities that the fictional company in the show banned.

In the actual New York outside the theater, the only public toilets you could find as stinky and unhygienic as the ones in the musical would have been those operated by some branch of government. Any self-respecting and profit-driven corporation would have promptly cleaned them up.

"Government Programs Offer the Only Remedy for Economic Downturns and Poverty"

"NO MORE EXCUSES!"

As part of her 2008 presidential campaign, Hillary Clinton made a bold pledge to appoint a new "secretary of poverty" who could promptly end the suffering of America's poor. Speaking in Memphis to honor the fortieth anniversary of the assassination of Dr. Martin Luther King Jr., the New York senator claimed that she, too, had a dream.

"I believe we should appoint a cabinet-level position that will be solely and fully devoted to ending poverty as we know it in America!" she cried, her voice rising in intensity. "A position that will focus the attention of our nation on the issue and never let it go. A person who I could see being asked by the president every single day, 'What have you done to end poverty in America?' No more excuses! No more whining, but instead a concerted effort."

Her former rival for the Democratic nomination John Edwards immediately endorsed the idea. "America's need to address the great moral issue of poverty demands strong action," he commented in a formal statement, "and a cabinet-level poverty position is exactly that kind of action."

To a pair of the nation's leading politicians, in other words, the mere gesture of creating a new job in the bureaucracy amounted to "strong action." They seemed altogether unconcerned with the fact that the only American sure to feel the impact of such "action" would be the individual hired to fill the position.

The call for a new Department of Poverty follows the less-than-inspiring national experience with a slew of other recent cabinet additions. Even the most fervent believer in ambitious and expensive federal initiatives must concede that President Carter's much-ballyhooed 1979 creation of the Department of Education never produced the promised renaissance in public schools—despite its current employment of five thousand full-time Washington bureaucrats and annual expenditures of more than $70 billion of the people's money.

Nevertheless, many Americans instinctively approve the concept of a new Department of Poverty because they accept the idea that government programs provide the best—and perhaps only—way to cope with economic hardship and the problems of the poor.

This conviction rests on a widely embraced narrative concerning the nation's past that's dramatic, inspiring . . . and wrong.

AFFECTIONATE, FALSE MEMORIES

Most Americans who claim to know anything at all about the Great Depression tend to recite the same familiar story line with reverence and gratitude.

First came the fat cats and speculators whose lusty, unrestrained greed characterized the Roaring Twenties, leading to a stock market crash and hard times. Banks closed, stockbrokers jumped out of upper-story windows, and once-prosperous workers sold apples on street corners or became hobos in shantytowns while Republican Herbert Hoover sulked in the White House and did nothing to aid his stricken country. Then FDR arrived on the scene, crippled in body but soaring in spirit, inspiring instantaneous new hope with his golden words ("the only thing we have to fear is fear itself") and a flurry of radical reforms in his first hundred days in office. While conservatives squealed, this "new deal for the American people" improved the lives of common people and got the economy humming again—just in time to face the challenges of World War II. No wonder a grateful nation rewarded Franklin Roosevelt with an unprecedented four terms—and a consistent ranking as one of our three greatest presidents (along with Washington and Lincoln).

Like most other baby boomers who arrived on the scene some time after the war, I learned this story from parents and grandparents who had lived it, not just from history teachers in school. My grandparents on my father's side, immigrants from Ukraine, became naturalized citizens in part to vote for Roosevelt, their idol and inspiration. In their cramped row-house home in a gritty neighborhood of South Philadelphia, they always kept a heroic black-and-sepia portrait of FDR over the mantelpiece, encased in a dime-store brass frame with a cracked pane of glass. My immigrant grandfather was a barrel maker who managed to keep working throughout the Depression, so he never benefited personally from New Deal programs, but he revered the thirty-second president for his general support for "the little guy" and apparent sympathy to newcomers to the country. My father recalled April 12, 1945, the day of Roosevelt's sudden, shocking death from a cerebral hemorrhage, as one of the darkest occasions of his life: FDR, who'd taken office shortly after my dad's seventh birthday, had been the only president he could remember. As a nineteen-year-old member of the U.S. Navy, my father joined other sailors at his San Francisco base in weeping openly at the loss of their commander in chief.

These affectionate memories of Roosevelt's undeniable charisma and charm have led all succeeding generations to learn false lessons about the right way to deal with hard times and poverty. These assumptions continue to shape political debate, especially at times of slow growth or recession, when Democrats love to recall the stirring days of the New Deal and to hail each "redemptive" leader as the second coming of FDR.

At fund-raisers for liberal candidates, Barbra Streisand regularly thrills Democratic donors with her yearning, slow-tempo, heart-wrenching, torch-song rendition of Roosevelt's campaign song, "Happy Days Are Here Again." The message suggests that if only governmental control returned to the enlightened heirs of FDR, then, yes indeed, "the skies above would clear again."

Campaigning for president in 1992, Bill Clinton promised to rescue the wounded nation from "the worst economy in fifty years," and twelve years later, John Kerry similarly claimed that we faced "the worst economy since the Great Depression"; both candidates explicitly compared their incumbent opponents to the hapless Herbert Hoover. In an attempt to recapture the magical impact of Roosevelt's First Inaugural Address, with its stirring declaration that "this nation asks for action, and action now," Bill Clinton announced in *his* First Inaugural Address in 1993, "To renew America, we must be bold," and he cited FDR's own commitment to "bold, persistent experimentation."

He also included one puzzling and singularly disturbing sentence: "We must provide for our nation the way a family provides for its children."

In other words, he viewed his fellow citizens—or at least many of his fellow citizens—as helpless kids who couldn't support themselves. But whom did Clinton have in mind when he said *"we* must provide"? The context suggests that he referred to his own new administration, elected officials who would play the role of hardworking parents devoting themselves to caring for kids who weren't yet ready to enter the workforce or to stand on their own.

The problem with the entire analogy is that real mothers and fathers engage in productive toil, creating wealth that they proudly use to support their own offspring. Politicos and bureaucrats, on the other hand, create no wealth through their governmental efforts but rather tax (that is, seize) the resources earned by others, then divert those funds to benefit their chosen "children." It's not an example of wholesome traditional values but rather a model of a deeply dysfunctional family.

During the Depression, Roosevelt played the role of that ultimate father figure, taking imperious control of money generated by society's most productive elements and then distributing it in an often arbitrary and quixotic manner to his government's favored factions. He launched so many new federal programs that were familiarly designated by their initials that commentators talked admiringly of FDR's "alphabet soup"— even though this potage offered only questionable nourishment.

According to conventional wisdom and nostalgic reminiscence, this unprecedented deployment of aggressive, sweeping governmental power restored vigor to the economy and confidence to the nation while improving the lives of the suffering masses. But such conclusions rest upon a foundation of myths, distortions, half-truths, and outright lies.

In truth, the New Deal shows the same disturbing results as other attempts to use the brute force of the federal government to provide economic advancement to the less fortunate (including, most notably, the Great Society's War on Poverty): higher tax burdens and a corresponding loss of liberty, with little gain—and sometimes serious damage—for the intended beneficiaries of bureaucratic largesse.

DELAYED RECOVERY, PROLONGED DEPRESSION

In 1931, in some of the darkest days of the Great Depression and the middle of the Hoover administration, the national unemployment rate stood at 17.4 percent. Seven years later, after more than five years of FDR and literally hundreds of wildly ambitious new government programs, after more than a doubling of federal spending, the national unemployment rate stood at—17.4 percent! As economist Jim Powell points out in his devastating book *FDR's Folly,* "From 1934 to 1940, the median annual unemployment rate was 17.2 percent. At no point during the 1930s did unemployment go below 14 percent. Even in 1941, amidst the military buildup for World War II, 9.9 percent of American workers were unemployed. Living standards remained depressed until after the war."

In his celebrated First Inaugural Address of March 4, 1933, FDR unequivocally declared: "Our greatest primary task is to put people to work. This is no unsolvable problem if we face it wisely and courageously."

But for the president and his economic planners, the task of putting people to work *did* remain an unsolvable problem—until world conflict led to sixteen million Americans leaving the workforce for the military, and millions more finding new jobs in humming defense plants. Considering Roosevelt's self-proclaimed priorities, the persistence of devastating unemployment (in an era when the typical family relied on only one wage earner and women for the most part stayed away from the workforce) should alone identify the New Deal as a wretched, ill-conceived failure.

Other measures of recovery show similarly dismal results. After the stock market crash and the beginning of the Great Depression, the Dow Jones Industrial Average hit 250 in 1930 under Hoover (it had been 343 just before the crash). By January 1940, after seven years of New Deal "experimentation," the market had collapsed to 151; it remained in the low 100s through most of Roosevelt's terms and didn't return to its 1929 levels until the 1950s. At the same time, federal spending as a percentage of the gross domestic product soared at an unprecedented rate: from 2.5 percent in 1929 to 9 percent in 1936 (long before the wartime spending began). In other words, the portion of the total economy controlled by Washington increased by a staggering 360 percent in the course of just seven years—without providing discernable benefit to the economy.

Such statistics look so disturbing, so incontrovertible, that they raise serious questions about the survival of the myth that the New Deal fixed the Depression.

How could reputable historians pretend that the vast expansion of government power between 1933 and 1941 somehow brought the nation out of its persistent, nightmarish economic misery?

Out of curiosity, I took from my shelf the college history textbook assigned to me at Yale in 1968. The relevant chapters had been written by Arthur Schlesinger Jr., the most acclaimed and authoritative of all New Deal historians. To my surprise, not even this fervent liberal, a onetime Kennedy aide and stalwart admirer of FDR, pretended that his hero's policies had solved the Depression. In *The National Experience*, published in 1963 (just eighteen years after FDR's death), Schlesinger wrote: "Though the policies of the Hundred Days had ended despair, they had not produced recovery. . . . The New Deal had done remarkable things, especially in social reform, but the formula for full recovery evidently still eluded it." He also wrote honestly about the devastating crash of

1937—in the midst of the "Second New Deal" and Roosevelt's second term. "The collapse in the months after September 1937 was actually more severe than it had been in the first nine months of the depression (or, indeed, than in any other period in American history for which statistics are available). National income fell 13 per cent, payrolls 35 per cent, durable goods production 50 per cent, profits 78 per cent. The increase in unemployment reproduced scenes of the early depression and imposed new burdens on the relief agencies."

In view of such acknowledged economic disaster after more than five years of vaunted reform, how can fawning historians still worship at the altar of Rooseveltian idolatry? Normal depressions or recessions last between one and three years; the Great Depression continued to hold down living standards and imposed severe hardships for more than a decade. A growing majority of economic historians now concede that the programs of the New Deal prolonged, rather than terminated, the Depression. In the Pulitzer Prize–winning account *Freedom from Fear*, Stanford history professor David Kennedy concluded: "Whatever it was, the New Deal was not a recovery program, or at any rate not an effective one."

The Depression proved to be a worldwide economic crisis, but in nearly all European nations it ended more quickly than it did in Roosevelt's America. In the words of economic historian Lester V. Chandler, "In most countries the depression was less deep and prolonged." Even at the time, experts understood the misguided nature of FDR's policies. In 1935, the Brookings Institution (then, as now, a left-leaning think tank) produced a nine-hundred-page report considering the impact of the New Deal's most ambitious and controversial program, the National Recovery Administration (NRA), and concluded that "on the whole it retarded recovery."

OLD-FASHIONED VOTE BUYING

To counter the inconvenient facts about the persistence of crippling unemployment and pervasive poverty in the face of huge increases in governmental spending and activism, New Deal apologists cite two positive results from the feverish emergence of new programs: the restoration of "hope" in place of despair, and the implementation of needed "reforms" that planted the seeds of justice even if they failed to bring economic recovery.

Concerning FDR's alleged conquest of fear, Amity Shlaes in her brilliant history of the Great Depression, *The Forgotten Man* (2007), points out that he achieved this change of mood through an old-fashioned vote-buying scheme in the style of the venal ward heelers and big-city bosses who still dominated the Democratic Party. She cites the nakedly political emphasis of the Public Works Administration (PWA), under the control of Secretary of the Interior Harold L. Ickes. This federal operation laid the groundwork for the current Washington mania for "earmarks"—in which congressional power brokers arrange for buildings, bridges, and other facilities to gratify their constituents back home. The PWA provided at least one project for all but thirty-three of the more than three thousand counties in America, spending a startling $3 billion in its first few years—this at a time when the total federal budget in any given year amounted to barely $6 billion. Secretary Ickes himself wrote concerning the expenditure for his program, "It helped me to estimate its size by figuring that if we had it all in currency and should load it into trucks, we could set out with it from Washington, D.C., for the Pacific Coast, shovel off one million dollars at every milepost and, at the end, still have enough left to build a fleet of battle ships." Jim Powell notes that "a disproportionate amount" of FDR's relief and public works spending "went not to the poorest states such as the South, but to western states where people were better off, apparently because these were 'swing' states which could yield FDR more votes in the next election."

Beyond the success of Roosevelt's programs in brightening the national mood (and, not incidentally, ensuring his perpetual reelection), New Deal defenders cite another justification for their costly and radical innovations. Schlesinger and others argue that even if the reforms failed to bring the promised economic recovery, their inherent "justice" made them nonetheless worthwhile. Roosevelt, the apologists say, empowered labor unions, pulled agriculture under federal control, imposed tighter supervision of banking, and made countless other "improvements." Regarding this argument, no less a leftist hero than the British economist John Maynard Keynes offered a tart response. He wrote FDR a letter published on December 31, 1933, in the *New York Times* in which he warned that "even wise and necessary Reform may, in some respects, impede and complicate Recovery. For it will upset the confidence of the business world and weaken their existing motives to action."

In other words, Keynes perceived at the very beginning of the New Deal its most damaging aspect: treating the nation's capitalists as an enemy— "the unscrupulous money changers," FDR called them in his First Inaugural Address, who "have fled from their high seats in the temple of our civilization." With new government regulatory schemes, lawsuits, and political attacks emerging every week, business leaders found it difficult to engage in the long-term planning that alone could restore investment and entrepreneurial energy and put Americans back to work.

ENDING RECESSIONS THROUGH GOVERNMENTAL RESTRAINT

The Great Depression occupies a unique position in the national imagination, but it constituted neither the first major collapse in U.S. economic history nor the last. The nation endured major contractions and sharply increased unemployment on many occasions, such as in 1815, 1837, 1873, 1893, 1920, 1958, and 1979. The record consistently shows that leaders who cut government to revive the economy succeeded far more quickly and painlessly than did the New Deal.

The punishing Panic of 1837 wrought havoc for American commerce and cost President Martin Van Buren his chances of reelection in 1840, but Powell points out that Van Buren responded in precisely the appropriate way: he cut federal spending from $37.2 million to $24.3 million and sharply reduced taxes (mainly tariff revenue). He determined "to make government cheaper and stay out of the way of the private sector." As a result, the young nation roared back to recovery and resumed its spectacular economic growth shortly after Van Buren left office.

Another serious downturn, the Depression of 1893, produced four million unemployed, violent strikes, and a colorful march on Washington by the dispossessed of "Coxey's Commonweal Army," who tramped en masse from Ohio behind a banner featuring an image of Christ and the legend HE IS RISEN!! BUT DEATH TO INTEREST ON BONDS!!! The marchers demanded interest-free advances from the government and a new program to hire the legions of unemployed to build highways across America. But the Democratic president, Grover Cleveland, refused to see them or to consider their pleas. Instead, he determined to reduce burdens on taxpayers, cutting tariffs and blocking an income tax. He even vetoed a bill (among more than three hundred "relief" measures he stopped) to distribute $10,000 in seed grain to drought-stricken Texas farmers. In his veto message, the president wrote: "Federal aid in such cases encourages an expectation of paternal care on the part of the Government and weakens the sturdiness of our national character."

Cleveland, in other words, explicitly denounced the "paternal care" that his Democratic successor Bill Clinton demanded in his First Inaugural Address a hundred years later. The stubborn and timeless integrity of "Grover the Good" won prompt vindication as the nation's gloomy economy sharply improved; the entire depression ended within two years.

Most striking of all, the reviled President Warren Harding proved himself a masterful manager of the recession he faced when he came to power in 1921. "Harding inherited from the comatose Wilson regime one of the sharpest recessions in American history," writes the great British historian Paul Johnson in *A History of the American People*. "By July 1921 it was all over and the economy was booming again." How did the president oversee such a quick turnaround? "Harding and [Treasury Secretary Andrew] Mellon had done nothing except cut government expenditure by a huge 40 percent from Wilson's peacetime level, the last time a major industrial power treated a recession by classic laissez-faire methods, allowing wages to fall to their natural level. Benjamin Anderson of Chase Manhattan was later to call it 'our last natural recovery to full employment.' The cuts were not ill-considered but part of a careful plan to bring the spending of the monster state which had emerged under Wilson back under control."

These cuts, and even sharper tax cuts under Harding's successor, Coolidge, produced the long period of growth and rising living standards associated with the Roaring Twenties.

The experience of the Reagan administration offered another striking example of an economic turnaround powered by governmental restraint rather than activism. Facing the crippling Carter legacy of "stagflation," President Reagan cut taxes dramatically and immediately, and began the longest peacetime expansion in American history.

President Eisenhower and both Presidents Bush managed to make other recessions short-lived without ambitious or expensive new government initiatives or interventions. Rather than depending on government programs to cushion us from the impact of inevitable economic downturns, the American people have benefited far more reliably by the proper instinct to cut government to allow the business cycle to take its course.

THE DEMOCRATS' FORGOTTEN HERITAGE

Today's activists for government programs to help the poor and the working class also overlook the fact that for much of this country's history the most celebrated advocates for the "little guy" argued for *less* government involvement in the economy, not more. From the time of America's founding at least through the end of President Cleveland's second administration in 1897, the Democrats (and their predecessors, Thomas Jefferson's Democratic-Republicans) favored limited government, low taxes, low tariffs, and the disentanglement of business from bureaucracy as the best way to ensure that ordinary citizens escaped the destructive impact of governmental favoritism for big business. It was their opponents, first Federalists and later Whigs, who favored an activist approach that would use federal power to assist business interests in building prosperity. The tariffs and other restrictions on free trade that they endorsed benefited business interests while increasing costs for the consumer.

Until the turn-of-the-century Progressive Era and its bastard spawn the New Deal, Democrats and other champions of the "common folk" understood that government powered by high taxes and stiff fees would much more likely impede rather than assist the chances of ordinary people to get ahead.

SMALL GOVERNMENT AND ECONOMIC MOBILITY

Despite the absence of federal programs to "help" the poor and downtrodden, the nineteenth century in America remained an unprecedented era of social and economic mobility. The Horatio Alger stories that became best sellers and inspired the nation reflected reality, as American families (including those of newly arrived immigrant masses) rose from abject poverty to middle-class status (or above) in one, two, or three generations.

Social programs didn't power this escalator to prosperity; economic growth did. In their 1963 book *A Monetary History of the United States, 1867–1960,* Milton Friedman and Anna Jacobson Schwartz write:

> The final two decades of the nineteenth century saw a growth of population of over 2 percent per year, rapid extension of the railroad network, essential completion of continental settlement, and an extraordinary increase both in the acreage of land in farms and the output of farm products. The number of farms rose by nearly 50 per cent—despite the price decline. Yet at the same time, manufacturing industries were growing even more rapidly, and the Census of 1890 was the first in which the net value added by manufacturing exceeded the value of agricultural output. A feverish boom in western land swept the country during the eighties.

Meanwhile, with government consuming a smaller portion of the gross domestic product in America than in other industrial powers (Britain, Germany, France), the United States emerged as the most open and mobile society on earth, providing opportunities for the penniless that more bureaucratic nations couldn't match.

CROWDING OUT CHARITY

These opportunities stemmed in part from the remarkable network of private charities that flourished for more than two hundred years, with no expectation that government should assist or interfere. Long before anyone contemplated federal "entitlements" funded by taxpayers, Professor Frank Dekker Watson of Haverford College wrote a fascinating chronicle of the emergence of private charity in the United States. Published in 1922, *The Charity Organization Movement in the United States: A Study in American Philanthropy* shows that voluntary groups worked tirelessly on behalf of the afflicted even in colonial times. He cites the Scots Charitable Society, organized in Boston in 1657, as one of the earliest benevolent organizations. Other nationalities boasted their own philanthropic groups, while some charities emerged to alleviate particular social ills, such as the Philadelphia Society for Alleviating the Miseries of Public Prisoners, formed in 1787; the Massachusetts Charitable Fire Society, incorporated in 1794, "for the purpose of relieving such as suffer by fire"; and the New York Dispensary, organized in 1791 for the care of the city's ill, diseased, and impoverished inhabitants. Philadelphia in 1800—with a population of less than fifty thousand—boasted eleven soup kitchens that offered food to all the city's hungry. Societies for widows proved especially prevalent: "The Widows' Society in Boston was started in 1816. . . . The records of the Widows' Society of Hartford, Connecticut, date from 1825."

Two assumptions shaped attitudes and activities regarding the unfortunate: that individuals bore a duty to band together to provide charity for those in need, and that each person must do whatever he could to avoid requiring assistance.

Watson devotes an entire chapter to the exemplary efforts of Unitarian clergyman Joseph Tuckerman, who in the early nineteenth century worked as a "minister at large" to unite disparate denominations in new organizations to help the poor. Reverend Tuckerman made a crucial distinction between "paupery"—a chronic condition of the homeless and destitute who at the time were largely drunken immigrants—and "poverty," affecting people who struggled to survive on low wages or faced temporary unemployment due to lack of jobs. Tuckerman also chastised the wealthy for offering wages inadequate for subsistence ("the evils of poverty grew out of the character of the more prosperous classes as well as of the poor"), but it never occurred to him or his fellow philanthropic activists that a governmental bureaucracy should remedy the situation.

When city, state, and finally federal officials began taking over responsibility for assisting the poor, private charities that had thrived for generations inevitably withered and retreated. Jonathan Gruber of MIT and Daniel Hungerman of the National Bureau of Economic Research have demonstrated that as government aid expenditures skyrocketed during the New Deal (increasing more than sixfold from 1933 to 1939), church-based private charity to the needy declined precipitously—by an estimated 30 percent.

This crowd-out represented a major problem because charities simply do a better job of uplifting the poor. In *The Tragedy of American Compassion* (1992), Marvin Olasky of the University of Texas explores the numerous reasons why private-sector efforts work better than governmental initiatives in meaningfully transforming the lives of the downtrodden. For instance, "a century ago, when individuals applied for material assistance, charity volunteers tried first to 'restore family ties that have been sundered' and 'reabsorb in social life those who for some reason have snapped the threads that bound them to other members of the community.' Instead of immediately offering help, charities asked, 'Who is bound to help in this case?' " This approach of course discouraged the extension of poverty as a semi-permanent status passed on from one generation to another.

As Olasky notes, faith-based and private aid organizations also maintained the crucial ability to make distinctions between "deserving" and "self-destructive" poor. "Charities a century ago realized that two persons in exactly the same material circumstances, but with different values, need different treatment. One might benefit most from some material help and a pat on the back, the other might need spiritual challenge and a push." This echoes the clear division Reverend Joseph Tuckerman proposed in his classification of the poor he served as victims of either "paupery" or "poverty"—the first more in need of moral refocusing and the second in need of aid. But bureaucratized and governmental interventions, no matter how well intentioned, do not—cannot—make such distinctions, or help to repair or encourage the family relationships so essential to escape from poverty and dysfunction.

The growth of government programs not only discouraged Americans from providing for their neighbors but also erased their need to provide for themselves. For example, Franklin Roosevelt imposed Social

Security taxes in 1935 and thereby discouraged individual saving. "Social Security—a pay-as-you-go program that does not save and invest—tends to replace savings that lower- and middle-income households otherwise would have accumulated," according to a 2006 report by the National Center for Policy Analysis. "This is because for these households, expected Social Security benefits replace retirement savings. As a result, they have little or nothing to leave to their children since these

---

"Free" Food from Uncle Sam

Every school day, the federal government feeds lunch to more than thirty million children—nearly 60 percent of all schoolkids in the United States. In Atlanta, 79 percent of public school children get federally funded lunch; in New York City, the figure is 72 percent; and for the whole state of Texas, 70 percent. How did distant bureaucrats in Washington, D.C., take on responsibility for feeding (at the taxpayers' expense) at least one meal a day to the majority of school-age children in the country? In the nineteenth century, private (generally religious) charities such as the Children's Aid Society operated extensive programs to bring food to malnourished kids in schools. During the Depression, FDR's Works Progress Administration (WPA) began operating federally funded school lunch programs in thirty-five thousand schools, using surplus food purchased from struggling farmers. In 1946, President Truman signed the National School Lunch Act, which Lyndon Johnson greatly expanded as part of his "War on Poverty." LBJ added a free breakfast program (which now serves seven million kids daily) and a summer meal program (now reaching two million more) to feed children even when school is out of session.

The "free" lunches provided by the federal government actually cost taxpayers $8.7 billion in 2007 alone. Despite the massive investment of public money over the course of sixty years, poor children continue to suffer from inadequate nutrition and, increasingly, a devastating and crippling epidemic of obesity.

benefits are not transferable." Social Security thereby limits the retirement resources of older Americans (by reducing both the ability and incentive to accumulate their own savings) at the same time it shrinks what they ultimately leave to heirs to help *their* economic mobility.

ERASING EMBARRASSMENT, ENCOURAGING DEPENDENCY

Charles Murray's pathbreaking 1984 book *Losing Ground* asks an obvious question about Lyndon Johnson's "Great Society" and its aftermath in the late 1960s: what caused the painful increase in poverty, illegitimacy, crime, and social dysfunction at the same time that government spending to address these pathologies vastly increased? He concluded that the well-intentioned and monumentally expensive programs of the period contributed to the problems, rather than to their solutions. As President Reagan trenchantly summarized the situation: "We had a War on Poverty. And poverty won."

The unmistakable failure of Great Society programs related to their underlying assumptions: they went far beyond the New Deal in erasing all distinction between the "deserving poor" and the "undeserving poor." The new welfare "entitlement" made all struggling citizens eligible for the same programs, regardless of the respectability or destructiveness of their behavior. Social workers and politicians aimed to obliterate the stigma once associated with receiving benefits from the government.

My barrel-maker grandfather never prospered in this society, but he always viewed the dole as an indication of failure and disgrace. Like most Americans of his generation, he would rather go hungry than lose his dignity as an honest workingman.

Great Society reformers worked hard to extirpate the sense of shame that previously kept the "working poor" from claiming government largesse, promoting "welfare rights" and insisting that the destitute bore no responsibility for their status. But an individual who bears no responsibility for his situation exerts no control over it—and must depend on outside forces (in this case the federal government) for his redemption. By removing the embarrassment previously associated with taking public money, antipoverty programs encouraged a culture of dependency and discouraged self-reliance.

The ultimate vindication for Murray's arguments came with federal welfare reform in 1996, which succeeded in cutting the number of dependent individuals by more than half and corresponded with a period of rapidly declining poverty.

WHO REALLY HELPED US CLIMB?

Rapid upward mobility remains a prominent factor in American life, but many families feel proud to exaggerate their own past destitution and somehow prefer to identify government rather than business as the source of their progress.

A few years ago I saw this principle at work when speaking to a Jewish temple in Florida. An angry questioner denounced my conservative politics by insisting that Jews in America owed our prosperity exclusively to liberal programs: were it not for the unions and their radical organizers and for the leftists and their compassionate initiatives, we'd all still be toiling in sweatshops and living in tenements.

In response to his impassioned declaration, I called for a show of hands in the crowd of some seven hundred people. I asked how many came from families in which labor unions played an important role in economic advancement. A few hands shot up, proudly—at most two or three dozen. Then I asked how many people in the audience came from families who had arrived in the middle class because of federal welfare programs. Members of the crowd looked at one another nervously, but only three people raised their hands in the entire temple. Finally, I asked the most telling question: how many in that crowd had come to their current state of comfort and opportunity because someone, a parent or a grandparent or the individual himself, had worked hard in business and achieved some measure of success? At this, the overwhelming majority of the audience lifted hands and laughed and applauded in recognition.

Whether the crowd happened to be Jewish, Irish American, Italian American, Mexican American, or black, the response wouldn't have been much different. The vast expansion of the middle class that occurred in the 1950s involved productive work in the private sector and only one prominent form of governmental assistance: the GI Bill, which helped countless veterans (including my father) pay for education and housing and the launching of businesses. The GI Bill—providing long-term reward for military service—hardly constituted a something-for-nothing welfare program.

"YOU'VE GOT TO HAVE THE BOOTS"

America has always been a compassionate society, finding various means—mostly private but occasionally involving state and local funds—to help those who required it. "Rugged individualism" never meant isolation from neighbors, family, or fellow congregants. In that context, attempts by left-leaning commentators to credit government alone for social and economic progress remain strained and unpersuasive.

Consider, for example, the argument offered by Al Franken, comedian, talk-show host, best-selling author, and Democratic candidate for the United States Senate from Minnesota. In his stump speeches, Franken often cites his wife's experience as proof for our dependence on benevolent government, and tells and retells "Franni's story" in these terms:

> When she was seventeen months old, her dad—a decorated veteran of World War II—died in a car accident, leaving her mother, my mother-in-law, widowed with five kids.
>
> My mother-in-law worked in the produce department of a grocery store, but that family made it because of Social Security survivor benefits. . . . Every single one of the four girls in Franni's family went to college, thanks to Pell Grants and other scholarships. . . . And my mother-in-law got herself a $300 GI loan to fix her roof, and used the money instead to go to the University of Maine. She became a grade school teacher, teaching Title One kids—poor kids—so her loan was forgiven.
>
> My mother-in-law and every single one of those five kids became a productive member of society. Conservatives like to say that people need to pull themselves up by their bootstraps—and that's a

great idea. But first, you've got to have the boots. And the government gave my wife's family the boots.

It's a moving tale, but it's hard to believe that without federal welfare programs Franni's family, with its obvious motivation and intelligence, would have found no way to become "productive members of society." Especially as the survivors of a decorated veteran, assistance would have been available—if not through the VA, then certainly through local or private agencies. Would the University of Maine truly (or properly) deny scholarship aid or educational loans to a widow of a war hero who's trying to raise five kids?

In any case, no one wants to wipe out the programs that benefited Franni and her family. Not even the most strident conservative seeks to remove Social Security survivor benefits; in fact, the partially personalized retirement accounts proposed by President Bush (and favored by most Republicans) would provide many grieving families with more resources, not less, since the accumulated funds would earn interest and be transferred (tax-free) to heirs and survivors. Pell Grants and GI loans are hardly controversial, and the real lesson of Franni's story is that hard-striving and goal-oriented people managed to make it without any of the expensive new government programs that Franken so fervently favors.

The notion that the poor can't make it without federal assistance dismisses (and undermines) the self-help potential of the needy at the same time as it ignores all those other sources of more personalized aid that might be available beyond the Beltway. Those who cherish the dubious belief that the president, Congress, and the federal bureaucracy bear primary responsibility for dealing with poverty not only underestimate the importance of private and local help but also greatly exaggerate the federal government's ability to control intractable human problems.

"SUBMIT OUR LIVES AND PROPERTY TO SUCH DISCIPLINE"

In this, they follow the example of FDR himself, whose public utterances remain a particularly painful example of governmental overreach. Everyone recalls the reassuring opening of his First Inaugural Address: "This great Nation will endure as it has endured, will revive and will prosper. So, first of all, let me assert my firm belief that the only thing we have to fear is fear itself." Unfortunately, the rest of the speech includes chilling language reminiscent of the fascist dictatorships simultaneously taking shape in Europe. "If we are to go forward," the new president declared, "we must move as a trained and loyal army willing to sacrifice for the good of a common discipline, because without such discipline no progress is made, no leadership becomes effective. We are, I know, ready and willing to submit our lives and property to such discipline."

Was the audience at this point supposed to raise arms and shout "Sieg heil"?

"With this pledge taken," FDR continued, "I assume unhesitatingly the leadership of this great army of our people dedicated to a disciplined attack on our common problems. . . . It is to be hoped that the normal balance of executive and legislative authority may be wholly adequate to meet the unprecedented task before us. But it may be that an unprecedented demand and need for undelayed action may call for temporary departure from that normal balance of public procedure."

Is it any wonder that conservatives gravely feared a grievous suspension of constitutional rule?

Roosevelt baldly announced: "I shall ask the Congress for the one remaining instrument to meet the crisis—broad Executive power to wage a war against the emergency, as great as the power that would be given to me if we were in fact invaded by a foreign foe."

In the speech's single most shocking (and altogether forgotten) passage, Roosevelt spoke of the need for a relocation program that might have pleased Mao, Stalin, or Pol Pot: "Hand in hand with this we must frankly recognize the overbalance of population in our industrial centers and, by engaging on a national scale in a redistribution, endeavor to provide a better use of the land for those best fitted for the land."

Fortunately, the New Deal never included a new alphabet agency to correct "the overbalance of population in our industrial centers" by driving people at bayonet point into the country, but the mere suggestion illuminates the mentality behind FDR's initiatives and all other sweeping liberal "reforms" over the years.

Under this thinking, the government and its planners make the crucial economic decisions for the people they command—the enlisted men in the "trained and loyal army" who are "willing to submit our lives and property to such discipline." The very idea that bureaucrats and politicos can direct economic advancement more reliably than individuals making millions of small decisions for themselves has not only reduced liberty but invariably threatened prosperity in the process.

The Lost Regiment in the War on Poverty

In 1964, as a cornerstone of his ambitious War on Poverty, President Lyndon Johnson launched the Job Corps to train disadvantaged young people for productive employment. Based on FDR's fondly remembered Civilian Conservation Corps, the Job Corps offers room and board to applicants between ages sixteen and twenty-four at one of its 122 residential centers across the country, as well as providing payments that increase the longer participants choose to remain. In forty-four years, more than two million Americans have taken part in the Job Corps, so naturally, the Labor Department authorized several studies to prove its effectiveness.

Unfortunately, the 2001 outcome study showed only trivial benefits to Job Corps graduates compared to nonparticipants: a weekly income difference of $25.20 four years after finishing the program. A 2003 report produced even more discouraging conclusions—so much so that the Labor Department waited until 2006 to make its findings public. The analysis showed "statistically insignificant" income increases for most Job Corps participants and an unexpectedly negative impact for one key group: female participants without children, who actually earned less than nonparticipants.

Nevertheless, Congress continues to authorize and reauthorize this dubious undertaking, with many Democrats calling for its expansion. Currently, sixty-two thousand young Americans take part in the Job Corps at a cost to the taxpayer of $21,500 for each enrollee in the eight-month program.

CLINICAL CRAZINESS

Seventy-five years later, left-leaning politicians express undiminished (and deeply dangerous) faith in the power of Washington initiatives—of "a disciplined attack on our common problems"—to remake society and transform private lives.

That faith underlies Hillary Clinton's astonishing confidence that her proposed Department of Poverty could "end poverty as we know it in America." Her language deliberately echoed her husband's 1992 pledge to "end welfare as we know it"—a pledge realized, thanks to the Gingrich-controlled Congress, with sweeping welfare reform in 1996.

There's a key difference, however: ending "welfare as we know it" meant terminating a government program, which is an undertaking well within the power of public officials. Ending poverty, on the other hand, means altering part of the human condition—which governments may attempt but never can achieve.

No secretary of poverty, no matter how dedicated or talented or lavishly funded, will be able to prevent suffering for a fourteen-year-old girl who gives birth to a baby and drops out of high school while functionally illiterate. This same official will similarly fail to rescue a heroin addict and gang member who goes to jail for burglary and assault and returns to a life of drugs and crime upon his release. An unskilled new immigrant with six children (even if all of them enter the country legally, with proper documentation) may need to go through several years (at least) of poverty, despite official determination to end inequality. There's also little chance to give security to a family with small children whose father gambles away all resources at local casinos, even while compiling prodigious credit card debt to live above his means.

In other words, much of today's poverty stems from bad choices and self-destructive behavior, rather than a lack of bureaucratic attention. The president may hector a new secretary of poverty (and every other cabinet official, for that matter) with the daily question "What have you done today to end poverty in America?" but it's safe to assume that poverty still won't end. It's a relative status in any event: today's "poor"— with their cell phones, color TVs, DVD players, air conditioners, cars,

Medicaid, free lunches, and food stamps—would have been considered middle class some fifty years ago.

At a time of looming bankruptcy for Medicare and Social Security, the apparently straight-faced idea of launching yet another cabinet department (to complement other worthy recent additions such as the briskly efficient Departments of Energy, Transportation, Housing and Urban Development, and Veterans Affairs) qualifies as a form of lunacy.

But then we've already got a secretary of health and human services to deal with such clinical craziness.

"America Is an Imperialist Nation and a Constant Threat to World Peace"

"A THREAT TO THE SURVIVAL OF THE PLANET"

The Reverend Jeremiah Wright, erstwhile pastor to Barack Obama, hardly rants alone in his ferocious denunciations of American imperialism, arrogance, corruption, and cruelty.

Though videotape of the rabid rev's "greatest hits" simultaneously shocked and fascinated the public in the heat of the 2008 presidential campaign, his volcanic eruptions (including the ever-popular "God damn America!" sermonette) actually reflected the views of leading academics, activists, literary figures, and celebrities in treating "USA" as a three-letter acronym for absolute evil.

On the first Sunday after September 11, 2001, Pastor Wright famously told his enthusiastically cheering congregation that guilty America deserved the devastating attacks we had received.

> We took this country by terror away from the Sioux, the Apache, the Arawak, the Comanche, the Arapaho, the Navajo. Terrorism! We took Africans from their country to build our way of ease and kept them enslaved and living in fear. Terrorism! We bombed Grenada and killed innocent civilians, babies, nonmilitary personnel. We bombed the black civilian community of Panama with stealth bombers and killed unarmed teenagers and toddlers, pregnant mothers and hard-working fathers. We bombed Gadhafi's home and killed his child. "Blessed are they who bash your children's head against a rock!" We bombed Iraq. We killed unarmed civilians trying to make a living. We bombed a plant in Sudan to pay back for the attack on our embassy. Killed hundreds of hard-working people—mothers and fathers who left home to go that day, not knowing they would never get back home. We bombed Hiroshima! We bombed Nagasaki, and we nuked far more than the thousands in New York and the Pentagon, and we never batted an eye! Kids playing in the playground, mothers picking up children after school, civilians—not soldiers—people just trying to make it day by day. We have supported state terrorism against the Palestinians and black South Africans, and now we are indignant, because the stuff we have done overseas has now been brought back into our own front yards!

Apologists for Dr. Wright attempt to explain (if not excuse) his diatribes with reference to "black rage," the righteous wrath inspired by four hundred years of slavery and racism, but similar sentiments emerge from other angry commentators with altogether dissimilar backgrounds.

The multimillionaire Hollywood filmmaker Michael Moore, for instance, regularly decries the horrible impact of America's global role and gleefully awaits the destruction of the American "empire." In his little-seen 1998 release *The Big One* (about the book tour for his best seller *Downsize This!*), the portly provocateur (and world's most successful documentarian) delivers the rousing punch line: "One Evil Empire down! One more to go!"

This same effort to equate today's United States with the old Soviet Union characterizes the work of Chalmers Johnson, professor emeritus of political science at the University of California, San Diego. Summarizing themes in his sunny, 2007 feel-good book *Nemesis: The Last Days of the American Republic,* Johnson declared: "When Ronald Reagan coined the phrase 'evil empire,' he was referring to the Soviet Union, and I basically agreed with him that the USSR needed to be contained and checkmated. But today it is the U.S. that is widely perceived as an evil empire and world forces are gathering to stop us."

Many domestic radicals, including tenured professors, proudly volunteer to join that international anti-American effort. Viewing the United States as a threat to world peace and a menace to the security and prosperity of other nations, they reject traditional notions of patriotism. Robert Jensen has taught journalism at the University of Texas since 1992, and on a half-dozen electrifying occasions he argued with me (and my listeners) as a guest on my radio show. In his 2004 book *Citizens of the Empire: The Struggle to Claim Our Humanity,* he baldly asserted: "It is time to scrap patriotism. More specifically, it is crucial to scrap patriotism in today's empire, the United States, where patriotism is not only a bad idea but literally a threat to the survival of the planet."

On a similarly sour note, in January 2006 *Los Angeles Times* columnist Joel Stein proudly announced: "I don't support the troops. . . . When you volunteer for the U.S. military, you're willingly signing up to be a fighting tool of American imperialism. . . . We shouldn't be celebrating people for doing something we don't think was a good idea."

The notion of a malevolent "American empire," of U.S. imperialism as a long-standing threat to all of humanity, has become such a common feature of "enlightened opinion" that an angry Nobel Prize acceptance speech advancing such ideas provoked scant controversy and attracted little attention. The British playwright Harold Pinter (author of joyless, often inscrutable dramas and screenplays of singular pomposity) won the Nobel Prize for literature and used the occasion to denounce the United States and all its works. In his "Pearl Harbor Day" Nobel lecture of December 7, 2005, Pinter launched his own sneak attack on his American cousins. "The crimes of the United States," he announced, "have been systematic, constant, vicious, remorseless, but very few people have actually talked about them. You have to hand it to America. It has exercised a quite clinical manipulation of power worldwide while masquerading as a force for universal good. It's a brilliant, even witty, highly successful act of hypnosis. I put to you that the United States is without doubt the greatest show on the road. Brutal, indifferent, scornful and ruthless it may be but it is also very clever. As a salesman, it is out on its own and its most saleable commodity is self love."

He went on to scold the United States for its "8,000 active and operational nuclear warheads. . . . Who, I wonder, are they aiming at? Osama bin Laden? You? Me? Joe Dokes? China? Paris? Who knows? What we do know is that this infantile insanity—the possession and theoretical use of nuclear weapons—is at the heart of the present American political philosophy. We must remind ourselves that the United States is on a permanent military footing and shows no sign of relaxing it."

While outspoken leftists such as Pastor Wright and playwright Pinter accuse the United States of a long history of exploitative, arrogant militarism going back to the early treatment of Native Americans and the very origins of the nation, a strain of anti-imperialist hysteria on the right suggests that our arrogant role in world affairs represents a recent, alien aberration imposed on a previously honorable republic by some vile conspiracy of "globalists" or "neocons." These impassioned critics of the current War on Terror conjure up images of an idyllic, noble, noninterventionist past, with Americans prospering peacefully and resisting entanglement in the Old World's corrupt and needless conflicts, and our judicious leaders displaying the good sense to avoid meddling in the business of other nations. Only recently, they argue, has the Republic involved itself in pointless, dangerous, and undeclared wars that sacrifice the true national interest for the sake of privileged but secretive economic elites.

"Why are we determined to follow a foreign policy of empire building and pre-emption which is unbecoming of a constitutional republic?" asked Congressman Ron Paul (R-Texas), whose 2008 presidential campaign made him something of a cult leader among angry activists who felt deeply disaffected from the aggressive internationalism of their government. In a February 2007 statement on Iraq policy that amounted to Dr. Paul's very own valentine to the Bush administration (and received wide Internet circulation under the heading "The Neoconservative Empire"), the indignant Texan complained:

> Those on the right should recall that the traditional conservative position of non-intervention was their position for most of the 20th Century. . . . Special interests and the demented philosophy of conquest have driven most wars throughout history. . . . In recent decades our policies have been driven by neoconservative empire radicalism, profiteering in the military industrial complex, misplaced do-good internationalism, mercantilistic notions regarding the need to control natural resources, and blind loyalty to various governments in the Middle East.

Both views of American imperialism badly misstate our history, distort our present policies, and require correction. No, the involvement in far-flung, often unpopular conflicts doesn't represent a recent innovation or the result of some conspiratorial takeover of U.S. foreign policy. Military involvement in remote corners of the globe characterized every stage of our emergence as a world power. And the purpose of these numerous conflicts and interventions bore little connection to colonialism or conquest or empire building in the classical sense, and more often displayed surprisingly and surpassingly unselfish intentions. Moreover, regardless of the true reasons or the often arguable wisdom behind these frequent military or diplomatic initiatives, their overall, long-term impact most often benefited the peoples involved as well as the world at large. Unlike other empires in human history, the powerful and globe-straddling American sphere of influence has generally promoted the cause of both prosperity and liberty.

NOTHING NEW IN FOREIGN FIGHTS

The United States fought its first war against Islamic extremism more than two hundred years ago, producing inspiring victories in exotic locales, a

Insurgents Play Politics—and Not Just in Iraq

Well before Iraq and even Vietnam, ruthless insurgents relied on anti-war agitation in the United States to provide victories they couldn't win in battle.

Between 1898 and 1902, some of America's most esteemed individuals condemned the punishing war in the jungles of the Philippines—including former president Grover Cleveland, labor leader Samuel Gompers, social reformer Jane Addams, and industrialist Andrew Carnegie (who offered $20 million to buy the Philippines to grant the islands their independence). Wily Filipino leader Emilio Aguinaldo deliberately intensified his guerilla activity in the months before the 1900 election in hopes of handing the presidency to "anti-imperialist" candidate William Jennings Bryan. Some of the Democrat's supporters explicitly hoped for Filipino victory "against our army of subjugation, tyranny, and oppression," while Mark Twain, condemning "atrocities" by U.S. forces, suggested redesign of the Stars and Stripes "with the white stripes painted black and the stars replaced by the skull and crossbones."

American soldiers in the Philippines deeply resented antiwar protests back home. Major General Henry Lawton, a Medal of Honor winner for his spectacular bravery in the War Between the States, grumbled, "If I am shot by a Filipino bullet, it might just as well come from one of my own men . . . because . . . the continuance of the fighting is chiefly due to reports that are sent from America." He received just such a fatal bullet a few weeks later, picked off by an insurgent sharpshooter.

Nevertheless, voters turned against antiwar politicians and gave the GOP ticket of William McKinley and Teddy Roosevelt a landslide victory. Less than seven years later, with the insurrection crushed, the Filipinos convened an elected legislature—the first anywhere in Asia. In 1946, the islands achieved final independence.

line in the first verse of the "Marines' Hymn" ("to the shores of Tripoli"), our first great post-Revolutionary military hero (Stephen Decatur), and his immortal toast ("Our country! In her intercourse with foreign nations, may she always be in the right; but our country, right or wrong!").

The first Barbary War (1801–5) lasted four years after President Thomas Jefferson sent the new Navy to the distant Mediterranean to protect American interests and honor. The semi-independent North African nations of Algeria, Tunisia, and Tripoli (today's Libya) functioned like modern day "state sponsors of terrorism," backing ruthless pirates who devastated U.S. shipping unless Washington delivered lavish tribute to the local authorities. When Jefferson stopped the bribes and made war successfully on the Barbary States and their fanatical rulers (without a formal declaration from Congress), he helped establish a long-standing tradition of small wars, or so-called low intensity conflicts. As Max Boot points out in his superb and eye-opening 2002 book *The Savage Wars of Peace:* "There is another, less celebrated tradition in U.S. military history—a tradition of fighting small wars. Between 1800 and 1934, U.S. Marines staged 180 landings abroad. The army and navy added a few small-scale engagements of their own. Some of these excursions resulted in heavy casualties; others involved almost no fighting. . . . Some were successful, others not. But most of these campaigns were fought by a relatively small number of professional soldiers pursuing limited objectives with limited means. These are the nonwars that Kipling called 'the savage wars of peace.' "

Ignoring the long record of American involvement in such conflicts in every region of the globe, those who question our current worldwide role express reverence for a simple-minded (and nonexistent) tradition of isolationism. They cite George Washington's words in his celebrated Farewell Address of 1796: "The Great rule of conduct for us, in regard to foreign Nations, is in extending our commercial relations to have with them as little political connection as possible. . . . 'Tis our true policy to steer clear of permanent Alliances, with any portion of the foreign world."

Jefferson also warned against "entangling alliances," at the same time he negotiated a vast expansion of U.S. territory with France (the Louisiana Purchase) and pursued the daring and difficult Barbary Wars.

Even Pat Buchanan, the three-time presidential candidate most often identified as a contemporary advocate of "isolationism," rejects the idea that the nation ever cowered behind its Atlantic and Pacific "water walls." In his provocative, beautifully written book *A Republic, Not an Empire* (1999), Buchanan argues:

> The idea that America was ever an isolationist nation is a myth, a useful myth to be sure, but nonetheless a malevolent myth that approaches the status of a big lie. . . . What is derided today as isolationism was the foreign policy under which the Republic grew from thirteen states on the Atlantic into a continent-wide nation that dominated the hemisphere and whose power reached to Peking. . . . To call the foreign policy that produced this result 'isolationist' is absurd. Americans were willing to go to war with the greatest powers in Europe, but only for American interests. They had no wish to take sides in European wars in which America had no stake.

Donald Kagan makes a similar case in *Dangerous Nation* (2006), insisting that many Americans remain misled or ill-informed about our purportedly isolationist past:

> This gap between Americans' self-perception and the perceptions of others has endured throughout the nation's history. Americans have cherished an image of themselves as by nature inward-looking and aloof, only sporadically and spasmodically venturing forth into the world, usually in response to external attack or perceived threats. This self-image survives, despite four hundred years of steady expansion and an ever-deepening involvement in world affairs, and despite innumerable wars, interventions and prolonged occupations in foreign lands. . . . Even as the United States has risen to a position of global hegemony, expanding its reach and purview and involvement across the continent and then across the ocean, Americans still believe their nation's natural tendencies are toward passivity, indifference and insularity.

This misconception helped to produce one of the most common (and ignorant) indictments of the Iraq war, with angry critics of Bush's policy emphatically insisting: "This is the first time in history we ever attacked any country that hadn't attacked us first." In fact, virtually all our major wars began without some clear-cut enemy attack on American soil: the French and Indian War, the Revolutionary War, the War of 1812, the Mexican War, the Spanish-American War, World War I, Korea, Vietnam, and the First Gulf War engaged the armed might of the nation based on incidents or interests, but not in response to sneak attack or mass assault. In 230 years of history only the Civil War (where Lincoln cleverly lured southern forces into the initial bombardment of federal property at Fort Sumter) and World War II (where Japan struck at precisely one of those outposts of empire in distant Hawaii that anti-imperialists often decry) brought our forces into battle in response to blatant enemy strikes.

TEMPORARY MISSIONS, NOT PERMANENT CONQUESTS

While America's record clearly clashes with the isolationist and quiescent stereotypes that many anti-interventionists revere, the nation's traditions also bear little resemblance to the colonialist and imperialist selfishness associated with the European powers. Britain, France, Spain, Portugal, Germany, the Netherlands, Italy, and even tiny Belgium established far-flung empires, planting their flags and seizing political control of subject peoples and territory in Africa, Asia, and the Western Hemisphere, but the United States generally avoided the temptations of conquest.

We fought our one frankly imperialist war (the Spanish-American conflict of 1898) primarily over the future of Cuba, just ninety miles from the shores of Florida, yet made no attempt to incorporate the promising island as part of American territory. Within four years of our quick, one-sided victory over the Spanish colonialists, we withdrew our troops and recognized Cuban independence. Even the bloodiest, most fiercely resisted, and longest-standing U.S. occupations (as in the Philippines at the turn of the twentieth century) resulted, ultimately, in the voluntary departure of American forces. Whatever the varied purposes of our many foreign adventures beyond the North American continent, conquest and territorial expansion played little role in shaping our policy.

The nation's lack of imperial designs revealed itself most clearly, perhaps, at the Versailles Conference following America's triumphant (and very costly) involvement in World War I. More than a hundred thousand U.S. servicemen perished in the conflict, and American entry into the war unequivocally turned the tide of battle and brought about the Allied victory. Despite the fact that President Woodrow Wilson clearly dominated the proceedings at the peace conference, hailed as a virtual messiah when he arrived in Europe after the war, the United States remained the only one of the major victorious Allied powers that sought no territorial or colonial enhancement at Versailles. France, Italy, and even Denmark, Belgium, Greece, and Romania won new territory in the negotiations, but the Americans asked only for enough land to bury their dead.

In 1942, the historian Rupert Emerson declared: "With the exception of the brief period of imperialist activity at the time of the Spanish American war, the American people have shown a deep repugnance to both the conquest of distant lands and the assumption of rule over alien peoples." In the more than sixty-five eventful years since Emerson's observation, this "deep repugnance" remains a prominent feature of American public opinion and has helped to shape foreign policy. The bloody (and seemingly innumerable) foreign wars of the twentieth century saw American troops deployed to every corner of the planet, but for the most part they came home at the earliest opportunity. President Wilson dispatched more than two million American soldiers to France to win World War I, but in less than two years they had all left the Old World behind.

The sixty-year presence of American forces in Europe and Japan following World War II not only decreased dramatically after the demise of the Soviet threat but continues today at the insistence of the host countries. Aside from the economic benefits to local economies from the numerous American bases, U.S. troops (for better or worse) provide a security shield that has allowed our European allies to scrimp on defense spending, making no attempt to develop military resources commensurate with their economic or political power. In any event, not even the most implacable anti-American could describe today's robust and reunited Germany as a restive, captive society crushed by Yankee imperialism because of the ongoing presence of the U.S. Army on its soil. By the same token, the twenty-nine thousand American troops who remain in South Korea for defensive purposes more than a half century after the armistice with the North hardly constitute an occupation force or have prevented the nation's dazzling prosperity and democratization.

These long-term military assignments represent prominent exceptions to the general American rule of quick, short-term interventions rather than permanent conquests.

In 1848, victorious troops marched into Mexico City after the crushing defeat of that nation's vaunted military machine. "Jingos" at home demanded the annexation of all of Mexico, but instead President James K. Polk accepted a treaty that added to the nation the sparsely populated territory of California, Arizona, New Mexico, Nevada, and Utah (Texas had achieved its own independence from Mexico eleven years before). Rather than simply imposing its will on a conquered neighbor, the United States agreed to assume Mexico's burdensome national debt of $3.25 million and to pay the government a surprisingly lavish sum of $15 million more. After the settlement, Washington made no attempt to maintain American forces or bases on Mexican soil.

The same pattern applied almost everywhere, with American withdrawal following even the bloodiest, most punishing military struggles. In *Dangerous Nation*, Robert Kagan discerns this same impatience in the Reconstruction of the American South after the War Between the States. In our nation's first exercise in "nation building," the federal government ultimately failed because it allotted only twelve years before withdrawing Union troops (as part of the compromise that settled the disputed election of 1876) and abandoning the ambitious effort to guarantee justice and security for former slaves.

This limited appetite for occupation and rebuilding has bedeviled postwar policies far more than any desire for permanent presence, leading to problematic and truncated missions in conflicts ranging from the Barbary Wars of the early 1800s to the First Gulf War and the Somali intervention of the early 1990s. Osama bin Laden pointed to America's humiliation in Somalia (where eighteen mutilated soldiers in the "Black Hawk Down" episode led to a hasty American withdrawal) as one of the incidents that led him to characterize the United States as a "paper tiger" with no staying power. Bin Laden also mentioned the U.S. departure from Lebanon after the 1983 Hezbollah suicide bombing that killed 241 Marines, and particularly noted the way that public impatience and exhaustion brought about the retreat from Vietnam.

Ironically, by focusing on the American penchant for quick withdrawals from the world's hot spots, our primary terrorist adversary undermined his own characterization of the United States as a ruthless imperialist power.

Even the long-standing and often bloody U.S. mission to the Philippines culminated in American decisions to forgo any imperial role and resulted in Filipino independence and (flawed) democracy. The United States seized the former Spanish colony with little difficulty at the outset of the Spanish-American War, but then suppressed a stubborn nationalist insurrection (1898–1902) that killed more than four thousand

Not Enough Tyrannizing

The extension of American power to distant territories and initially hostile cultures never depended on military force alone. In the grueling struggle in the Philippines, for instance, the United States succeeded through generous policies during the occupation as much as through courage on the battlefield. Max Boot describes U.S. efforts in *The Savage Wars of Peace:* "Soldiers built schools, ran sanitation campaigns, vaccinated people, collected customs duties, set up courts run by natives, supervised municipal elections, and generally administered governmental functions efficiently and honestly. A thousand idealistic young American civilians even journeyed to the Philippines to teach school in a precursor of the Peace Corps." Manuel Quezon, who became the first president of the "autonomous commonwealth" of the Philippines in 1935, once served as a major in Aguinaldo's army and lamented the American kindness that undermined the insurrection. "Damn the Americans!" he wailed. "Why don't they tyrannize us more?"

American troops and some two hundred thousand Filipinos. This nightmare didn't stop the American authorities from setting up an elected legislative assembly five years later, with a U.S.-style bicameral legislature by 1916. In 1935, the Philippines achieved full internal self-government and, after a brutal Japanese occupation during World War II, gained complete independence (together with massive U.S. reconstruction aid) in 1946. America's renunciation of any colonial role in the Philippines, even after massive sacrifices over the course of nearly a half century, in no sense demonstrates a typically imperialist approach.

Above all, those enraged voices that tirelessly damn the United States as a rapacious, insatiable imperialistic power must somehow explain the continued independent existence of the nation of Canada.

Alongside our allegedly land-hungry and bellicose empire, the Maple Leaf Republic has flourished for more than two centuries—vast, underpopulated, resource-rich, and virtually defenseless. Unlike our Mexican neighbors to the south, the Canadians presented no substantial cultural or linguistic differences to sour the prospect of swallowing the Great White North. On three different occasions, Americans attempted or considered a push to absorb all or part of Canada: during the Revolutionary War, the War of 1812, and the complicated Venezuela Boundary Crisis with Great Britain in 1895. Nevertheless, the Yankee imperialists stopped well short of conquest, and in the twenty-first-century era of unchallenged U.S. hegemony, Canada has gone its own quirky way more notably than ever before, reveling in its separate destiny and distinctive institutions.

The history of U.S. respect for Canada's continued sovereignty hardly comports with the prevailing anti-American clichés that suggest Americans long to impose on all the world the same "genocidal" approach we deployed against the Indians.

CONQUEST BY AMERICANIZATION, NOT AMERICANIZATION BY CONQUEST

As to the territories the United States added as part of its ongoing westward expansion in North America, none of these acquisitions followed the normal colonial pattern of invasion and subjugation of hostile native populations. In all cases, America annexed or negotiated for sparsely populated tracts of land in which U.S. settlers had already established flourishing communities.

Before the United States acquired West Florida from Spain, or Oregon and Washington from Great Britain, or California, Texas, and the Southwest from Mexico, or even the Louisiana Purchase from France, U.S. citizens had already rushed into these territories and to some extent Americanized them. For example, more than thirty thousand Americans settled in Texas with the permission of the Spanish colonial and Mexican governments, and by 1835, the time of the War for Texas Independence, they outnumbered their Mexican neighbors by at least eight to one.

Even the annexation of Hawaii confirmed, rather than began, U.S. domination. American traders and whalers played a prominent role in the islands beginning in the 1780s, and the arrival of U.S. missionaries in the 1820s led to the rapid spread of Christianity, literacy, and civil institutions. As early as 1854, the native Hawaiian government formally applied to Congress for admission to the Union as an American state—bypassing the normal territorial phase. Because the Hawaiians insisted on joining the Republic as a free state, the slaveholding South blocked their bid for instant statehood. Robert Kagan writes that some thirty years later, "Hawaii had become a virtual 'economic colony' of the United States. Hawaiian products sold to the United States, mostly sugar, constituted 99 percent of all the islands' exports, while the United States supplied three-fourths of all Hawaii's imports. American-born settlers, the sons and daughters of missionaries and whalers, had over the years become a dominant economic and political force on the islands. Over time the 'American' and other influential light-skinned merchants in Hawaii agitated for political rights and a political system more closely attuned to their political and economic interests." This led to an elected legislature, the decline of the monarchy, the establishment of a republic in 1894, territorial status in 1900, and statehood in 1959.

As in the other permanent additions to U.S. territory, it wasn't invading armies that made Hawaii part of the nation, but independent-minded immigrants and settlers—acting for their own advancement, without governmental sponsorship or sanction, and establishing American communities—that made U.S. acquisition not only possible but inevitable.

NO LUST FOR DOMINANCE

The notion of America as liberator of the world animated the Republic and its politics long before the globe-girdling wars of the twentieth century. As onetime Jefferson biographer Christopher Hitchens noted in a column on "imperialism" for *Slate:*

> When founders like Alexander Hamilton spoke of a coming American "empire," they arguably employed the word in a classical and metaphorical sense, speaking of the future dominion of the continent. By that standard, Lewis and Clark were the originators of American "imperialism." Anti-imperialists of the colonial era would not count as such today. That old radical Thomas Paine was forever at Jefferson's elbow, urging that the United States become a superpower for democracy. He hoped that America would destroy the old European empires.

As early as 1838, a Jacksonian newspaper called the *Democratic Review* published a soaring description of America's destined international role that might bring a blush to the cheek of even the most visionary neocon:

> The far-reaching, the boundless future will be the era of American greatness. In its magnificent domain of space and time, the nation of many nations is destined to manifest to mankind the excellence of divine principles: to establish on earth the noblest temple ever dedicated to the worship of the Most High—the Sacred and the True. Its floor shall be a hemisphere—its roof the firmament of the star-studded heavens—and its congregation the Union of many Republics, comprising hundreds of happy millions, calling and owning no man master, but governed by God's natural and moral

law of equality, the law of brotherhood—of "peace and goodwill among men."

Otto von Bismarck might boast of building his German Reich on the basis of "blood and iron," but the United States consistently viewed its international mission in deeply Christian, messianic terms. After deciding on an ongoing American role in the Philippines, President William McKinley granted a White House interview to the General Missionary Committee of the Methodist Episcopal Church. "I walked the floor of the White House night after night until midnight," the president revealed,

and I am not ashamed to tell you, gentlemen, that I went down on my knees and prayed to Almighty God for light and guidance more than one night. And one night late it came to me this way—I don't know how it was but it came . . . that there was nothing left for us to do but to take them all, and to educate the Filipinos, and uplift them and civilize and Christianize them, and by God's grace do the very best we could by them, as our fellow-men for whom Christ also died. And then I went to bed, and went to sleep, and slept soundly, and the next morning I sent for the chief engineer of the War Department and I told him to put the Philippines on the map of the United States and there they are, and there they will stay while I am President!

One can scoff at such naïveté and sentimentality, just as many Americans scoffed at the soaring rhetoric of George W. Bush in his second Inaugural Address with its promise to eliminate tyranny and promote democracy around the world. Nevertheless, such ideals about the U.S. obligation to less fortunate peoples have always played a role in shaping American policy and mobilizing public support for our most risky and costly international initiatives. The sincerely held notion of an American mission helps to explain the apparent contradictions in the U.S. approach to the world: we're reluctant and embarrassed to pursue raw power for its own sake, but we can be shockingly aggressive, even militant when it comes to promoting democracy, free markets, and Christianity.

Not surprisingly, this restless and sometimes misapplied idealism led to the worldwide categorization of the United States as "a very dangerous member of the society of nations" (in the 1817 phrase of America's ambassador in London, John Quincy Adams), feared and distrusted as much for its ideological and cultural distinctiveness as for its burgeoning power. Donald Kagan (who paraphrased Adams for the title of his influential book *Dangerous Nation*) writes: "But aggressive territorial expansionism was not the only quality that made the young American republic dangerous in the eyes of others. Of equal if not sometimes greater concern was the danger posed by America's revolutionary ideology, as well as by the way its liberal, commercial society seemed to swallow up those cultures with which it came into contact."

This tendency to devour less vital systems and societies not only reflected the nation's democratic assertiveness but also brought obvious financial benefits. In a fascinating 2007 book called *Day of Empire,* about the emergence of a succession of "hyperpowers," Professor Amy Chua of Yale Law School writes that "America built its world dominance not through conquest but commerce," creating "an informal empire based on trade and influence." Chua cites economic historian John Steele Gordon, who writes, "If the world is becoming rapidly Americanized as once it became Romanized, the reason lies not in our weapons, but in the fact that others want what we have and are willing, often eager, to adopt our ways in order to have them too."

While the "soft power" of U.S. culture and corporations ultimately wields more influence than our military strength, America has pursued numerous humanitarian interventions over the centuries that in no way serve either our financial or strategic self-interest. The recent military missions in Haiti, Somalia, Bosnia, and Kosovo brought scant reward to the United States while managing, with varying degrees of success, to save lives. Nearly a century earlier, the Boxer uprising shook China and, as Max Boot writes, "America joined in a multinational expedition to rescue the besieged legations in Peking. While the Europeans and Japanese participants were determined to carve out their own spheres of influence in China, the United States pointedly committed itself to maintaining free trade for all—the Open Door."

Unlike other dominant powers in world history, the United States today remains less focused on enhancing its own sway than on promoting the stability and institutions that have allowed it to flourish. As Amy Chua concludes: "Even when the United States invades and occupies other countries, the goal today is never annexation but, at least ostensibly, an eventual military withdrawal, leaving behind a constitutional (and hopefully pro-American) democracy."

ENERGIZED AND ENRICHED BY AMERICA

The strongest, most direct evidence against the indictment of America as a destructive imperial power comes from a consideration of the progress of those nations most closely involved with the United States.

It is no accident that the two nations of East Asia with the most vibrant economies and most robust democratic institutions—Japan and South Korea—are precisely those two nations with the most intimate association with the United States and with, in fact, the continued presence of thousands of American troops on their native soil.

In the long term, the states and peoples who aligned themselves with America in world affairs, and even those nations that experienced lengthy American occupations, prospered economically and developed functioning democratic institutions. Just consider the experience of America's Western European allies, and even of our onetime enemies in Germany, Italy, and Japan. The phrase "The Yanks are coming! The Yanks are coming!" (featured in George M. Cohan's stirring World War I rabble-rouser "Over There") most often signaled a nation's immediate liberation and never meant its long-term destruction or conquest.

It's also revealing to note the fate of divided nations split between a pro-American segment and an anti-American counterpart. The United States surely deserves credit for the vastly more fortunate circumstances of South Korea over North Korea: according to UN statistics, South Korea boasts a per-capita gross domestic product twenty-five times greater than North Korea's ($25,840 versus $1,007)—an astonishing ratio for two neighboring, ethnically identical countries. America's influence also contributed to the relative freedom and prosperity of the former West Germany compared to East Germany, and even to the superior

development and free institutions in small, pro-Western Chinese en-
claves (Taiwan, Hong Kong) compared to mainland China.

Moreover, developing states that have realigned from an anti-American
position to a policy of cooperation and commercial connection with the
United States have gained enormous benefits. Most notably, the former
states of the Soviet sphere in Eastern Europe—the Baltic republics (Lithua-
nia, Latvia, Estonia), Poland, Hungary, the Czech Republic, and others—
entered periods of dramatic growth and democratization after the collapse
of the Russian empire.

By the same token, nations that shifted from affiliation with the West
to a posture of anti-Americanism—Cuba in 1959, Iran in 1979—suffered spectacularly. It's far more than a matter of U.S. power rewarding
our friends and punishing our enemies; the record in every corner of
the world suggests that the incorporation of American ideas of self-
government and free markets leads to higher standards of living and
more stable free institutions.

Hawaii, the singularly favored "Aloha State" beloved by tourists and
locals alike, provides a particularly striking example of the blessings
America imparts. Agitators who push for some form of native Hawaiian
"sovereignty" or even a restoration of the nineteenth-century monarchy
ignore the basis for the state's distinction as by far the most prosperous,
functional, and dynamic society in all the Polynesian islands. Fiji and
Tahiti also feature stunning beaches and breathtaking landscape, but
they're racked by chronic poverty, poor health, shaky institutions, and
unreliable infrastructure. The undeniable success of the Hawaiian island
chain when compared to every other Pacific nation east of New Zealand
stems not from resources or historical accidents but from the benevolent
influence of American institutions and values.

THE REAL AMERICAN CRIME:
SURRENDER, NOT INTERVENTION

To a surprising extent, the welfare of the world depends on American
success. Other nations benefit through U.S. prosperity and power, just as
the rest of humanity suffers from American reverses and defeats.

The war in Vietnam remains a hotly debated topic among historians, with powerful recent arguments from Michael Lind *(Vietnam: The Necessary War)* and Mark Moyar *(Triumph Forsaken)* challenging the conventional wisdom that the United States blundered into a useless and unwinnable conflict. The hideous suffering of the people of Southeast Asia, and their long-term oppression by cruel totalitarian regimes, resulted from the ultimate defeat of U.S. policy aims, not from the original decision to support pro-Western governments in the region. The myth that American intervention *caused* the slaughter in Southeast Asia runs counter to the brute fact that the death rate (especially in Cambodia) intensified once U.S. troops went home.

The Korean counterexample helps make the point that America's greatest crime in Vietnam involved Congress's 1975 decision (over the fervent objections of President Gerald Ford) to abandon our allies to our vicious enemies. In Korea, the people also suffered unspeakable casualties, but the perseverance of the United States preserved South Korea's independence and security, to the eternal benefit of the fifty million who now inhabit an economic dynamo and flourishing democracy.

The Vietnam experience showed the tragically high cost to our allies of American surrender. The most important argument for continued U.S. involvement in Iraq hinges on the importance of preventing the struggling Iraqi government from mirroring the Vietnam experience. Withdrawal would ensure a continued and even worsening regional bloodbath, with obvious consequences for American security.

With all the danger and deprivation in the Middle East, the most wretched conditions in today's world still occur almost entirely in sub-Saharan Africa, where impoverished and violence-ridden nations complain far more frequently of too little U.S. involvement than they do of too much. The Clinton administration drew widespread criticism for its handling of the genocidal conflict in Rwanda: though no one could blame the United States for provoking the slaughter, America earned ferocious denunciation for its failure to intervene.

"CRIMES" AND CONTEXT

In 1959, the hilarious Peter Sellers comedy *The Mouse That Roared* charmed audiences around the world by mocking America's long-standing reputation for prodigious generosity—especially to nations who've fought the United States and lost. The movie (based on a droll and sprightly novel by Leonard Wibberley) tells the story of the fictional Duchy of Grand Fenwick, which decides to cope with imminent financial collapse by declaring war on the United States. The grand duchess and her prime minister (both played by Sellers) unleash the full might of a Fenwickian expeditionary force for an invasion of New York City, storming Manhattan with a twenty-man army equipped with medieval armor and bows and arrows. The scheming Europeans naturally plan in advance for a speedy, abject surrender, after which they expect to benefit from the bountiful foreign aid and reconstruction assistance that America traditionally lavishes on its beaten foes.

This good-natured spoof connected with moviegoers of the era precisely because they recognized elements of truth in its portrayal of America's bounteous naïveté—satirizing a notorious national instinct to spread Yankee wealth even to obscure, powerless, and hostile nations. Ironically, the film appeared in the midst of the Cold War period regularly characterized by revisionist historians and commentators (William Appleman Williams, Howard Zinn, Noam Chomsky, and many more) as the very height of U.S. arrogance and imperialism, when the American colossus needlessly menaced the appropriately frightened Soviet Union and ruthlessly imposed its will on allies and unaligned alike.

Critics of the United States support their dark vision of its role in the world by concentrating on specific instances of bullying or brutality, trotting out their favorite horror stories from Indochina or Chile, Vietnam or Iraq, or dozens of other cases where American involvement imperfectly exemplified the nation's high ideals.

These arguments lack perspective and ignore context. They emphasize details over destiny, appalling but isolated incidents over fateful long-term struggles. Anti-American scholars and agitators love to cite random crimes and blunders by U.S. troops and diplomats in order to smear the larger goals of the nation's policies, no matter how noble or necessary.

No one, for instance, questions the righteous nature of America's determination to crush Hitlerism, but even in that epic struggle our armed forces proved themselves capable of appalling cruelty. As Stanford professor Norman Naimark noted in the *Weekly Standard:*

> Some five million Germans died during World War II, including 1.8 million civilians. Allied bombing campaigns, including the firebombing of Dresden and Hamburg, destroyed German cities and killed hundreds of thousands of their inhabitants, among them 75,000 children under 14. . . . Many thousands of Germans starved to death, especially in the American *Rheinwiesenlager* (Rhine Meadow camps); others were beaten and horribly tortured. American soldiers sometimes shot Germans, usually SS and other uniformed Nazis, where they were found, and executed others without trial in detention camps. No American (or German) should have any illusions about the violence carried out by GIs and their officers against disarmed and interned German soldiers, policemen, and even civilians at the end of the war. The "greatest generation" committed crimes against captured Germans that make Abu Ghraib look like child's play.

Naimark readily concedes, however, that it makes no sense to consider such atrocities outside the context of the wider war, just as it makes no sense to condemn the U.S. atom bombs against Hiroshima and Nagasaki (are you listening, Reverend Wright?) without reference to their ultimate lifesaving role for both Americans and Japanese (who otherwise would have perished by the millions in a fight-to-the-death defense against a conventional invasion of the home islands).

In the same way, it's impossible to indict America for its vigorous and sometimes overweening international role in the period 1945–89 without consideration of the multigenerational, worldwide struggle against the aggressive force of worldwide Communism.

In his Nobel Prize lecture, Harold Pinter slimed the United States for causing "hundreds of thousands of deaths" with its support for "every right-wing military dictatorship in the world"—in "Indonesia, Greece, Uruguay, Brazil, Paraguay, Haiti, Turkey, the Philippines, Guatemala, El Salvador, and, of course, Chile." At no point, however, did Pinter remind his listeners that every one of these "dictatorships" played a role in the larger struggle against the Soviet Union and its repeatedly announced intentions to destroy the United States and its way of life ("We will bury you," warned Nikita Khrushchev).

America bashers may insist that the Russian empire never constituted a real threat to the West and that militant anti-Communists merely conjured up the specter of the "Red menace" to serve their own power-mad ends, but the corpses piled high in much of Europe, Asia, and Latin America provide unimpeachable evidence to the contrary. *The Black Book of Communism: Crimes, Terror, Repression,* the 1997 compilation of research edited by French academician Stéphane Courtois, counts some one hundred million victims of Communist murder during the twentieth century. This horrifying record, ignored by too many contemporary Americans, may not excuse American misdeeds of the Cold War period, but it certainly can help to explain them.

Chile constitutes a favorite demonstration of American perfidy, as Pinter's speech showed ("The horror the United States inflicted upon Chile in 1973 can never be purged and can never be forgiven"). But that nation faced dire and increasingly violent divisions even before the CIA-directed coup in 1973. In 1970 Dr. Salvador Allende had become the world's first democratically elected Marxist president and immediately launched a radical program of nationalization, wealth distribution, and social reform. More moderate Chileans feared the imminent imposition of a Castro-style dictatorship. Instead, Chile endured seventeen years of authoritarian, right-wing, pro-American rule from General Augusto Pinochet, with ruthless persecution of suspected dissidents combined with audacious free-market reforms. For all his brutality, Pinochet created the most dynamic economy in Latin America, and under American pressure he allowed a referendum on his own rule in 1988, then gave up power altogether less than two years later. Today Chile continues to benefit from a growing economy and stable democratic institutions, with a freely elected socialist (and female) president.

While the international Left regularly blames the United States for installing Pinochet, America gets no credit for its decisive role in his removal. In the same way, critics assault the United States for backing the

Filipino strongman Ferdinand Marcos but never praise American policy makers for securing his peaceful removal and supporting the more democratically minded "People Power" revolution of Corazon Aquino.

When it came to supporting even the earth's most loathsome dictator in order to achieve victory in a fateful struggle, liberal hero Franklin D. Roosevelt led the way. During World War II, the United States provided massive shipments of war matériel to Stalin himself so that the Russian mass murderer could use the equipment against our common enemy, Hitler. Without the context of the ongoing life-and-death battle to destroy the Third Reich it would have made no sense whatever to back one of the bloodiest tyrants in human history, but within the framework of the ongoing war that backing proved decisive and indispensable.

It's a mistake to evaluate a foreign policy or, for that matter, a military campaign by emphasizing its tactical failures while ignoring its strategic successes. Those who concentrate on Cold War blunders by U.S. policy makers miss the most significant point of them all: America's strategies and sacrifices, doctrines and deceptions resulted in the most remarkable victory in our history, with nearly five hundred million human beings liberated from Stalinist tyranny. The results everywhere, in terms of vastly improved living standards and fresh blessings of freedom, should speak for themselves.

So should the USA's restraint, modesty, and generosity in responding to the collapse of its longtime Soviet rival. With America for the first time enjoying matchless power in a suddenly unipolar world, the new "hyperpower" made no attempt to abuse its standing. As Amy Chua writes:

> Here was a society with unthinkable destructive capacity, facing no countervailing power. Yet it seemed to go without saying that the United States would not use its unrivaled force for territorial expansion or other aggressive imperialist ends. . . . When it came to U.S. military might, the most controversial issues were whether the United States should intervene abroad for purely humanitarian reasons (as in Kosovo or Rwanda) and what America should do with its "peace dividend," the billions of dollars the United States would no longer be spending on its military.

No Alternative to America

"Yes, it is not perfect, this republic of ours. But the possibilities for emancipation and self-improvement it offers are unmatched in other lands.... It is one thing to rail against Pax Americana, but after the pollsters are gone, the truth of our contemporary order of states endures. We live in a world held by American power—and benevolence. Nothing prettier, or more just, looms over the horizon."

—Fouad Ajami, Lebanese-born scholar
at the School of Advanced International Studies
at Johns Hopkins University, June 2008

THE BEDFORD FALLS EXPERIMENT

After the Cold War, American power represents the one indispensable element in sustaining hopes for an ordered and peaceful world. Christopher Hitchens writes:

> The plain fact remains that when the rest of the world wants anything done in a hurry, it applies to American power. If the "Europeans" or the United Nations had been left with the task, the European provinces of Bosnia-Herzegovina and Kosovo would now be howling wildernesses, Kuwait would be the 19th province of a Greater Iraq, and Afghanistan might still be under Taliban rule. In at least the first two of the above cases, it can't even be argued that American imperialism was the problem in the first place. This makes many of the critics of this imposing new order sound like the whimpering, resentful Judean subversives in *The Life of Brian*, squabbling among themselves about "What have the Romans ever done for us?"

Donald Kagan, reviewing the nation's ongoing struggle in April 2008 in the *New Republic*, notes that China and Russia may threaten American hegemony with a new axis of autocracy, but they understand and recognize the continued dominance of the United States:

> For all their growing wealth and influence, the twenty-first-century autocracies remain a minority in the world. As some Chinese scholars put it, democratic liberalism became dominant after the fall of Soviet communism and is sustained by "an international hierarchy dominated by the United States and its democratic allies," a "U.S.-centered great power group." The Chinese and the Russians feel like outliers from this exclusive and powerful clique. "You western countries, you decide the rules, you give the grades, you say 'you have been a bad boy,'" complained one Chinese official at Davos this year. Putin also complains that "we are constantly being taught about democracy."

The best way to put America's place in the world in proper context is to call to mind a famous sequence from the most beloved Hollywood movie of them all.

In *It's a Wonderful Life*, small-town banker George Bailey (Jimmy Stewart) contemplates a Christmas Eve suicide before guardian angel Clarence provides the ultimate life-affirming vision. He provides the disheartened hero with a dark, dysfunctional view of the town of Bedford Falls as it would have been if he'd never drawn breath, the community taking shape without his good deeds and benevolent influence. With that sharper perspective, George can go home to his loving family to celebrate the holiday with gratitude and joy.

Those who condemn the United States should perform a thought experiment involving a global "Bedford Falls vision."

Imagine that the United States had never become a world power, or never existed at all.

Would the ideals of democracy and free markets wield the same power in the world?

Would murderous dictatorships have claimed more victims, or fewer?

Would the community of nations strain under the lash of Nazism, Communism, or some vicious combination of both?

Would multiethnic, multireligious democracy flourish anywhere on earth without inspiration from the groundbreaking example of the USA?

Would the threat of jihadist violence and resurgent Islamic fundamentalism menace humanity more grievously, or not at all?

No one can provide definitive, authoritative answers to such hypothetical questions, but merely confronting the questions should help put the American role in more complete perspective. Just as George Bailey's view of an alternative reality convinced him that "it's a wonderful life," even the briefest contemplation of a world without America should persuade us that "it's a wonderful nation"—and an indispensable boon to all of humanity.

"The Two-Party System Is Broken, and We Urgently Need a Viable Third Party"

NOT EVEN CLOSE

The persistent American fascination with third parties and fringe candidates defies every lesson of history, logic, human nature, and common sense.

No minor-party candidate has ever won the presidency or, for that matter, even come close. For the most part, these ego-driven "independent" adventures in electoral narcissism push the political process further away from their supporters' professed goals, rather than advancing the insurgent group's agenda or ideas.

Nevertheless, prominent leaders in business, media, and even politics regularly declare that the two-party system has been irretrievably broken and that the United States urgently needs a viable third party. Opinion surveys suggest that such arguments have found enthusiastic public support. A clear majority of Americans (58 percent) in September 2007 told the Gallup Poll that the two major parties "do such a poor job that a third major party is needed," while only 39 percent agreed with a statement that the established parties "do an adequate job of representing the American people." A Rasmussen Survey (May 2007) produced similar results, with 58 percent agreeing that "it would be good for the United States if there were a truly competitive third party," and only 23 percent disagreeing.

Douglas E. Schoen, longtime campaign consultant for Bill and Hillary Clinton, has read these numbers and told my radio audience that he's now committed himself to changing the organization of our politics. In his 2008 book *Declaring Independence: The Beginning of the End of the Two-Party System,* Schoen notes that "evidence that voters are generally unhappy with today's Democratic and Republican parties is mounting everywhere. . . . Two out of five Americans cannot name anything they like about the Democratic Party, and nearly half of those polled cannot name anything they like about the Republicans . . . According to a poll taken by the firm I founded, Penn, Schoen & Berland, 61 percent of voters say the two major parties are failing and that having an independent on the ballot in the 2008 election would be good for America."

CNN's pompous pontificator Lou Dobbs expressed similar sentiments in his 2007 best seller *Independents Day.* "I don't know about you," he harrumphed, "but fundamentally I don't see much of a difference between Republicans and Democrats. The creation of a third, independent choice, one that has the concerns of American working people as its basis, is the way we must proceed." In a column on CNN.com a year before the 2008 presidential election, Dobbs went so far as to predict that an unconventional candidate, "an independent populist" who shunned the two major parties, would sweep to victory and seize the White House. "I believe next November's surprise will be the election of a man or woman of great character, vision and accomplishment, a candidate who has not yet entered the race."

Much to the disappointment of the fans of his rabidly anti-immigrant TV show, Dobbs himself declined to join the race—as did New York mayor Michael Bloomberg, whose reported willingness to spend up to $500 million of his personal fortune would have made him a vastly more formidable candidate. By the time the major-party candidates had been chosen, ardent advocates for independent candidacies and minor parties still lacked the figure of "great character, vision and accomplishment" they noisily craved. Instead, they settled for rounding up the usual suspects, such as three-time loser Ralph Nader, disgraced former congresswoman Cynthia McKinney, former congressman Bob Barr, perennial candidate Alan Keyes, radio preacher Chuck Baldwin, Las Vegas oddsmaker Wayne Allyn Root, and other assorted odd ducks with no chance of carrying even a single state.

As the 2008 situation powerfully demonstrated, the ever-present call for some political third force remains not just a forlorn hope but a cruel hoax. The unquenchable enthusiasm for new parties and marginal, cult-of-personality candidacies rests on a foundation of unassailable ignorance and relentless historical illiteracy. Even a glancing review of lessons from the electoral past reveals uncomfortable but incontrovertible facts regarding independent or minor-party campaigns.

THIRD PARTIES ALWAYS LOSE—AND RUIN THEIR LEADERS' POLITICAL CAREERS

Consider the fate of the bonkers billionaire Ross Perot, the most formidable minor-party candidate of the past ninety-six years. In 1992, against Bill Clinton and George H. W. Bush, he invested some $65 million of his own funds and at one time emerged as the leader in national surveys, polling close to 40 percent. On Election Day, after arbitrarily suspending and then relaunching his campaign, Perot still drew an impressive 19 percent of the popular tally (though he failed to win even a single electoral vote).

Four years later, he tried again but this time spent only $22 million of his own money and relied on federal matching funds. More than half of his former supporters abandoned him, and he polled a scant 8.4 percent. The Reform Party he had assembled as a personal vehicle for his quixotic quest quickly collapsed when Perot lost interest in it: in 2000, "Pitchfork

Pat" Buchanan claimed the party's nomination and drew a spectacularly pathetic 0.4 percent—even fellow fringie Ralph Nader topped his sad vote total by an astonishing ratio of six to one.

If anyone today recalls Ross Perot and the Reform Party, they do so only as a punch line or as a factor in allowing Bill Clinton to win the White House twice without ever winning a majority of the popular vote. Perot's credibility as a political commentator all but evaporated in the wake of his campaigns—and Buchanan's stature also suffered major damage, even after he returned to the Republican fold to back George W. Bush in 2004.

Other conservatives similarly destroyed once-promising careers with their third-party obsessions. Howard Phillips, twice elected president of the Student Council at Harvard, qualified as a rising Republican star when he headed two federal agencies in the Nixon administration. In 1992, however, he succumbed to the temptation of running for president as candidate of the U.S. Taxpayers Party (later rebranded as the Constitution Party), and then ran again in 1996 and 2000. Each of these inept and incurably self-righteous campaigns drew less than 0.2 percent of the vote and made Phillips an object of pity more than admiration to most of his colleagues in the movement.

Time and again, prominent leaders wasted their time and shattered their reputations with their third-party misadventures. Henry A. Wallace, the supremely charismatic and widely admired chief of two cabinet departments (Agriculture and Commerce) under FDR and vice president of the United States (1941–45), ran as the standard-bearer of the leftist Progressive Party in 1948 and won a surprisingly paltry 2.4 percent—not nearly enough to damage the reelection drive of his archrival, Harry Truman. Former president Martin Van Buren drew a humiliating 10 percent as a Free Soil candidate in 1848 (seven years after leaving the White House), and in 1856 another former president, Millard Fillmore, drew 22 percent as the anointed champion of the anti-immigrant American (or "Know-Nothing") Party. As a result of their fringe-party escapades, both onetime chief executives ended their careers in embarrassment and irrelevance.

Even Theodore Roosevelt, a wildly popular ex-president and war hero, damaged his national standing when he launched his ill-fated Progressive (or "Bull Moose") campaign in 1912. Yes, TR managed the best showing for any third-party candidate in American history, with 27 percent of the popular vote and 88 electoral votes. But he still finished more than 14 percent behind the victorious Woodrow Wilson (a man he thoroughly despised), while falling a full 178 votes short of earning an electoral college majority, and carrying only six states to Wilson's forty. After his long, bitterly frustrating campaign to return to the White House (capped by receiving a bullet in the chest from an anti-third-term fanatic during a campaign speech in Milwaukee two weeks before the election), TR dropped his association with the "Bull Moose" Progressives and scuttled back toward the Republican Party. Fuming with impatience during eight years of Wilsonian rule, he dreamed of making a last run for the White House—as a Republican—and might well have won his party's nomination in 1920 except for his untimely death at age sixty in January 1919.

While not even a genuinely adored Mount Rushmore figure such as Teddy Roosevelt could shake the third-party curse when it came to a presidential race, some prominent independent candidates have defied the odds and won statewide elections. Professional wrestler Jesse Ventura came to power as Minnesota's governor in 1998, winning a three-way race as the Reform Party (and later Independence Party) candidate, but his stalled, ineffectual governance—with no party colleagues in the legislature to support him—made him a one-term wonder. After leaving office he retreated to the desert and concentrated on riding his motorcycle, until he returned briefly to the public eye in 2008, peddling a hastily written book full of conspiracy theories about 9/11 as an inside job.

A far more worthy candidate achieved similarly short-lived third-party glory: James Buckley, brother of the great conservative intellectual William F. Buckley Jr., won a stunning electoral upset in 1970 as New York's Conservative Party candidate for U.S. Senate. He prevailed in a three-way split against a liberal Democrat and a liberal Republican (who'd been appointed just months before to replace the assassinated Senator Bobby Kennedy). After this unexpected victory in extraordinary circumstances, Buckley also lasted only one term: he lost his reelection bid (even though he ran this time as candidate of both the Conservative Party *and* the GOP) in a crushing landslide to moderate Democrat Daniel Patrick Moynihan.

Other minor-party "success stories," in races for governor, senator, congressman, and mayor, faced comparably brief careers—even among

The First Fringe Party Fights "Lowly Reptiles"

America's first significant third party emerged in the aftermath of the suspected murder of a hard-drinking bricklayer in upstate New York. William Morgan disappeared in 1826 after quarreling with fellow Masons of the local lodge and threatening to publish a scandalous book exposing Freemasonry's "dark secrets." Though authorities never found a body, and Masons denied all wrongdoing, an impassioned new political movement promoted lurid conspiracy theories and demanded the suppression of Freemasonry.

So many prominent leaders identified as Masons—including Presidents George Washington, James Monroe, and Andrew Jackson, Chief Justice John Marshall, House Speaker Henry Clay, and New York governor DeWitt Clinton—that the Anti-Masonic Party readily mobilized general resentment toward the privileged and the powerful. The party published thirty-five newspapers in New York alone, and elected governors of Pennsylvania and Vermont. Future Republican leaders such as William Seward and Thaddeus Stevens got their start in the Anti-Masonic Party; Stevens summed up the organization's subtle approach by characterizing Masons as "a feeble band of lowly reptiles" and describing the Masonic Grand Lodge as "a chartered iniquity, within whose jaws are crushed the bones of immortal men, and whose mouth is continually reeking with human blood, and spitting forth human gore."

The Anti-Masons themselves spat forth a major political innovation: convening the first national presidential nominating convention in 1832. They chose former U.S. attorney general William Wirt as their standard-bearer; ironically, he was a former Mason who defended Freemasonry in his acceptance speech. Running against high-ranking Masons Jackson and Clay, Wirt drew 8 percent of the popular vote and carried Vermont. Despite this impressive showing, the party faded after Wirt's retirement—though as late as 1884 Jonathan Blanchard (president of Wheaton College) ran his own quixotic presidential campaign on the Anti-Masonic ticket.

the surging Populists of the 1890s. In 1896, they reached a high-water mark with 21 seats in the House of Representatives (compared to 204 Republicans and 113 Democrats), but just two years later their representation plummeted to 4. In 1902, only six years removed from their glory days, the Populists elected not a single member of Congress—and never again made serious races for federal office.

NO, REPUBLICANS NEVER CONSTITUTED A THIRD PARTY

Whenever I take the time on the radio to discuss the obvious and inevitable futility of minor-party campaigns, some smug caller will try to play "gotcha" by reminding me that my own beloved GOP began its political life as a minor party and managed to elect an underdog nominee named Lincoln in the fateful election of 1860. It makes for a good story, and I know it allows misled minions to reassure themselves that at least one minor party of the past beat the odds to emerge as a significant electoral force, but it's not in any sense true that Republicans *ever* operated as a third party.

By the time of the very first Republican county convention (in Ripon, Wisconsin, on March 20, 1854) the Whig Party had already collapsed and shattered, hopelessly divided between its northern antislavery branch and the southern "Cotton Whigs." The quickly organized Republicans came into being as replacements, not rivals, for the dissolving Whigs. Refugees from the old party (including thirty sitting congressmen, several senators, and others) determined to fill the vacuum, and, joined by a few antislavery Democrats and former Free Soilers, they launched their new state organizations, which instantly cooperated on a national basis.

Candidates first appeared on ballots with the designation of the new Republican Party in the congressional elections of 1854, and the fresh organization won stunning success from the very beginning. In part, Republicans prevailed because in many races they replaced the Whig candidate and faced only Democrats as their opponents. That very first year the Republicans won the largest share of seats in the House of Representatives (108, compared to 83 for the Democrats), along with 15 Senate seats, including the majority of those contested in that election. After an eight-week struggle, the Republicans even elected the Speaker of the House (Nathaniel P. Banks of Massachusetts) scarcely a year after the party's initial organization.

In other words, the Republicans began their existence not as a third party, or even a second party, but as the instantly dominant party in American politics. The future "Grand Old Party" showed itself a grand young party not only with its congressional candidates but also with its first-ever presidential nominee—John C. Frémont, the "Great Pathfinder"—in 1856. With no Whig candidate on the ballot, he never counted as a third-party contender and his rousing slogan, "Free speech, free soil, free press, free men / Frémont and victory!" stirred massive support in the northern states. Far from the traditionally indulgent and pointless gestural politics of minor-party candidacies, Frémont made a real race of it against the Democrat James Buchanan, losing the popular vote 45 percent to 33 percent and the electoral vote 174 to 118. The real third-party candidate was former president Fillmore, whose anti-immigrant Know-Nothing campaign (150 years too early to benefit from the support of Lou Dobbs) drew a few remnants of the Whigs and took just enough votes away from Frémont in New Jersey and Pennsylvania to give Buchanan narrow victories and the electoral majority.

The last pre–Civil War election of 1860 did witness a shake-up of the normal political order, with a campaign that resembled a European multiparty election, but the Republicans never represented an upstart third-party effort. By this time they commanded clear majorities in nearly all the northern states and fully expected to sweep more than enough of those states (especially in light of Democratic divisions) to capture the White House. Sure enough, the Republican nominee, Abraham Lincoln, won a clear majority of the electoral vote (59 percent) and a comfortable plurality (40 percent) of the popular vote.

The third party in this fateful campaign—actually, a third party *and* a fourth party—grew out of the Democratic Party, not the Republican. Southern Democrats abandoned their national nominee, Stephen A. Douglas, and rallied behind the sitting vice president, John C. Breckinridge (a future Confederate general), while former Cotton Whigs and pro-Union Democrats from border states launched a campaign for former Speaker of the House John Bell of Tennessee. Breckinridge won 18 percent of the popular vote and 72 electoral votes, and Bell claimed 13 percent of the popular vote and 39 electoral votes.

For the only time in American history, the two-party system clearly broke down in 1860—and that breakdown contributed significantly to the outbreak a few months later of a devastating four-year war that claimed 600,000 American lives.

In other words, no one can look at the four-way race in 1860 and feel encouraged by the results of the experiment. The experience of that campaign offers no proof of the positive value of third (and fourth) parties, but rather illustrates their dangers. The four-way competition in the presidential race contributed to the splitting of the Union and the explosion of the national party consensus that had previously kept a divided assemblage of very different states from flying apart.

IT'S EASIER TO WIN OVER A PARTY THAN A NATION

Though third-party purists and fantasists find it difficult to come to terms with the truth, the essence of political success involves persuading enough people to vote for you or your point of view so that you're actually able to win elections. In this context, it makes no sense whatever to believe that it's somehow easier to reach and convince the large number of voters in a general election than to win over the relatively small number of voters in party primaries.

In general elections, any new party faces huge challenges getting on the ballot, raising money, earning press attention, and competing with the established parties in terms of substance or credibility.

But the greatest obstacle to minor-party success isn't difficult ballot access, exclusion from debates, or even residual loyalty to the Democrats and the GOP. It is, rather, the obvious, incontrovertible fact that it's vastly easier to win races within one of the major parties than it is to set up the structure to compete against them.

Consider a hypothetical race for state assembly, with a total electorate of one hundred thousand voters. Let's say you're a prominent but controversial member of the community who can count on the support of twenty thousand hard-core voters but stands little chance of persuading many more. In this situation, there's no possibility you can win as a third-party contender—even with a three-way split, 20 percent won't carry the day. But if you enter one of the party primaries, you stand an excellent chance of victory, since your committed core represents a much higher percentage (perhaps even a majority) of those casting ballots. Not only do primary elections divide Republicans and Democrats, but independents often don't participate and turnout always proves less robust. That means that your little army of twenty thousand, badly outnumbered in a general election, becomes a formidable, even intimidating force on the limited battlefield of a primary.

Primary elections, in other words, provide far more openings for challenging and unorthodox candidates and ideas. And if such candidacies succeed in winning Republican or Democratic nominations, they inevitably draw additional votes in November from those citizens who instinctively and automatically support their party's nominee.

This simple logic obliterates the most frequent justification for third parties: the claim that we're "shut out" of one (or both) of the established parties so we have no choice but to run an insurgent, independent campaign.

But if you don't have enough support to win a party primary, how will you ever draw the backing to beat the far more formidable competition, among a far larger universe of voters, in the general election? If you can't mount a persuasive campaign for the Republican or Democratic nomination, how can any rational politico expect to conduct a successful campaign among the voters at large?

These questions apply just as forcefully to major issues as they do to political personalities. Take, for instance, the intense agitation in 2007–8 regarding government policies toward illegal immigration. After a successful populist battle against a bipartisan congressional reform bill, Congressman Tom Tancredo of Colorado ran for the Republican presidential nomination as an unapologetic, outspoken anti-immigration contender and offered himself as a virtual one-issue candidate. His failure to attract substantial support (he polled below 2 percent in all primaries and caucuses) convinced him, however, that it made no sense to launch the third-party campaign some of his backers desired. If he couldn't mobilize the troops within the Republican Party, where secure-the-borders sentiment predominates, what chance did he have with a more indifferent and divided general electorate?

Outsiders will always enjoy greater viability in competing for nominations rather than contesting the final battle in November, and this enhanced accessibility becomes particularly pertinent in presidential campaigns. Because of the disproportionate importance of small-state contests in Iowa and New Hampshire, a candidate can conceivably ensure himself the nomination with a tiny number of votes: in a split field, a combined total of a hundred thousand backers in both states can easily carry the day in either major party. In 1992, Ross Perot almost certainly could have won the Democratic (or perhaps even the Republican) contest in independent-minded New Hampshire, gained traction in states that followed, and gone on to become the nominee of a major party and (heaven help us) president of the United States.

If you mean to mobilize an army of committed activists to advance your political prospects, it's inarguably more plausible to do so in specific primary states than in general election contests in fifty separate states all across the continent.

Consider the baleful example of Pat Buchanan, who enjoyed some primary success as a protest candidate against President George H. W. Bush in 1992 and then actually won the GOP New Hampshire primary (in a tight three-way race with Bob Dole and Lamar Alexander) in 1996. As a Republican, Pitchfork Pat managed to mobilize the "Buchanan Brigades" and to draw literally hundreds of thousands of supporters (if not a majority). When he left the party in 2000, however, his appeal quickly disintegrated, and the hard core of enthusiasts that had made him competitive in Republican primaries counted for nothing in the general election (and yes, 0.4 percent—despite taking $12 million in federal campaign funds—counts as just about nothing).

THIRD PARTIES: LESS RELEVANT THAN EVER

The classic justification for any candidate to walk out of his party and to launch an independent bid involves the charge that arrogant bosses have blocked his path to the nomination and thwarted the will of the people.

That claim clearly animated Theodore Roosevelt's powerful third-party challenge in 1912. The former president had become disillusioned with the conservative policies of his hand-picked successor, William Howard Taft, and battled him in all available primaries. TR won handily almost everywhere, with majorities in Illinois, Minnesota, Nebraska, South Dakota, California, Maryland, and Pennsylvania. He even won a landslide victory in Taft's home state of Ohio. Nevertheless, Taft loyalists controlled the credentials committee at the GOP convention in Chicago and seated just enough of their supporters to renominate the president. Furious at the transparent defiance of the clear popular preference for TR, the former president walked out of his party and summoned his own "Bull Moose" convention to seal his third-party nomination some six weeks later, instantly ensuring easy victory for Democrat Woodrow Wilson.

Fifty-six years later another Chicago convention raised similar issues for Democrats. At the height of the Vietnam era, antiwar candidates Eugene McCarthy and Bobby Kennedy won every primary between them; Vice President Hubert Humphrey, the loyalist choice of embattled president Lyndon Johnson, never bothered to contest a single one of the primary states. Nevertheless, after Kennedy's assassination, Humphrey won the nomination (while bloody riots convulsed the streets of Chicago) because of his solid support from the party establishment.

After this nightmarish experience in 1968, the Democrats chartered the McGovern Commission to open up and reform the nomination process, and the Republicans soon followed suit. Never again could a candidate become his party's standard-bearer without competing in primaries; never again could a group of bosses in a "smoke-filled room" (or even today with superdelegates in a politically correct fern-filled room) choose a nominee who hadn't battled his way through dozens of well-publicized electoral battles in various corners of the country. The new openness of the primary process provided a number of bizarre surprises, including the 1976 nomination (and ultimate election) of an obscure, one-term governor of Georgia named Jimmy Carter, or the shocking 2008 upset of the heavily favored Hillary Clinton by a previously little-known candidate, Barack Obama, with less than three years' Washington experience.

The new importance of primaries also facilitated the abrupt ideological shifts that third-party advocates invariably demand. In 1964, for instance, the process allowed conservative grassroots activists in the GOP to throw out the "Eastern Republican establishment" (even booing its leader, Nelson Rockefeller, at the convention) and to nominate outspoken conservative Barry Goldwater. To signal the depth of the change he heralded, Goldwater's acceptance speech explicitly rejected the party's traditional centrism, with its ringing declaration: "Extremism in the defense of liberty is no vice; moderation in the pursuit of justice is no virtue."

Eight years later, the Democrats experienced a similar transformation, when the antiwar left took over the party with the nomination of George ("Come home, America!") McGovern and trumpeted its thoroughgoing contempt for the moderate establishment. The "new politics" antiwar insurgencies of 1968 and 1972 moved the party forcefully and permanently to the left, repudiating the long-standing anti-Communist, socially conservative, pro-military slant that had characterized the Democrats since World War II.

Finally, in 1976 conservative ideologues rallied behind Ronald Reagan and came within a few convention votes of taking the nomination from incumbent president Gerald Ford. Four years later, the Reaganites swept to victory, capturing the whole machinery of the Republican Party, completing the work of the Goldwater revolution—and demonstrating that with today's nomination process, true believers who disdain compromise and equivocation can not only nominate their candidates of choice but also shift the ideological orientation of our great political parties.

The old argument that party bosses stymie insurgent or issues-driven campaigns no longer applies to political reality—not in an era when campaigns in both parties cater so obviously to enthusiastic activists who dominate the early primaries.

FRINGE PARTIES DISCREDIT
THE ISSUES THEY EMBRACE

Apologists for minor parties regularly defend their eccentric activism with the claim that they're gradually, inexorably building support for their unconventional ideas. The Libertarian Party in particular insists that it has made steady progress for its philosophy of limited government with its thirty years of tireless campaigning.

In fact, the electoral record shows dramatic deterioration in the party's electoral appeal rather than any discernable increase in influence, as the once trendy Libertarians have morphed into the goofy and sophomoric Losertarians. The party reached its all-time peak of success with its second major presidential campaign under Ed Clark in 1980. Running against Ronald Reagan, Clark drew 921,000 votes and a rousing 1.06 percent of the electorate. The next time out, the Libertarians did barely half as well, and after that the party's fortunes continued to slide. In 2000, Libertarian nominee Harry Browne won only 0.36 percent, and in 2004, the hapless Michael Badnarik did even worse, with less than 0.33 percent.

In other words, after a quarter century of fund-raising, propaganda, and party building, the Libertarians succeeded in alienating two-thirds of their never significant support—their 1 percent showing of twenty-eight years ago representing a golden moment that's never even come close to replication. After so much frustration, futility, and consistent public rejection, on what basis do Losertarians suddenly expect a brighter future?

Among the faceless cavalcade of Libertarian losers, one of their presidential candidates manages to stand out—not because of his strong showing (he drew only 0.47 percent of the vote) but because he drew the right message from his embarrassing experience. Texas obstetrician Ron Paul carried the fringe party's banner in 1988 but soon thereafter returned to the Republican Party, won election to Congress, and conducted a dynamic, much publicized, and lavishly funded (to the tune of $30 million) campaign for the GOP presidential nomination in 2008. As a Republican contender, Dr. Paul garnered vastly more attention for his ideals and proposals (his book *The Revolution: A Manifesto* became a number one best seller) than he ever did as the Libertarian nominee—a living demonstration of the ill-considered idiocy of fringe-party campaigns.

Rather than advancing unconventional ideas, minor parties most often discredit them through association with quirky political organizations far outside the political mainstream. The Prohibition Party, for instance, took opponents of alcohol out of the major parties and concentrated them in a marginal political organization that, during 134 years of fielding candidates, elected one congressman from California (1914) and one governor of Florida (1916) but almost nothing else. In terms of presidential politics, the party managed its best showing ever in 1892 (2.25 percent), some twenty-seven years before temperance advocates finally achieved Prohibition through the Eighteenth Amendment to the Constitution. Predictably, Republicans—rather than members of the Prohibition Party—finally brought about this historic change. The Prohibition platform succeeded, in other words, only when true believers left the fringe and entered one of the established parties.

The Transcendental Politics of the "Natural Law Party"

Dr. John Hagelin, a physicist trained at Dartmouth and Harvard, ran for president three times as the nominee of the Natural Law Party. In 1992 he nearly carried his home county in Iowa (drawing 23.9 percent of the vote against Clinton, Bush, and Perot), and in 1996 he reached his political zenith, appearing on the ballot in forty-four states and persuading 113,668 of his fellow citizens to vote for him.

These were impressive feats given that the Natural Law Party promoted Transcendental Meditation as the solution to the world's problems. In fact, Dr. Hagelin has been a prominent member of the faculty at Maharishi International University, specializing in the "Maharishi Effect"—using "advanced meditation techniques" to cure social ills. Dr. Hagelin once imported four thousand meditators to Washington, D.C., and then cited crime records to show the beneficial result.

In 2004, the Natural Law Party endorsed the Democratic presidential juggernaut of leftist firebrand Dennis Kucinich. Dr. Hagelin himself returned to teaching and to an esteemed position as minister of science and technology of the Global Country of World Peace, an organization that Maharishi Mahesh Yogi authorized "for preventive, invincible administration for the whole world."

By the same token, Populists saw meaningful progress for their national agenda only after the party largely collapsed and its most gifted members migrated into the Democratic Party beginning in 1896. Somehow, even crackpot ideas (such as the bizarre Populist obsession with "free silver") look less menacing when they're advocated by leaders of a well-established political organization rather than by a turbulent fringe group.

YOU CAN'T INFLUENCE A PARTY BY LEAVING IT

One of the most bizarre arguments for third parties suggests that walking out of one of the established parties will force it to move in your direction.

This reasoning constitutes sheer madness, of course: what sort of maniac honestly believes that he'll exert greater impact on a political organization after he's abandoned his membership?

In 2000, when Pat Buchanan deserted the Republicans for his disastrous Reform Party race (in which he selected a former L.A. high school teacher with a history of mental disability as his running mate), he took with him some of his fellow GOP advocates of a more protectionist trade policy. The result, predictably enough, was a Republican Party more unanimous than ever in support of free trade. Why should Republicans take protectionist arguments more seriously when the few supporters of such arguments had already left the party?

Party walkouts don't produce some sudden desire for reconciliation any more than marital walkouts strengthen a fraying relationship. If you unilaterally separate from your wife or husband, can you expect to come back to greater love and standing if you decide to reconcile after four years?

When a faction abandons its major-party home, it's rarely welcomed back into the fold—especially when the party disloyalty has produced a major defeat. Take the case of Ralph Nader, with his incontestably destructive impact on Al Gore's 2000 presidential bid: even if the gadfly wanted to make a place for himself in the Democratic Party, the deep resentment of his role in the election of George W. Bush would make it impossible for him to assume a position of respect or influence.

LOSING CAMPAIGNS DON'T SHAPE GOVERNANCE OR POLICY

For third-party true believers, rejection by the general public confirms their sense of moral superiority and martyrdom: winning 0.03 percent with uncompromising principles feels somehow nobler than winning an election through the normal compromises and actually changing the direction of politics. In this sense, fringe-party activism represents the ultimate in masturbatory politics: giving intense pleasure and passing thrills to the individual participants but exerting no impact whatever on anyone else.

On those rare occasions when third parties play some decisive role in close elections, they almost always damage the candidates who more closely resemble the independent contenders. Former Republican Ross Perot, for example, destroyed Republican George H. W. Bush; leftist Ralph Nader damaged Al Gore; and "limited-government" Libertarian Senate candidates in Montana, Washington, Georgia, and other states recently swung elections to big-government Democrats (and in 2006 tilted at least three close elections to give Harry Reid his one-vote Senate majority).

By taking votes from the major-party contender who's ideologically most similar and rewarding those opponents who agree with them the least, independent candidates move the political process away from their professed goals, not toward them.

"NOT A DIME'S WORTH OF DIFFERENCE"?

Despite all the logical and historical arguments against third-party campaigns, insurgent candidates claim that they're compelled to run to give the people a "real choice." Ignoring the increasingly profound ideological gulf between Republicans and Democrats on foreign policy, economics, social issues, and much more, minor-party activists dismiss these old political organizations as "Tweedledum and Tweedle-dumber," indistinguishable "Republicrats and Demicans"—power-hungry hacks who serve the same corporate masters and only *pretend* to disagree. Former Alabama governor George C. Wallace ran his entire 1968 campaign (as standard-bearer for the hastily assembled American Independent Party) based on the slogan that "there's not a dime's worth of difference" between his two opponents, Nixon and Humphrey, claiming they both kowtowed to the same "pointy-headed intellectuals."

In retrospect, any comparison of the careers, character, and ideology of Richard Nixon and Hubert Humphrey reveals that even in that pre-inflation era, the value of their differences amounted to more than ten cents. But aside from the substance of Wallace's complaint, the impact of his relatively successful backlash-to-civil-rights campaign (he won 13.5 percent of the vote and carried five southern states) shows the futile na-ture of the third-party strategy. Four years later he rejoined the Demo-crats and competed successfully in several primaries, though a would-be assassin's bullet cut short his campaign. In the end, the Democrats nom-inated ultraliberal George McGovern, underlining their big differences with Nixon by moving further away from, not closer to, Wallace's right-wing, blue-collar position.

Other "give 'em a choice" campaigns produced similarly negligible long-term results. "Outsider" Ralph Nader claimed in 2000 that he could see scant difference between insiders Bush and Gore, and so he drew a crucial 2.7 percent of the electorate. Four years later, Republican Bush and Democrat Kerry utterly ignored Nader's issues while each drawing millions more votes than their parties had won four years before, but Nader himself got less than one-sixth the ballots he had claimed in 2000.

If major-party candidates tend to sound similar themes in the last weeks before an election, it's because they're competing for the same moderate, centrist swing voters who end up deciding every close race. Third-party "choice" candidates can't magically mobilize mass support by positioning themselves outside the political mainstream.

In fact, many recent third-party movements have criticized Republi-cans and Democrats not because they're too similar but because they're too different—too polarizing, partisan, and extreme. Middle-of-the-road independent contenders such as John Anderson in 1980 and Ross Perot in 1992 and '96 made no attempt to push the parties to the left or the right, but rather schemed to attract the incurably undecided—

confused voters who waffle and dither, somewhere between donkey and elephant. Dreams of running various above-the-fray, vaguely postpartisan figures (such as Colin Powell or Mike Bloomberg or Chuck Hagel) persistently animate minor-party activists who don't hope to give voters a new choice but instead want to help them avoid any choices at all by offering ill-defined, split-the-difference candidates.

The apparent and appalling contradictions in popular pleas for a new national party—pleas that simultaneously attack the big parties as too close and too far apart—expose the essential silliness of the fringe-candidate compulsion.

THIS CRUEL AND DANGEROUS GAME

Most Americans have come to understand this cruel and dangerous game, so even the most ballyhooed fringe candidates fail to live up to their promising poll numbers. In 1980, moderate Republican John Anderson believed the surveys and pundits who said he could establish himself as an alternative positional in between the outspoken conservative Ronald Reagan and the failed liberal standard-bearer, Jimmy Carter. At one point in the race, Anderson (with a former Wisconsin governor as his running mate) polled an attention-getting 24 percent, but in the end he drew only 6.6 percent, fading fast in the last days before the election as the American people began to focus on the true stakes in the choice before them.

This pattern repeats itself in almost every election: even the most intriguing third-party flirtations abruptly turn sour in the "getting serious" phase that precedes a final decision. With an evenly divided electorate providing seesaw victories for Democrats and Republicans, an individual can change history far more readily by voting for one of the major candidates than by giving his support to a laughably irrelevant fringie. A shift of 0.5 percent can alter the outcome of many elections, but it changes nothing if a Constitution Party candidate gets 0.7 percent or 0.2 percent.

In this context, the American people remain too sensible to accept the fulminations of brain-dead blowhards such as Lou Dobbs. "All that seems to remain of the Republican and Democratic parties is their partisanship, their labels, and their records of intransigence and ineffectiveness over the past forty years."

Over the past forty years, Mr. Dobbs? Really?

The Reagan Revolution, which won the Cold War and slashed top tax rates from 70 percent to 28 percent, represented only "intransigence and ineffectiveness"? Welfare reform, balanced budgets, and a booming economy, achieved by the Gingrich Congress in collaboration with Bill Clinton's administration, amounted to nothing more than "partisanship"?

The suggestion that the past forty years brought only misery and darkness counts as only slightly less ridiculous than the conviction that redeeming the Republic requires a new political organization built from the ground up to shatter, once and for all, the (amazingly durable) two-party system.

Third-party purists say they refuse to accept a choice between "the lesser of two evils"—a wretchedly misleading line that suggests that any public servant with whom we disagree is, indeed, evil and not merely wrong. In truth, very few working politicians, Republican or Democrat, honestly qualify as utterly "evil": the process of winning and retaining office won't by any means eliminate all mediocrities, but it almost always rids us of truly malevolent individuals. The notion that electoral opponents constitute "evil" of any kind—either the lesser or greater variety—only poisons our politics and prevents mature choices between major-party candidates who, while invariably flawed, give us a chance to serve our country by selecting the better of two imperfects.

Advocates for "independent candidates" and eccentric parties claim an obligation to "vote their conscience" even if they acknowledge that this decision means they will play no role in the election of an office-holder. There is, however, nothing conscientious in discarding your precious franchise for a self-righteous gesture; indeed, it is unconscionable to refuse to play a meaningful role in resolving the key issues of our time.

"A War on the Middle Class Means Less Comfort and Opportunity for the Average American"

"A NATIONAL NIGHTMARE FOR ALL OF US"

There's no place like Las Vegas for coming to terms with the horrifying "national nightmare" of a disappearing and devastated American middle class.

In November 2007, after considerable grumbling, I finally gave in to my radio producers and associates at Townhall.com and made a quick, dutiful trip to "Sin City" to participate in a panel at a bloggers' convention. I arrived on a Wednesday night to find the gambling utopia utterly jammed—so much so that my hotel, insisting that every room in town had been booked or overbooked, made me wait several hours for the accommodations I had reserved weeks in advance.

Settling myself and my luggage on a sofa near the front desk, I waited for my room and made a sincere effort to focus on a book, despite the distractions of the vast, crowded casino that bustled and dinged and buzzed a few steps away. Ironically enough, the title I tried to read while diverted by the comings and goings of leggy cocktail waitresses and beefy tourists turned out to be yet another best-selling jeremiad by Lou Dobbs, the carefully coiffed Cassandra of CNN.

In *The War on the Middle Class* (2006), this Harvard-educated, multimillionaire broadcaster offered the conclusion that "our political, business, and academic elites are waging an outright war on Americans, and I doubt the middle class can survive the continued assault by forces unleashed over the past few years if they go on unchecked. . . . In my opinion we are on the verge of not only losing our government of the people, for people, and by the people, but also standing idly by while the American Dream becomes a national nightmare for all of us. . . . Middle-class working men and women and their families have been devastated."

Somehow, these mournful and alarming words comported poorly with the glitzy scene that unfolded before me in Las Vegas, with masses of my fellow Americans (most of them very clearly the "middle-class working men and women" invoked by Mr. Dobbs) thronging to the casino floors day and night, depositing their hard-earned cash into high-tech machines cunningly devised to induce gambling addiction.

Statistics from the local tourist authorities indicate that more than forty million visitors found their way to Las Vegas in 2007. Most of these tourists—87 percent—were American (average age: forty-eight), and their socioeconomic status was undeniably middle-class. Only 24 percent of all visitors boasted household incomes above $100,000 a year; 46 percent never graduated from college; 15 percent were nonwhite. These everyday Las Vegas thrill seekers still managed to spend an average of $662 on their hotel packages, $261 on food and drink, $141 on shows and shopping, and a startling $652 (in net losses) on what the local businesses so tenderly call "gaming."

On the other side of the country, the nation's other gambling mecca, Atlantic City, drew thirty-three million pilgrims of its own, with an even more modest median household income of $51,000. Only 60 percent of these devotees stayed overnight at the seashore resort, and yet they sustained gaming losses that averaged $406 per trip.

Given the steadily increasing popularity of such indulgent amusements among a clientele that overwhelming identifies itself as "middle class," it seems difficult to credit the Dobbsian declarations that ordinary families have been "devastated" and now find themselves trapped in blighted, broken lives.

Nevertheless, major elements of the media and popular culture enthusiastically affirm the curious notion of a diabolical cabal bent on impoverishing the badly squeezed bourgeoisie. The Eddie Becker Band, a popular Maryland group with a devoted cult following, released a hard-driving R&B number in 2007 with the catchy title "There's a War on the Middle Class," which described Americans toiling for "the Elites for a slave's pay" and about "to live in third-world poverty." Meanwhile, a bumper sticker sold on liberal blogs declares: AT LEAST THE WAR ON THE MIDDLE CLASS IS GOING WELL.

Such messages resonate because the most influential voices in the press remain so fixated on the story line of middle-class anguish that they fail to see the ironies in their own reporting. On May 7, 2007, *USA Today* ran a compassionate feature story under the headline "Gas or Gamble? Economy Forces Some to Choose." The worried account began with a heart-rending story: "Carlos Bueno and his wife, Mayra, drove three times last year from their home in Houston to a casino in Lake Charles, La., but they won't be making the two-hour drive this summer. 'Gas prices are the main reason,' says the 32-year-old father of three children who works for a utility company and also is canceling the family's annual vacation to the Dominican Republic. 'The economy is harsh right now and the little money saved for vacation will have to be spent on fuel for our vehicle.' "

It's easy to feel sympathetic toward presumably hardworking family men such as Mr. Bueno, but if a 32-year-old utility company employee could previously afford three annual casino trips (costing, he said, $1,500) *plus* yearly vacations with his wife and three kids to the Caribbean, then how "harsh" could the economy really be? Gambling may constitute a cherished recreation for millions of middle-class Americans, but cutting back on that activity during an economic slowdown hardly amounts to evidence of suffering or oppression.

Leading newspapers breathlessly picked up the story of setbacks for the gambling interests. "Debt-Laden Casinos Squeezed by Slowdown," warned a *Wall Street Journal* headline, while *USA Today* lamented, "Airline Woes Cause Pain for Las Vegas Casinos." But official figures well into the rocky year of 2008 told a less disturbing story, with overall Nevada gaming revenue down only 0.5 percent from the previous year.

Of course, leading politicians still prefer to portray everyday Americans as hapless victims of implacable and malevolent forces, just one step away from loading meager possessions into shopping carts and camping out in alleys. Most famously, the fabulously wealthy trial lawyer John Edwards regularly warned on the campaign trail: "Over the last twenty years, American incomes have grown apart. . . . The result is Two Americas, one struggling to get by and another that has everything it could want."

Stressing similar themes, Senator Hillary Rodham Clinton (who reported income with her husband of $109 million over the previous seven years) campaigned in Iowa in a bus labeled "The Middle Class Express," telling her eager audiences that "America's middle class is under siege and ready for a change. People are working harder and longer for less and less. . . . For six long years, it's like America's middle class and working families have been invisible to our president. He's looked right through them."

Barack Obama, shortly before he won the Democratic presidential nomination, announced that families "all across America" were "suffering in very real ways" and, emphasizing his own messianic vocation, explained that "I'm running for president to start doing something about that suffering."

Such rhetoric plays an inevitable role in every campaign season, demonstrating that the idea of a sinking, suffering middle class, victimized by callous if not downright hostile corporate forces, has taken on a stubborn life of its own. This self-pitying and paralyzing notion has, in fact, managed to survive all statistical evidence to the contrary, regular attempts at logical rebuttal, numerous shifts in the business cycle and political leadership, and the real-life experience of tens of millions of actual middle-class Americans.

PUBLIC GLOOM VS. PRIVATE HAPPINESS

While demagogues and doomsayers sound the alarm about the dire impact of the "war on the middle class," most Americans stubbornly refuse to see themselves at risk in the alleged assault.

In April 2008 the *New York Times* announced the results of a new poll with a typically alarming headline: "81 Percent in New Poll Say Nation Is Headed on Wrong Track." But immediately below that disturbing proclamation, a series of graphs showed the respondents maintaining far more optimistic attitudes regarding their personal status. When asked, "How would you rate the financial situation in your household?" an amazing 72 percent said "good"; only 27 percent said "bad." In fact, the Pew Global Attitudes Project found that satisfaction with family income *increased* between 2002 and 2007, from 74 percent to 76 percent—more than three-quarters of those surveyed.

The "declinists," who warn of the disappearance or destruction of the middle class, love to cite surveys showing big majorities who offer grim evaluations of the general state of the nation, but they fail to note that the same polls report far greater optimism about the respondents' personal status.

For instance, a July 2007 Harris Poll found that a staggering 94 percent of respondents considered themselves satisfied with their lives (with a majority—fully 56 percent—choosing the highest rating, "very satisfied"). More striking still, crushing majorities saw no evidence at all that their personal conditions had suffered in recent years. Asked the question "If you compare your present situation with five years ago, would you say it has improved, stayed about the same or gotten worse?" fully 82 percent said it had improved or held steady (with a majority—54 percent—reporting improvement). Only 17 percent saw their situations worse, despite all the alarmist reports about the "devastated middle class."

Similarly, in response to the question "In the course of the next five years, do you expect your personal situation to improve, to stay about the same or to get worse?" people overwhelmingly expected a sunny future. Sixty-two percent anticipated improvement, with only 7 percent expecting their conditions to "get worse"—an optimistic ratio of nine to one.

The blatant contradiction between public gloom and private confidence has been a consistent feature of national public opinion for nearly a quarter of a century. We display a distinctively American tendency to view ourselves as dwelling on isolated sunlit islands of good fortune while surrounded by turbulent seas of generalized misery. In place of the old "I'm OK, you're OK" self-help formula of forty years ago, we now seem to assert "I'm OK, but everybody else is in a mess of trouble."

Obviously American majorities can't be simultaneously correct about their own good fortune and correct about the miserable condition of society at large, and there's good reason to take them more seriously when they rate their own status or prospects. Every American can speak most authoritatively about his or her own life, but we know much less about our neighbors or the residents of other cities, and least of all about the abstraction called the generalized "state of the nation." Instead of reporting impressions digested from personal experience or even the stories of friends, we naturally rely on messages conveyed by television, newspapers, or politicians we respect. Those accounts in turn stress dysfunction and negativity: when it comes to placing expert guests on TV talk shows, Chicken Little ("The sky is falling!") will always get more bookings than Pollyanna. And when it comes to getting elected, the party out of power will invariably claim the worst economic conditions since the Great Depression.

Given the prevalence of this message, most Americans see no contradiction in reporting their own satisfaction and progress at the same time that they perceive general decline and decay. No one wants to be branded a simple-minded boob, an agenda-driven hack, a starry-eyed America booster, or, worst of all, a malleable dupe—and so bright individuals are motivated to acknowledge regular pronouncements of the horror and menace of the crisis of the month. There's another payoff to expressing indignation over the presumed prevailing misery, even while acknowledging personal success: such sentiments help to alleviate any sense of guilt by indicating compassion for, even solidarity with, the less fortunate.

There are powerful reasons, in other words, why negative statistical indicators always get more play and acceptance than encouraging data. This preference for pessimism leads to endless recycling of a few misleading statistics that can cause even some families who ought to know better to doubt their own good fortune.

Hard Work Makes You Happy

In his illuminating book *Gross National Happiness,* Professor Arthur C. Brooks of Syracuse University shows that happiness produces economic success more reliably than economic success produces happiness. Despite common assumptions that most Americans hate their jobs and long, above all, for more time off, the studies cited by Brooks provide powerful backup for your grandmother's assumption that hard work keeps people happy—and uncomplaining. An astonishing 89 percent of Americans who are employed ten hours a week or more say they are "very satisfied" or "somewhat satisfied" with their jobs, while only 11 percent are "not very satisfied" or "not at all satisfied." Amazingly enough, as Brooks notes, there "is no difference at all in job satisfaction between those with below-average and above-average incomes."

SEEING IS DISBELIEVING

According to an ancient joke from the "Borscht Belt" of the Catskill Mountains in the 1940s and '50s, a wife came to her husband's office unexpectedly and saw him making love on his desk with his secretary.

"You're having an affair with your secretary!" she wailed. "How could you!"

"No, you're wrong," he insisted. "We're just taking care of some important work. Nothing's going on."

"But I saw you!" she moaned. "You were having sex with her."

"Look," the indignant executive declared. "Who are you going to believe in a situation like this? Me, your husband of thirty years? Or your own eyes?"

In the same tradition, people who accept "end of the world" pronouncements about the collapse of the middle class choose to ignore the evidence of their own eyes. They elect to believe the arguments and statistics of various experts and activists, and to ignore what they can learn from their own experiences.

Whenever I've had the opportunity to confront some of the alarmists about their conclusion that ordinary Americans have been losing ground for decades, I make it a point to pose the same questions: Does your theory apply to your own family history? Do you and your siblings live less comfortably than your parents? Do your various cousins enjoy more—or less—comforts and opportunities than your aunts and uncles?

I've engaged in literally hundreds of such conversations—on the radio, at lectures, and in private interchanges—and not once has anyone said, *Yes, I'm worse off than my parents and grandparents.* When it comes to reflection on the nation's economic conditions, there's an instinctive resort to the old "I'm OK, you're screwed" paradigm.

For most of us with clear memories of childhood or previous stages in our careers, the progress is simply impossible to ignore or deny.

My own experience reflects the path of more than a few of my fellow baby boomers. My grandfather, a barrel maker, came to this country in 1910 and worked hard as a manual laborer all his life without ever accumulating property or savings. His son, my father, came home from World War II and attended college and grad school through scholarships and the GI Bill. After my dad earned his Ph.D. in physics, he got a job in the defense industry and my parents bought their first home—a stucco, ranch-style palace of 1,000 square feet where they raised four rambunctious boys.

Growing up, we received constant reminders of our limited circumstances. My mother, may she rest in peace, never allowed us to go out for dinner more than twice a year and even discouraged fast food such as hamburgers as a shameful waste of money. For vacations, my parents preferred camping trips because of the money saved on motels; the first time in my life I ever stayed at a four-star hotel came at age twenty-seven, during the promotional tour for my first book.

Yes, the four Medved brothers all benefited from loving and hardworking parents, wonderful educations, and countless opportunities (which we occasionally managed to seize), but our circumstances also reflect the general improvement for America's middle class. We regularly experience luxuries and options that my grandparents could scarcely imagine and that we never dared to expect as children.

GIZMOS FROM *THE JETSONS*

Middle-class consumers have established a burgeoning market for high-tech gizmos that we saw as children only on *The Jetsons* or *Star Trek*—BlackBerries, iPods, HDTVs, digital cameras. Ten years ago, public figures (prominently including Vice President Al Gore) warned the country of the potentially devastating impact of the "digital divide"—with black children at special risk because they were less likely to become familiar with personal computers. Today, PCs have become so ubiquitous in every segment of society that the very term "digital divide" draws only blank stares from tech-savvy young people of all races (and income levels).

A time traveler from the 1960s or '70s might also feel shocked to look around today at the rapidly spreading middle-class suburban neighborhoods in every corner of the country and the simultaneous transformation of former districts of blight and desperation. For the first time in American history, gentrification looms as a more dreaded, widespread threat than the spread of slums. Moreover, this neighborhood improvement—with new construction, renovation, the arrival of prosperous new neighbors, and the corresponding rise in property values—"menaces" even some of the most destitute urban areas in the nation.

Statistics on housing actually confirm the conclusions of anyone who travels the country with open eyes and open mind. On November 19, 2007, National Public Radio reported: "The average American house size has more than doubled since the 1950s. Consider: back in the 1950s and '60s, people thought it was normal for a family to have one bathroom, or for two or three growing boys to share a bedroom." The figures from the National Association of Home Builders show that in 1950 the average new single-family home offered only 983 square feet. In 2004 (the most recent year for available statistics) that number stood at 2,349 square feet—an increase of 240 percent at the same time family size dramatically declined.

New homes today also include features and comforts all but unknown fifty years ago—central air-conditioning, garages, dishwashers, built-in stoves, fireplaces, microwaves, and so forth.

The recent foreclosure crisis may menace millions at the edge of the middle class, but in the new century, home ownership still reached and maintained record levels (more than 80 percent of Americans over the age of forty now own their own home) and at least 95 percent of mortgage holders have avoided default. No wonder that overwhelming majorities of Americans express satisfaction, even pride, in the lives they have built for themselves.

EXPANDING THE "JET SET"

In a pungently effective 2008 video essay for Reason TV, a project of the libertarian Reason Foundation, the popular comedian Drew Carey takes mirthful note of the enormous gap between the "woe is me" reporting on the state of the middle class and easily observable reality. A camera crew visited Castaic Lake, north of Los Angeles, on a sunny Saturday and "confronted some fat cats as they played around in the water with hardly a care in the world."

Boaters brag about their craft, including a speedy $50,000 vessel described by its owner as "a special boat for wakeboarding." Carey speculates that "this guy sees the world through rose-colored designer glasses. Probably a trust fund kid who doesn't even have a job. What do you do for a living?" With a broad smile, the interviewee responds: "I'm a gardener."

Other boaters, who drove to the lake in Hummers and Escalades, identify themselves as "a cop," "a guy who sells building materials," and "a truck driver." A friend of the trucker, an auto mechanic, explains that he only uses his buddy's boat because "I've got motorcycles. Hondas, Harleys, Suzukis. Got 'em all."

Carey then interviews W. Michael Cox, economics professor at Southern Methodist University and chief economist of the Federal Reserve Bank of Dallas. "That's America's middle class today," Cox notes about the boaters at Castaic Lake. "It's amazing what they're able to own and the consumption levels they're able to achieve today compared to the past."

The secret, according to Cox, involves the startling, rapid, and continuing decline in the real cost of most consumer goods because of soaring technology and enhanced productivity. "Really the best way to measure cost is work time: how long do I have to work in order to afford to buy something. So let's take a product—for example, the cell phone." The video shows a huge, boxy, "antique" phone from 1984—"a $4,200 brick." Dr. Cox then holds up a sleek, versatile, contemporary cell phone that costs $50, and explains that for the typical worker, today's device can be purchased with 3 hours of work, while in the 1980s it took *460 hours* of work to buy a cell phone. "Huge declines in prices enabled these things to be afforded by the middle class," he notes. "And many other products too."

Similarly, only the wealthy could afford automobiles when they first became available, but the price—in terms of hours of labor for a typical worker in order to purchase a typical car—has fallen 70 percent in a century. Food counts as 84 percent cheaper in those terms, and clothing 87 percent less expensive. As Drew Carey comments: "The falling cost of living allows regular Joes to own boats, vacation at lakes, and fly around the world. Just check it out: the cost of a cross-country flight has plummeted by 95 percent between 1930 and 2007." Dr. Cox notes: "When flights first came out, they were the exclusive purview of the rich, the 'jet set.' But now the jet set includes—just get on a plane and look! The people there are of all income levels."

LIFE-CYCLE ADJUSTMENTS

The reduced cost for most goods and services helps to explain the apparent contradiction between undeniable improvements in living standards and misleading statistics (beloved by alarmists) that show falling household income in recent years.

Economist Stephen Rose, affiliated with the "progressive" Third Way strategy center in Washington and a fan of Barack Obama, points to numerous ways in which frequently cited income figures fail to reflect reality. Most obviously, they don't include the value of benefits—particularly employer contributions to retirement savings plans and health insurance premiums—which have risen far more rapidly than wages.

Rose, writing in the *Washington Post,* also shows that the statistics for household income ignore the changing size of American households— namely, many more people live in single-adult households now than thirty years ago. (The increase in life expectancy produces more widows living alone, and the rise in the marriage age brings greater numbers of single adults.) This means that even the same reported household income supports fewer people, resulting in more money per person and a higher standard of living. Rose adjusts income numbers to account for the shift in household size and the boost in employer benefits and determines that "the real middle class median income has risen 33 percent, or $18,000, since 1979."

The numbers, in short, show steady and continuing improvement in the status of typical Americans, rather than a "war on the middle class." Placing the figures in the context of the normal life cycle brightens the picture even further. In a *Huffington Post* piece titled "What's the Income of the Typical American?" Rose notes that most Americans earn less at the beginning and end of their adult lives without necessarily suffering in terms of living standards. "Many graduate students have very low incomes for several years," he writes. "But few would classify this group as poor given their long term prospects (and probably back-up income help from their parents). At the opposite end of the age spectrum, retired people have much fewer direct expenses, often have paid off their mortgage, have a home filled with furniture and appliances, and are not likely to have to subsidize their adult children. Consequently, a retiree's income of $40,000 translates into a very different standard of living than a young couple with a new born child."

With this in mind, Rose focuses on "prime-age" adults between the ages of twenty-five and sixty-two and finds a median income of $60,000. "Your typical husband-wife couple in this age range," he adds, "has a median income of over $70,000; and couples in which both husband and wife work at least part of the year had a median income of $81,000."

Most remarkably, a full half of all adults reported at least one year in which their total household incomes were greater than $100,000. No wonder Drew Carey could find an abundance of boats and Hummers at a Southern California lake.

Reviewing historical trends in March 2008, economics professor Brad

Schiller of American University writes: "When you look at the really big picture, it's apparent that living standards are rising across the entire spectrum of incomes. Just since 2000, GDP has risen by 18 percent, while population has grown by 6 percent. So per-capita incomes have clearly been rising. The growth of per-capita income since 1980 or 1970 has simply been spectacular."

Cruises, Second Homes, and the "Vanishing Middle Class"

If the American middle class is, in fact, shrinking, there's little doubt as to why: more middle-income people become increasingly prosperous, not impoverished. The official poverty rate has declined from 22.4 percent in the 1950s (remembered as the golden age of middle America) to well below 13 percent in recent years. Meanwhile, two news items provide important perspective on the status and future of middle-income Americans:

- In 2007, a total of 9.57 million Americans took cruise vacations, and a 2008 national survey for the Cruise Lines International Association showed that 34 million plan to take a cruise within the next three years.
- With the foreclosure crisis sweeping the country, numerous news reports noted that second homes were disproportionately hard hit—that's the bad news. But the good news from the Federal Reserve is that a stunning 12.5 percent of *all* households still own a second home; among families with household heads between ages 55 and 75, that figure rises to 20 percent.

These numbers reinforce the idea that when Americans no longer qualify as middle-class, they usually leave that designation for the world of vacation homes and luxury cruises, not hunger and homelessness.

The statistical evidence for a rising standard of living for every seg-ment of the population is so overwhelming that charges of a "vanishing middle class" rely on sleight of hand that grossly distorts Census Bureau numbers.

It's true that between 1979 and 2006, the percentage of middle-income households ($30,000 to $75,000 in inflation-adjusted dollars) went down sharply, by 13.1 percent. But lower-income households (below $30,000) also went down slightly (0.6 percent).

What happened to these formerly middle-income and poor people? They got richer.

As a matter of fact, the only income group that increased at all was households earning more than $100,000, which rose by nearly 15 per-cent, from 13 percent to 28 percent of the population. In other words, a major chunk of the middle class disappeared into relative affluence, not poverty.

MORE EDUCATION, MORE WORRIES

These encouraging numbers provide small comfort to stressed families struggling with the rising costs of gas, health care, and college tuition. There's also no doubt that our increasingly complex and sophisticated economy offers drastically reduced opportunities for workers with low skills and limited education—and a great deal of the concern about the "middle-class squeeze" focuses on the dimming horizons for these hard-working Americans, particularly in the manufacturing sector. Nearly every commentary on our economic future makes clear that new jobs and enterprises will require a more educated workforce.

Few Americans realize, however, how much progress we've already made in this arena. In 1960, 51 percent of all workers had not finished high school; by 2006, only 10 percent lacked a high school diploma or a GED. In 1960, only 11 percent had earned four-year college degrees; forty-six years later, that number had exactly tripled to 33 percent, with another 28 percent who earned two-year/community college degrees or attended college without graduating. This means that a solid majority—61 per-cent—now pursue some form of education after high school. As Stephen

Rose writes: "There is another disconnect between the images of our economy being diminished by low-skill, low-paid service jobs ('McJobs') and a work force where 60 percent have some post-secondary education."

The cost of college tuition worries Americans far more intensely than ever before in part because so many more of our children manage to attend college.

SPECIALIZATION AND WOMEN'S WORK

The hugely increased chances for higher education offer one powerful reminder of the openings provided by a dynamic and ceaselessly growing economy. A wealth of data on every aspect of our lives shows that we enjoy more choices, more comfort, more recreational pursuits, more food, more buying power, bigger houses, better cars, and longer lives. These numbers don't prove that we're better or happier people than our parents or grandparents, or that our nation has solved all or even most of its problems. They do indicate, however, that there's no decline in living standards for the great American middle class, which still includes a clear majority of the populace.

When pressed, gloom-and-doomers may acknowledge the enhancements in material well-being in the past generation, but they insist that we've achieved these gains only by working harder—particularly by sending women into the workforce. Callers to my radio show regularly bemoan the fact that two-income households have become the norm, with fewer women playing the role of stay-at-home mom.

Professor Cox provides a brilliant response to laments about the new prevalence of working women. "Both adults have always worked," observes Cox, writing with business journalist Richard Alm. "Running a household entails a daunting list of chores: cooking, gardening, child care, shopping, washing and ironing, financial management, ferrying family members to ballet lessons and soccer practice." In the 1950s, the average workweek of the *Leave It to Beaver* housewife amounted to 52 hours, far more labor than the 39.8 hours her husband devoted to the office.

Cox and Alm explain: "The idea that people at home don't work isn't just insulting to women, who do most of the housework. It also misses how specialization contributes to higher and higher living standards. At one time, both adults worked exclusively at home. The man constructed buildings, tilled the land, raised livestock. The woman prepared meals, preserved food, looked after the children. Living standards rarely rose above the subsistence level." But as men went to work outside the home— "gaining specialized skills and earning an income that allowed the family to buy what it didn't have the time, energy, or ability to make at home"— living standards rose. Cox sees a similar improvement in living standards associated with women choosing to work outside the home, as households with more disposable income now hire professionals for the specialized jobs of painting, cleaning, home repair, gardening, laundry, tax preparation, cooking, and child care.

Contrary to the idea that the "middle-class squeeze" forces women to go to work against their wishes and interests, Stephen Rose notes that "the rise in hours has been greatest for women whose husbands have the highest earnings." Meanwhile, National Public Radio reported in 2008 that more than 80 percent of mothers with infants manage to remain at home full-time. This indicates that for most women, balancing work and child care stems at least as much from choice as from compulsion, with options for in-home assistance previously available only to the wealthy.

INCREASING LEISURE, NOT WORK

Despite the endlessly repeated charge that Americans work longer hours for less and less pay, the numbers actually show sharp long-term increases in both disposable income and leisure time. Economists Mark Aguiar of the Federal Reserve Bank of Boston and Erik Hurst of the University of Chicago examined five decades of time diary surveys administered by research universities and the government. James Sherk of the Heritage Foundation reports the economists' key findings:

- "Since the mid-1960s, the amount of time that the typical American spends working fell by almost eight hours per week, while the time spent on leisure activities rose by just under seven hours per week."

- "This additional leisure time is equivalent to an extra seven to nine weeks of vacation per year."
- "Leisure has increased unequally. Less educated and lower-income Americans now work less and enjoy more leisure than Americans with higher incomes. This explains part of why they have lower incomes."

Meanwhile, all Americans spend more time and vastly more money on recreational pursuits. The Census Bureau reports that inflation-adjusted spending on recreation per capita soared from $854 in 1970 to $2,551 in 2005, an increase of nearly 300 percent. Even as a percentage of total consumption, recreation went up dramatically—from 6.5 percent in 1970 to 8.7 percent in 2005.

This reallocation of time and resources to the pursuit of fun and pleasure helps explain why hotels and casinos in Las Vegas fill up in all seasons with middle-class and working-class visitors (even at times of economic stress). The pricey theme parks in Orlando, Florida (where Disney World has become the world's most visited tourist attraction), drew 45.1 million guests in 2007. Average household income of these Orlando vacationers (and most of these households supported multiple children) was $73,389.

In terms of even more expensive vacations, the percentage of American adults who traveled overseas in a given year has more than tripled since 1970 (to 12.4 percent of all adults from 3.7 percent).

Closer to home, we eat out at an unprecedented rate, regularly patronizing elegant restaurants or shopping center food courts several times each week. The average American household now spends $2,634 on meals away from home—a sharp increase of more than 10 percent (in inflation-adjusted dollars) in just the three years between 2003 and 2006. As Lou Dobbs himself ruefully admits in his book *Independents Day:* "Americans are spending as much on meals outside the home as we do for health care—a little over $2,600 per family. We spend almost as much to buy and operate our cars as we do to pay for our homes—about $8,000 a year on each."

These priorities don't necessarily represent wise economic decisions—nor does the $426 spent per year on "alcoholic beverages," or the $319 on "tobacco products and smoking supplies," or all the hundreds if not thousands a year in gambling losses in Vegas, Atlantic City, Indian casinos, and heavily hyped state lotteries. Nevertheless, the fact that Americans feel free to make frivolous or even self-destructive spending decisions contradicts the portrait of a helpless, choiceless middle class in the grip of powerful, exploitative elites perversely committed to destroying the very workforce that makes possible corporate prosperity.

THE MYTH OF PERMANENT MISERY

The media, always eager to command public attention by emphasizing bad news, indulge a destructive and dishonest instinct to portray America's poor, working-class, and minority citizens as locked into permanent misery—despite undeniable evidence to the contrary.

A November 2007 *Washington Post* story by Michael A. Fletcher offered an especially baleful example. When the report appeared in the *Seattle Times* it bore the alarming headline "Many Blacks Earn Less than Parents, Study Finds." Anyone who took time to read the article, however, encountered the following revelation in paragraph seven: "Overall, four out of five children born into families at the bottom 20 percent of wage earners surpassed their parents' income. Broken down by race, nine in 10 whites are better paid than their parents were, compared with three out of four blacks."

If 75 percent of low-income blacks are better paid than their parents (and another 15 percent earn the same as their parents), then how could any responsible news outlet choose the headline "Many Blacks Earn Less than Parents, Study Finds"? The answer involves an anomaly in the original study (performed by the Pew Charitable Trusts). Only a tiny percentage of black families counted as "solidly middle class" (in the language of the study) in 1968, with inflation-adjusted median income of $55,000. Among children of this small group, a surprising number (45 percent) did indeed fall to the lowest fifth of the nation's earners, with a median family income of $23,100. But the disappointing performance of a handful of offspring in a major study did nothing to invalidate the most important conclusion: that 75 percent of African American children (and 80 percent of the overall sample) who began life in poverty ended up with higher incomes (and often substantially higher incomes) than their parents.

A similar distortion occurred in another misleading story from the same month. The front page of *USA Today* featured the headline "Poll: Blacks Grow More Pessimistic" and then the boldfaced subhead "Fewer than Half Expect Their Lives to Improve." Actually, by a ratio of two to one the African American respondents in the Pew research poll *did* expect their lives to improve: 44 percent said "life for blacks will be better in the future" and only 21 percent guessed it would be worse. With 31 percent saying life would remain the same, that means 75 percent were convinced that circumstances for American blacks would either remain unchanged or improve.

The lead sentence in the article also emphasized the negative: "Black Americans are more dissatisfied with their progress than at any time in the past twenty years." Yet in the poll a total of 69 percent of black respondents said that they were doing either "the same" as (49 percent) or "better" than (20 percent) they were five years earlier. Moreover, the article quoted experts who talked about a "great deal of anxiety, cynicism and pessimism today" while barely noting that the majority of those surveyed in the study said "that blacks who don't get ahead are mainly responsible for their own situation."

A much more extensive, revealing, and encouraging study by the U.S. Department of the Treasury received much less media attention—precisely because it failed to fit the preconceived notion of a stratified, static, unjust economic order. The November 2007 Treasury report, based on 96,700 tax returns from 1996 and 2005, discovered that 58 percent of filers who found themselves in the poorest income group (the bottom 20 percent) in 1996 moved into a higher income category in just ten years. In fact, after inflation, the median income of all tax filers increased by a solid 24 percent in the decade. Two out of three workers had a real income gain since 1996—contradicting the common charge that the working class has steadily lost ground.

In terms of the American dream of reliable advancement, there's been no nightmarish transformation. The Treasury Department explains: "The basic finding of this analysis is that relative income mobility is approximately the same in the last ten years as it was in the previous decade." There you have it, in the unadorned conclusion of the federal bureaucracy itself: despite terrorist attacks, war expenditures, and hysterical denunciations of the Bush administration's alleged devastation of the working class, ordinary Americans retained the same ability to climb the economic ladder that they enjoyed between 1986 and 1995—the last years of the Reagan boom and the opening years of the Clinton expansion.

A May 2007 report by the nonpartisan Congressional Budget Office (CBO) reached similar conclusions. Covering a fifteen-year period, the CBO found that low-wage households with children had incomes after inflation that were more than one-third higher in 2005 than in 1991. Among all families with children, in fact, the poorest fifth had the fastest overall earnings growth—with increases even higher than the richest 20 percent. The median family with children saw an inflation-adjusted 18 percent rise in earnings from the early 1990s through 2005—representing $8,500 in additional purchasing power.

In the face of these realities, doomsayers and pity prophets transparently manipulate statistics to try to support their theme of downward mobility. A twenty-six-year-old author, Anya Kamenetz, provides a particularly notable example in her book-length whine *Generation Debt*. She contends that today's young people "are much more likely to remain in the working class than previous generations," and then offers her cockeyed evidence: "Youths eighteen to twenty-four are the most likely to hold minimum-wage jobs, giving them a poverty rate of 30 percent in 2000, according to the U.S. Census; that's the highest of any age group. For those aged twenty-five to thirty-four, the poverty rate is 15 percent, compared with 10 percent for older working adults."

In other words, the economy functions exactly as it should—providing greater rewards for those with more experience in the workforce. There's no evidence whatever that today's young people constitute the first generation in American history to fail to advance as they move forward into their prime earning years; in fact, Kamenetz's own numbers provide evidence to the contrary.

NO CONSPIRACY TO TAX THE MIDDLE CLASS
AND SPARE THE RICH

According to the most recent CBO figures (from tax year 2004), the poorest fifth of the population (with an average annual income of $15,400) pays only 4.5 percent of their income in federal taxes. The middle fifth (with income of $56,200) pays 13.9 percent. The highest fifth (with reported income of $207,200) coughs up 25.1 percent—some 600 percent of the rate paid by those at the bottom. The richest 1 percent of taxpayers (earning lavish salaries of $1,259,700) pay even more: 31.1 percent of overall income to the federal government.

With these higher tax rates, high-income taxpayers shoulder a hugely disproportionate share of the overall tax burden. The CBO figures indicate that the top 10 percent of all taxpayers (those earning more than $87,300) paid 70.8 percent of all income taxes. A quarter century ago, before the Reagan and Bush tax cuts that allegedly favored the rich, this top 10 percent paid much less of the overall burden—only 48.1 percent.

Simply put, conspiracists who rail against the "war on the middle class" are flat-out wrong when they suggest that part of that assault involves a bigger share of the tax burden. "While corporations are paying lower taxes than ever before, and tax breaks for the wealthy are expanded," Lou Dobbs falsely fulminates, "the middle class is forced to shoulder ever more of the tax burden."

Actually, the middle fifth of the income scale paid 10.7 percent of the nation's income tax in 1979 (under Jimmy Carter) but only 4.7 percent in 2004 (after two rounds of Bush tax cuts).

TRUTH, HAPPINESS, AND THE CHANCES
FOR SUCCESS

Rejecting the self-pitying lies about middle-class oppression and powerlessness isn't just a matter of defeating demagoguery for the sake of the political health of the country; grasping the essential truths about today's

American economy also represents a prerequisite for personal content-
ment and future advancement.

Professor Arthur C. Brooks of Syracuse University cites a fascinating
question asked by the National Opinion Research Center's General Social
Survey: "The way things are in America, people like me and my family
have a good chance of improving our standard of living—do you agree
or disagree?" An encouraging two-thirds of the population agreed, and
this group, Brooks reports, was "44 percent more likely than the others to
say they were 'very happy,' 40 percent less likely to say that they felt 'no
good at all' at times, and 20 percent less likely to say that they felt like failures. In other words, those who don't believe in economic mobility—for
themselves or for others—are not as happy as those who do."

This happiness not only matters in a personal and familial sense
(greatly increasing the chances, for instance, of marital stability) but also
brings economic consequences. As Jim Holt argued in a January 2007
piece in the *New York Times Magazine,* a wealth of psychological data
suggests that pessimism produces poor commercial outcomes, whereas
optimism helps to ensure success. Holt writes: "In a recently published
study, researchers in the Netherlands found that optimistic people—
those who assented to statements like 'I often feel that life is full of
promises'—tend to live longer than pessimists. Perhaps, it has been speculated, optimism confers a survival advantage by helping people cope
with adversity."

Politicians and pundits who rail endlessly (and dishonestly) about the
"Two Americas" or the "vanishing middle class" may therefore do serious
damage to the prospects of precisely those hardworking folks they claim
to want to help. Misleading whining about falling living standards and
the end of economic mobility may serve as a self-fulfilling prophecy for
those who embrace the underlying message of powerlessness and self-
pity. If you buy the idea that corporate exploiters and corrupt politicians
have poisoned your life and stolen your ability to create a better life for
your family, you've obviously damaged your own ability to get ahead.

There's no real "war on the middle class," but there is a media war on
middle-class values. Popular culture shows little respect for the simple
virtues our grandparents taught—saving, deferred gratification, reliabil-
ity, self-control, family loyalty. All the hysteria about economic apoca-

lypse treats these qualities as quaint and irrelevant. According to this logic, our dire circumstances demand a response of indignation and protest rather than stoicism and hard work. In fact, it's self-reliance—not self-pity—that's always been the most important middle-class value.

Meanwhile, the demagogues and deceivers try to advance their own well-paid careers with their increasingly shrill and gloomy dispatches. Though these messages clearly influence perceptions about the state of the nation at large, they haven't yet shaken the confidence and gratitude of most working Americans regarding their personal situation. In an odd combination of real cynicism and fake compassion, declinists try to portray Americans in the middle as the latest victim class. Fortunately, most members of the real middle class are too smart, and too busy counting blessings and seizing opportunities, to believe the lie that they are losers.

"America Is in the Midst of an Irreversible Moral Decline"

"THE END IS NEAR"

As a boy I became fascinated with frequent *New Yorker* cartoons (the only part of that magazine I actually read) depicting bearded, robed, and sandaled figures marching down city streets with placards proclaiming THE END IS NEAR.

In recent years, some of the nation's most thoughtful social conservatives have embraced this apocalyptic message as their own, identifying America's undeniable cultural decay as a steep, irreversible slide.

In 1996, Judge Robert Bork, an old friend and impeccably provocative professor from my days at Yale Law School, issued a best-selling denunciation of national decline entitled *Slouching Towards Gomorrah*. Possess-

ing the requisite beard and robes (though he'd actually hung up his judicial garb eight years before), Judge Bork described the United States as a "degenerate society," "enfeebled, hedonistic," "subpagan," and headed for "the coming of a new Dark Ages." He urged his readers to "take seriously the possibility that perhaps nothing will be done to reverse the direction of our culture, that the degeneracy we see around us will only become worse."

Three years later, Paul Weyrich, one of the widely admired founding fathers of the modern Religious Right (and the originator of the term "Moral Majority"), published a despairing open letter to his fellow conservatives. "The culture we are living in becomes an ever-wider sewer," he wrote in February 1999, in the midst of the Clinton impeachment crisis. "In truth, I think, we are caught up in a cultural collapse of historic proportions, a collapse so great that it simply overwhelms politics. . . . I no longer believe there is a moral majority. I do not believe that a majority of Americans actually shares our values. . . . I believe that we probably have lost the culture war."

In the same era, the redoubtably conservative *Insight* magazine ran an article with the headline "Is Our Society Worth Saving?" and, after reviewing omnipresent signs of rot, allowed that the answer might well be no.

More recently, John F. MacArthur, the influential California pastor, president of the Master's College, and author of some fifty books on the Bible and contemporary life, declared: "There comes a point in God's dealing with men and nations, groups of people, when He abandons them. . . . Sin is so rampant in our country, it is so widespread, it is so tolerated by people in leadership and even people in the church, it is so widely tolerated it is pandemic: it is endemic; that is, it is in the very fabric of our life that I believe God has just taken away the restraining grace that might preserve our nation, and has let our nation run to its own doom."

Dr. MacArthur brings an unapologetically Christian perspective to his pronouncements of impending catastrophe, while the perpetually enraged talk radio ranter Michael Savage joins the Loony Left in predicting the coming onset of Nazism. "I am more and more convinced that we have a one-party oligarchy ruling our nation," he warned in *The Savage Nation,* his 2002 best seller. "In short, the 'Republicrats' and 'Demicans'

have sacked our Constitution, our culture, our religions, and embarrassed the nation. . . . The last years of the Weimar Republic of pre-Nazi Germany come to mind—where decadence completely permeated a free society."

While most Americans remain untroubled by the prospect of imminent Hitlerism, it's impossible for any fair-minded observer to ignore or deny the abundant indications of long-term cultural decline. A review of major changes in American society over the past half century provides powerful evidence of moral decay: the collapse of family norms, an appalling coarsening of the popular culture, and the fraying of any national consensus on standards of right and wrong.

In March 1993, William J. Bennett, who previously led the battle against demons of decadence as secretary of education and "drug czar," published his first "Index of Leading Cultural Indicators," identifying "substantial social regression." Since 1960, out-of-wedlock births had increased by 400 percent, violent crime by 500 percent, and teen suicide by 300 percent. Even my unflappable friend Bennett, by no means an alarmist or doomsayer, looked at the data at the time with something like despair and concluded that "the forces of social decomposition are challenging—and in some instances overtaking—the forces of social composition."

The most pertinent question for today's parents and policy makers is whether that process of decomposition will continue, and whether the destructive trends identified in the 1990s have become unstoppable.

Most recently one of Dr. Bennett's associates on the "Cultural Indicators" project, Peter Wehner, raised the possibility that most of the distressing phenomena they identified fifteen years ago have already reversed themselves, providing significant signs of social revival. Wehner, now a senior fellow at the Ethics and Public Policy Center, prepared a stunning update for the December 2007 issue of *Commentary* magazine. Writing with Yuval Levin, Wehner declared: "Just when it seemed as if the storm clouds were about to burst, they began to part. As if at once, things began to turn around. And now, a decade-and-a-half after these well-founded and unrelievedly dire warnings, improvements are visible in the vast majority of social indicators; in some areas, like crime and welfare, the progress has the dimensions of a sea-change."

It's impossible to evaluate this apparent change of direction, or its relevance to the most recent pronouncements that the end is near, without placing the debate in its proper historical perspective. As it turns out, worried moralists have railed against corruption, sinfulness, and the end of American civilization since the very beginning of American civilization—the earliest days of colonial settlement.

FOUR HUNDRED YEARS OF IMMINENT DOOM

We prefer to think of William Bradford, the longtime leader of Plymouth Colony, as a courageous man of faith who calmly overcame every obstacle to establish the Pilgrims' settlement in the Massachusetts wilderness. Some twenty-five years after taking shore at Plymouth Rock, however, Bradford became the first major American commentator to see evidence of deadly moral decay and a betrayal of his society's heroic past.

In 1645, he made one of the last significant entries in his journal while in an obviously mournful mood:

> O sacred bond, which inviolably preserved! How sweet and precious were the fruits that flowed from the same! But when this fidelity decayed, then their ruin approached. O that these ancient members had not died or been dissipated (if it had been the will of God) or else that this holy care and constant faithfulness had still lived, and remained with those that survived, and were in times afterwards added unto them. But (alas) that subtle serpent that slyly wound himself under fair pretenses of necessity and the like, to untwist these sacred bonds and ties. . . . It is now a part of my misery in old age, to find and feel the decay and want thereof (in a great measure) and with grief and sorrow of heart and bewail the same. And for others' warning and admonition, and my own humiliation, do I here note the same.

Historians argue about the reasons Bradford looked so harshly at his own prospering and secure settlement. A few years earlier, in the "horrible" year of 1642, a Plymouth youth named Thomas Granger had to be executed for the unspeakable sin of bestiality (along with all the animals he had defiled). Whatever the cause, virtually every subsequent generation echoed Bradford's certainty that new attitudes, sins, and shortcomings proved unworthy of a sacred, noble past.

One of the old Pilgrim's spiritual successors, the great preacher (and president of Princeton) Jonathan Edwards, wrote that the 1730s represented "a far more degenerate time . . . than ever before." In his immortal 1741 sermon "Sinners in the Hands of an Angry God," he riveted the devout Puritan churchgoers in Northampton, Massachusetts, and Enfield, Connecticut, by telling them: "Yea, God is a great deal more angry with great numbers that are now on earth: yea, doubtless, with many that are now in this congregation, who it may be are at ease, than he is with many of those who are now in the flames of hell. . . . The wrath of God burns against them, their damnation does not slumber; the pit is prepared, the fire is made ready, the furnace is now hot, ready to receive them; the flames do now rage and glow. The glittering sword is whet, and held over them, and the pit hath opened its mouth under them."

Almost exactly a century later another New England preacher, anti-slavery firebrand William Lloyd Garrison, deplored the impiety, hypocrisy, and degradation of his own temporizing generation: "I accuse the land of my nativity of insulting the Majesty of Heaven with the grossest mockery that was ever exhibited to man." He also denounced the Constitution as "a covenant with death and an agreement with Hell" and frequently burned copies of the nation's founding document to signify God's righteous wrath.

Billy Sunday, former major league outfielder (for the Philadelphia Phillies and other teams) and famous revivalist, led another moral crusade against the decadence of early-twentieth-century America. Proclaiming himself "the sworn, eternal, and uncompromising enemy of the Liquor Traffic," he fervently pledged that "I have been, and will go on, fighting that damnable, dirty, rotten business with all the power at my command." The evangelist also opposed public dancing, card playing, attending the theater, reading novels, and baseball games on Sunday. Even before the "loss of innocence" associated with America's entry into World War I, he asked one of his huge audiences: "Did you ever know a time in all history when the world was worse than it is now? People are passing up the Church and the Prayer Meeting for the theatre, the leg show, and the movies. Oh, Lord, how we need someone to cry aloud, 'Return to God!' "

These thundering denunciations by yesterday's revivalists should remind twenty-first-century culture critics that they by no means count as the first of their countrymen to sound the alarm over rampant self-indulgence and imminent moral collapse. Even the most heroic generations in American history fell short of the one-dimensional, statues-in-the-park righteousness we love to impute to the supposedly simpler world of the glorious past.

Colonial birth records confirm, for instance, that in the decades before the American Revolution a shockingly high percentage of first children (at times as high as 30 percent in some regions) arrived less than seven months after the wedding ceremony—a powerful indication that strict self-control escaped young Americans of more than two hundred years ago much as it escapes too many young people today. Even the noble and spectacularly gifted Founding Fathers struggled with the same temptations and foibles afflicting politicians (and others) of our era: Benjamin Franklin fathered an illegitimate son from an unidentified mother, married a woman who lacked a proper divorce, and conducted numerous flirtations during diplomatic missions to France; Thomas Jefferson (as a widower) carried on a deep love affair with a beautiful married woman and probably indulged in a long-term relationship with his own slave Sally Hemings beginning when she was thirteen; Alexander Hamilton engaged in a torrid connection with a married woman while paying blackmail to her husband; and Aaron Burr enjoyed literally scores of passionate affairs and faced persistent rumors of incest with his glamorous daughter.

In at least one area, today's citizens display better discipline and higher moral standards than our Revolutionary forebears. In their essay "Drinking in America," historians Mark Lender and James Martin report: "One may safely assume . . . that abstemious colonials were few and far between. Counting the mealtime beer and cider at home and the convivial drafts at the tavern or at the funeral of a relative or neighbor, all this drinking added up. . . . While precise consumption figures are lacking, informed estimates suggest that by the 1790s an average American over fifteen years old drank just under six gallons of absolute alcohol a year. . . .

The comparable modern average is less than 2.9 gallons per capita." This consumption created worrisome problems with public drunkenness in Philadelphia, Boston, New York, and other colonial centers that mirrored, though never equaled, the appalling alcoholism that plagued London.

Such details from the historical record serve as a useful corrective to

"Show Me Something Worse!"

Each generation of Americans sees its own era as uniquely corrupt, but when it comes to prostitution and the mass degradation of women, the last years of the nineteenth century stood out as especially shameful. In *City of Eros* (1992), historian Timothy J. Gilfoyle looks at surviving records and suggests that as many as one out of six female New Yorkers may have worked full-time as prostitutes. With cities teeming with lonely, homesick, and predominantly male immigrants, young women who arrived from Southern Europe, Eastern Europe, or Asia either got snapped up as brides or, too often, found themselves forced into brutal "white slavery."

In 1892, Reverend Charles Parkhurst of Madison Square Presbyterian Church went undercover to expose New York's savage "underworld" and confirm his charges of corruption against city officials. At each stop, Parkhurst ordered the private detective guiding him, "Show me something worse!" and encountered excesses of sadism and pedophilia (involving both girls and boys) to disgust observers of any century. When he went public with his revelations, the press and legal establishment (including a committee of the legislature) joined his crusade against vice. A reform ticket swept Tammany Hall out of office in the next city election at the same time that Emma Willard of the Women's Christian Temperance Union intensified her campaign against white slavery everywhere. By the end of World War I in 1918, reformers had made noteworthy progress against forced prostitution, emphasizing hygienic arguments and warning of the impact of venereal disease.

nostalgia for earlier eras of allegedly effortless moral purity. They also give the lie to the common assumption that social degradation is a one-way street that leads year by year, generation by generation, only downhill. When it comes to measures of morality, it would be more accurate to say that America has experienced a dizzying roller coaster of steep ups and downs, zigzags, climbs and reverses, and even loop-the-loops.

GREAT DISRUPTIONS, GREAT REDEMPTIONS

Francis Fukuyama of Johns Hopkins University, author of *The Great Disruption,* writes trenchantly: "While conservatives may be right that moral decline occurred over the past generation, they cannot be right that it occurs in every generation. Unless we posit that all of human history has been a degeneration from some primordial golden age, periods of moral decline must be punctuated by periods of moral improvement." Impassioned scolds such as Bradford, Edwards, Garrison, and Sunday actually helped facilitate such "periods of moral improvement," pushing and prodding toward the various awakenings and revivals that changed American society for the better.

Religious historians refer to four distinct "Great Awakenings" that profoundly influenced the course of history and the ethical outlook of the populace. The first, from the 1730s through the 1750s, was led by fiery preachers such as Jonathan Edwards and British visitors George Whitefield and the Wesley brothers, and spread from rural districts to the largest cities, helping lay the groundwork for the American Revolution. The second, from 1800 through the 1830s, brought camp meetings that drew tens of thousands even in remote frontier settlements, the founding of pious, nonconformist sects (including the Mormon Church), and new energy for the antislavery and women's suffrage movements. The Third Great Awakening, from the 1880s through the 1900s, brought the Holiness Movement, the beginnings of American Pentecostalism, Christian Science, the Social Gospel, Progressive politics, and the resurgent temperance crusade against alcohol. Many sociologists and theologians see a Fourth Great Awakening beginning in the late 1970s and continuing to the present day, evidenced by the power of the so-called Religious Right, the growth of evangelical "megachurches," and an immensely expanded Christian influence in popular culture. Regardless of how one evaluates the significance and lasting impact of each of these periods of revival, they suggest that the nation's moral and religious history has never followed a straight line toward degeneracy and shattered traditions.

In her supremely valuable book *The De-Moralization of Society*, historian Gertrude Himmelfarb focuses on the British model to show that faith-based reformers can exert a potent impact on a nation's manners and morals, virtues and values. The Victorian era, popularly identified with restrictive and judgmental codes of behavior, actually represented a conscious reaction to the excesses and debauchery of the 1700s. The raising of social standards—readily apparent in statistics on illegitimacy, drunkenness, crime, abandonment of children, and more—resulted from conscious efforts by mobilized moralists. Himmelfarb writes:

> In addition to societies for the promotion of piety and virtue, others were established for the relief of the poor and infirm—for destitute orphans and abandoned children, aged widows and penitent prostitutes, the deaf, dumb, blind, and otherwise incapacitated. . . . The idea of moral reformation also extended to such humanitarian causes as the elimination of flogging in the army and navy, the abolition of the pillory and public whipping, the prohibition of cockfighting, bull-baiting, and bearbaiting, and, most important, the abolition of the slave trade . . . Less formally, but no less effectively, they promoted those manners and morals that have come to be known as "Victorian values." . . . The "moral reformation" initiated in the late eighteenth century came to fruition in the late nineteenth century.

The reformers refused to see moral failings as inevitable, intractable, or imposed by a higher power. In fact, the Victorian "remoralization" represents one of the most spectacular examples of self-conscious social betterment in all of human history—an improvement in which the

United States ultimately followed Britain's example. As Himmelfarb concludes: "At the end of the nineteenth century, England was a more civil, more pacific, more humane society than it had been in the beginning. 'Middle-class' manners and morals had penetrated into large sections of the working classes."

Francis Fukuyama notes the same wholesome transition as a prime example of a "great redemption" following one of history's periodic "great disruptions." He notes that "in both Britain and the United States, the period from the end of the eighteenth century until approximately the middle of the nineteenth century saw sharply increasing levels of social disorder. Crime rates in virtually all major cities increased. Illegitimacy rates rose, families dissolved, and social isolation increased. The rate of alcohol consumption, particularly in the United States, exploded. But then, from the middle of the century until its end, virtually all of these social indicators reversed direction. Crime rates fell. Families stabilized, and drunkards went on the wagon. New voluntary associations—from temperance and abolitionist societies to Sunday schools—gave people a fresh sense of communal belonging."

In addition to such sweeping changes of direction, the United States has experienced more limited periods of disruption or renewal. In the twentieth century, two world wars undermined the stability of family life and traditional mores, while the 1950s and its era of American dominance, prosperity, and religiosity saw dramatic improvements in divorce rates, criminality, drug and alcohol addiction, and access to higher education.

The countercultural explosions of the 1960s, viewed by many as an altogether fatal blow to parental authority, sexual self-discipline, sobriety, and the work ethic, gave rise in less than twenty years to the era of Reaganism and "Morning in America." Some of the same baby boomers who turned on, tuned in, and dropped out, or traveled to Woodstock in 1969 "to get themselves back to the garden," found their way home to church and suburb within twenty years, enrolling their children in religious schools and honoring the patriotic and entrepreneurial values the hippie era so colorfully scorned.

The rapid discrediting and dissolution of some of the most pernicious, drug-soaked notions of the once-celebrated youth culture (when's the last time anyone glamorized a free-love commune or cult leader's "family"?) demonstrated that major changes in manners and mores often prove ephemeral. While the most prominent and portentous Beatles-era philosophers, such as Charles Reich (*The Greening of America*), proclaimed a seismic shift in consciousness that would alter human attitudes forever, as it turned out, the big transformation didn't even last past the 1970s.

Dr. Allan C. Carlson and Paul T. Mero, authors of *The Natural Family: A Manifesto,* see these advances and setbacks as part of a long, indecisive struggle to preserve "the natural family—part of the created order, imprinted on our natures, the source of bountiful joy, the fountain of new life, the bulwark of ordered liberty." Industrialization brought the decisive break that undermined "the natural ecology of family life" when "family-made goods and tasks became commodities, things to be bought and sold," with the factory and "mass state schools" taking children away from their previously home-centered lives. When the French Revolution gave ideological basis to these changes, "advocates for the natural family—figures such as Bonald and Burke—fought back. They defended the 'little platoons' of social life, most of all the home. They rallied the ideas that would show again the necessity of the natural family. They revealed the nature of organic society to be a true democracy of free homes." This intimate restoration, they argue, made possible the sweeping reforms of the Victorian era.

Of course, other pendulum swings rapidly followed—with the totalitarian state power associated with Communist and Fascist ideology declaring open war on the family. When 1960s free spirits intensified their own struggle, Carlson and Mero report, they never won the expected easy or comprehensive victory. "As the culture turned hostile, natural families jolted back to awareness. Signs of renewal came from the new leaders and the growth of movements, popularly called 'pro-life' and 'pro-family,' which arose to defend the natural family. By the early twenty-first century, these—our—movements could claim some modest gains."

Such gains, which many social conservatives perversely refuse to recognize, need to be acknowledged and solidified to facilitate further progress.

IRREVERSIBLE, OR *ALREADY* REVERSED?

Those who insist on the definitive moral collapse of the United States as an unchallenged article of faith need to consider a shocking report in the *New York Times* in late November 2007:

> New York City is on track to have fewer than 500 homicides this year, by far the lowest number in a 12-month period since reliable Police Department statistics became available in 1963.
>
> But within the city's official crime statistics is a figure that may be even more striking: so far, with roughly half the killings analyzed, only 35 were found to be committed by strangers, a microscopic statistic in a city of more than 8.2 million.
>
> If that trend holds up, fewer than 100 homicides in New York City this year will have been strangers to their assailants. In the eyes of some criminologists, the police will be hard pressed to drive the killing rate much lower, since most killings occur now within the four walls of an apartment or the confines of close relationships.

The trend did hold up: throughout 2007 a total of 494 murders were committed in New York City, and well under 100 involved victimizing strangers.

The stunning enhancement of public safety in America's largest city represents a stinging rebuke to those who persist in viewing the nation as a victim of ongoing moral breakdown and spreading anarchy. The change could hardly be more dramatic: New York recorded its greatest number of killings in a single year in 1990, with 2,245, and strangers committed a majority of those homicides. Seventeen years later, the city's murder rate had fallen by more than three-fourths.

Other major cities may boast less spectacular progress than New York (with its two successive—and successful—crime-fighting Republican mayors), but they all show less violent and property crimes from their peaks some twenty years ago. While FBI crime statistics demonstrate an unfortunate uptick in criminal violence in the past two years (concentrated in cities such as Philadelphia and Washington, D.C.), the overall rate remains well below its peak. The criminal ethos regularly associated with social chaos and moral disorder has retreated across the country, and other indicators show a nation struggling to improve its spiritual and cultural health.

As Peter Wehner and Yuval Levin report in *Commentary:*

> Teenage drug use, which moved relentlessly upward throughout the 1990s, declined thereafter by an impressive 23 percent, and for a number of specific drugs it has fallen still lower. Thus, the use of Ecstasy and LSD has dropped by over 50 percent, of methamphetamine by almost as much, and of steroids by over 20 percent. . . . Teen use of alcohol has also fallen sharply since 1996—anywhere from 10 to 35 percent, depending on the grade in school—and binge drinking has dropped to the lowest levels ever recorded. The same is true of teens reporting that they smoke cigarettes daily.

In July 2007, the National Center for Health Statistics released more encouraging numbers involving the next generation of Americans. The Associated Press summarized the center's findings: "Fewer high school students are having sex these days, and more are using condoms. The teen birth rate has hit a record low. More young people are finishing high school, too, and more little kids are being read to."

Despite lurid publicity about a new "hookup culture" of casual sex among young people, the actual incidence of intercourse has markedly declined. The center's study revealed that in 1991, 54 percent of high school students reported having had sexual intercourse, but by 2005, that number had dropped to 47 percent.

Even the Guttmacher Institute, affiliated with Planned Parenthood, reported similar declines in teenage sexual activity. In September 2006, the institute observed that "teens are waiting longer to have sex than they did in the past. . . . The proportion of teens who had ever had sex declined . . . from 55% to 46% among males" in just seven years between 1995 and 2002.

The reduced sexual activity has also brought about a sharp reduction in abortion rates. The Guttmacher Institute acknowledges that abortion rates peaked in 1981, just as our most outspokenly pro-life president, Ronald Reagan, entered the White House. In that year, doctors and clinics performed 29.3 abortions per 1,000 women aged 15 to 44. Twenty years later, after tireless efforts by pro-life activists and educators, that number had dropped steadily, year by year, all the way to 21.1, a reduction of nearly 30 percent. Meanwhile, the number of U.S. abortion providers went down by 11 percent in just four years between 1996 and 2000 and, according to all recent reports, continues to decline.

In April 2008 the U.S. Centers for Disease Control and Prevention released a report showing that between 1990 and 2004, the estimated abortion rate declined by a full 24 percent. In no single year did the rate even inch upward. Among the most vulnerable teenage mothers between the ages of fifteen and seventeen, the abortion rate fell a staggering 55 percent—at the same time that rates of teen pregnancy and live births also retreated.

In terms of family structure, the most common assumptions about the breakdown of marriage bear little connection to current realities. Professors Betsey Stevenson and Justin Wolfers of the University of Pennsylvania write in the *New York Times*:

> The great myth about divorce is that marital breakup is an increasing threat to American families, with each generation finding their marriages less stable than those of their parents. . . . In fact, the divorce rate has been falling continually over the past quarter century, and is now at its lowest level since 1970. . . . For instance, marriages that began in the 1990s were more likely to celebrate a tenth anniversary than those that started in the 1980s, which, in turn, were also more likely to last than marriages that began back in the 1970s. . . . The facts are that divorce is down, and today's marriages are more stable than they have been in decades.

Despite deeply troubling increases in out-of-wedlock birth (a status now claimed by more than a third of newborn Americans), that phenomenon also may have begun to level off in recent years (most notably in the African American community). Moreover, the figures for children born outside of marriage do not register the widespread phenomenon of mothers and fathers who decide to marry and form a conventional family after the birth of their child. Though the white-picket-fence, "honey, I'm home" family looks far less solid and dominant than it did fifty years ago, the Census Bureau's most recent statistics (2003) show a surprising total of 68.4 percent of all children below the age of eighteen (of all races) currently living in households with two parents; among white children that number reaches 74.2 percent. Despite its battering in the media, the family remains the normal, prevalent unit of social organization for the purpose of child rearing.

If the idealized family TV shows of the 1950s *(Ozzie and Harriet, Father Knows Best, Leave It to Beaver)* failed to portray the imperfections and complexities of real-life relationships, the lusty and lonely libertines of *Desperate Housewives* represent today's realities just as poorly. In their enormously helpful book *The First Measured Century,* scholars from the American Enterprise Institute report: "The declining incidence of extramarital sex may seem implausible to television viewers who see a world of wholesale promiscuity in which marital fidelity is the exception rather than the rule. The data tell a different story." The authors point out that "the most authoritative study of American sexual practices," the 1992 National Health and Social Life Survey, reveals "an unmistakable decline in extramarital sexual activity during the latter part of the century, especially among married men."

Finally, the progress on welfare, with its grim associations with dysfunction and dependency, has been nothing short of breathtaking. As Wehner and Levin summarize the situation, "Since the high-water mark of 1994, the national welfare caseload has declined by over 60 percent. Virtually every state in the union has reduced its caseload by at least a third, and some have achieved reductions of over 90 percent. Not only have the numbers of people on welfare plunged, but in the wake of the 1996 welfare-reform bill, overall poverty, child poverty, black child poverty, and child hunger have all decreased, while employment figures for single mothers have risen."

The various numbers and analyses hardly paint a portrait of some golden age of moral rectitude or even of functional families—not at a time when, according to 2005 census figures, a record 37 percent of all American children enter the world without the benefit of married parents, or when cohabitation before marriage (despite indisputably increasing the likelihood of divorce) has become significantly more common (and even the norm to many young people).

Nevertheless, the claim that the nation faces irreversible moral decline can't survive the incontrovertible evidence that some of the decay of previous decades has already been reversed. The effort to "remoralize" America after the disruptions of the 1960s has met with some success, and its future will depend to a great extent on the continued vitality of traditional religious faith.

Pledging Purity

Appalled by frightening rates of teen pregnancy, abortion, and sexually transmitted diseases, in 1993 a Nashville-based ministry of the Southern Baptist Convention launched an ambitious new program called "True Love Waits." Participating youngsters took a public pledge, and signed a card, making "a commitment to God, myself, my family, my friends, my future mate, and my future children to a lifetime of purity including sexual abstinence from this day until the day I enter a biblical marriage relationship." Within a year, more than 100,000 young people took the pledge, often in ecstatic and joyful public gatherings. By 2008, the *Journal of Adolescent Health* was reporting that an impressive 23 percent of American females between the ages of twelve and seventeen, and 16 percent of males, made public commitments to avoid sex before marriage. Some researchers questioned the efficacy of such pledges, but a 2008 study by the RAND Corporation showed that those adolescents who committed themselves to virginity oaths "were less likely to be sexually active over the three-year study period than other youth who were similar to them, but who did not make a virginity pledge."

KEEPING THE FAITH

During the heralded New Age of the Beatles generation ("We're more popular than Jesus now"), various celebrities and influential intellectuals pronounced the death of old-style American religiosity and trumpeted its replacement with assorted cults, fads, and crackpots. *Time* magazine ran a cover story in 1966 that featured a black background with red lettering boldly asking, "Is God Dead?" A generation later, a comparison of church attendance and magazine circulation figures suggests that the Almighty may possess considerably more vitality than *Time* itself.

The United States remains an incurably God-centered society, with levels of belief and participation dramatically higher than in Western Europe. British journalist Geoffrey Wheatcroft in the *Wall Street Journal* reported regular attendance at religious services in the United Kingdom at 7 percent, and a pathetic 2 percent for the official Church of England. The *lowest* comparable figures for the United States, as Professor Robert Wuthnow of Princeton has noted, range between 30 and 35 percent of the adult population.

Meanwhile, the Gallup Organization offers its own "Index of Leading Religious Indicators," measuring a variety of variables: belief in God, the importance of religion in lives, membership in churches, weekly worship attendance, confidence in organized religion, confidence in ethics of clergy, and relevance of religion in today's society. Gathering data on these issues going back to 1941, Gallup (like other surveys) shows 1957–58 as a peak year for religiosity, followed by precipitous declines, then another rise between 1977 and 1985. After a thirty-point decline between the Reagan era and the middle of the Clinton era (1996), religion resumed its upward march, with a twenty-point rise in the past ten years.

The most demanding and scripturally rigorous denominations show the greatest vitality of all. Professor Wuthnow, generally skeptical of all talk of a religious revival, unequivocally acknowledges the swelling influence of conservative forces in scriptural interpretation:

First, as a proportion of the entire U.S. public, evangelical Protestant affiliation grew from around 17 to 20 percent in the early 1970s to between 25 and 28 percent in more recent surveys. Second, because the affiliation with the more liberal or moderate mainline Protestant denominations was declining during this period, the relative strength of conservative Protestantism was even more evident. For example, conservative Protestantism had been only about two-thirds as prominent as mainline Protestantism in the early 1970s but outstripped it by a margin of 2 to 1 in some of the more recent surveys.

The chief growth in religious commitment, in other words, has come in precisely those strict and enthusiastic denominations (evangelical Christianity, Mormonism, traditional Catholicism, Orthodox Judaism) that provide the structure and the communal institutions to connect personal faith to the broader regeneration of social capital and functional values.

Francis Fukuyama notes that the current vitality of religious institutions confounds all expectations of the past:

> A generation or two ago, social scientists generally believed secularization was the inevitable byproduct of modernization, but in the United States and many other advanced societies, religion does not seem to be in danger of dying out.

He sees the reconnection to religious institutions as motivated more by rational self-interest than by selfless faith:

> Religion may serve a purpose in reestablishing norms, even without a sudden return to religious orthodoxy. Religion is frequently not so much the product of dogmatic belief as it is the provider of a convenient language that allows communities to express moral beliefs that they would hold on entirely secular grounds. . . . In countless ways, modern, educated, skeptical people are drawn to religion because it offers them community, ritual, and support for values they otherwise hold.

In his view, religion may be an instrument for the revitalization of values rather than the driving force behind it, but the connection between faith and cultural revival remains indispensable.

ENDORSING DEGENERACY

While faith-based communities constitute a potent factor in remoralization, they face a uniquely powerful opposing force in today's society: the influence of mass media and the arts.

In the past, few authority figures glorified radical challenges to the established ethical order. In Hogarth's eighteenth-century London, many residents of every rank and station drank to excess, abused or abandoned their families, frequented houses of ill fame, contracted grotesque and incurable diseases, and then collapsed as pustulating refuse among the foraging pigs in the fetid and rubbish-ridden streets. At the time, however, no novelists or musicians or pamphleteers troubled to celebrate such behavior or to hail the miscreants as courageous avatars of some new consciousness. In previous generations, even at moments of thoroughgoing moral breakdown, the attitude of leading institutions remained sternly disapproving. Corruption might infect the church, the government, the aristocracy, the press, and the universities, but none of these official establishments ever attempted to endorse degeneracy.

Today, on the other hand, Yale and other elite institutions host "sex fairs" for undergraduates to learn about the diverse joys of group sex, transvestitism, bestiality, masochism, and even necrophilia. Legislatures in several states have passed laws making it illegal to "discriminate" against behaviors classified as felonious just one generation ago. Cable television and satellite radio offer prurient material every day and, in fact, every hour that would have provoked prosecution for obscenity in an earlier age.

The obstacles to a sweeping restoration of values remain ubiquitous and overwhelming. Any effort to roll back immorality faces formidable government bureaucracies, official regulations, the smug assurance of nearly all of academia, and ceaseless special pleading in mass media meant to protect and glamorize the most deeply dysfunctional values.

THE POWER OF CHOICE

In 1992, I decried the corrosive impact of media's visceral hostility to faith and family in my controversial book *Hollywood vs. America:*

> The dream factory has become the poison factory. Hollywood ignores the concerns of the overwhelming majority of the American people who worry over the destructive messages so frequently featured in today's movies, television, and popular music. . . . It's not "mediocrity and escapism" that leave audiences cold, but sleaze and self-indulgence. What troubles people about the popular culture isn't the competence with which it's shaped, but the messages it sends, the view of the world it transmits. Hollywood no longer reflects—or even respects—the values of most American families.

Considering the current caliber of offerings from the entertainment conglomerates, it's difficult to discern evidence of redemption that would require a revision of this verdict. It's true that big studio films and network TV have somewhat deemphasized the exploitation of graphic violence, but the salacious focus on bodily functions and witless, joyless raunch continues to typify an industry once considered the international arbiter of glamour and class.

Even without literally hundreds of readily available university studies to make the point, the influence of popular culture remains potent and inescapable, especially in light of the fact that the average American views twenty-nine hours of TV weekly (without calculating the many additional hours of DVDs, video games, theatrical films, the Internet, and pop music). Given this prominence of media distractions in our lives, the question for the nation's moral health becomes obvious: how could the public provide significant evidence of reformation and restoration when the most prominent and popular entertainment offerings continue to drag consumers in the opposite direction?

The answer provides both encouragement for the present and hope for the future, and centers on the single word *choice.*

L. Gordon Crovitz, former publisher of the *Wall Street Journal,* effectively sums up the most positive and dynamic aspects of our cultural landscape. "Technologists are optimists, for good reason," he writes. "My own bias is that as information becomes more accessible, individuals gain choice, control and freedom."

The one great improvement in our media and even educational landscape involves the proliferation of unprecedented alternatives, often tied to new technologies. With cable and satellite and Internet options, the nation has become less dependent than ever before on the dreary array of network programming. Not only do neighborhood video stores provide literally thousands of DVDs delivering the best (and worst) offerings in Hollywood history, but they do so with the addition of exclusive (and often educational) features never seen in theaters. The Internet, with literally countless diversions and downloads on offer, lends its own unimaginable power to breaking the tyranny of film company bosses and network programmers.

A restless and disillusioned public can't, in the end, control the release schedule of any major studio, but each consumer can shape the schedule of what he chooses to see. Beleaguered families won't succeed in determining the new fall lineup of any TV network, but they get the final say in what they decide to watch.

With the help of the information revolution and dramatic improvements in communication, Americans have developed their own networks and affinity groups and subcultures, largely independent of bureaucratic or corporate control. In Milton Friedman's famous phrase, we are now "free to choose" and to defy the overwhelming forces that purportedly drove society only in a downward direction.

This new freedom even facilitates the basic approach advocated by Paul Weyrich in his despairing "we have lost the culture war" letter of 1999. "Therefore," he wrote, "what seems to me a legitimate strategy for us to follow is to look at ways to separate ourselves from the institutions that have been captured by the ideology of Political Correctness, or by other enemies of our traditional culture . . . I think that we have to look at a whole series of possibilities for bypassing the institutions that are controlled by the enemy." The rapid development of home schooling, with practitioners gaining unprecedented access to curricula and expertise through the Internet, provides one example of bottom-up expressions of do-it-yourself conservatism that already play a role in the ongoing revival.

The power of choice and the exercise of free will can inject wholesome energy into a troubled society and begin the process of regeneration, but the decentralization and, ultimately, democratization of decisions and authority make it unthinkable to return to an era of unquestioned, top-down moral absolutes. As Fukuyama writes:

> What would the remoralization of society look like? In some of its manifestations, it would represent a continuation of trends that have already occurred in the 1990s, such as the return of middle-class people from their gated suburban communities to downtown areas, where a renewed sense of order and civility once again makes them feel secure enough to live and work. It would show up in increasing levels of participation in civil associations and political engagement.

The predicted surge in political engagement constituted one of the most notable aspects of the campaign year 2008. But Fukuyama cautions that the improvement in the moral climate can only go so far:

> Strict Victorian rules concerning sex are very unlikely to return. Unless someone can figure out a way to un-invent birth control, or move women out of the labor force, the nuclear family of the 1950s is not likely to be reconstituted in anything like its original form. Yet the social role of fathers has proved very plastic from society to society and over time, and it is not unreasonable to think that the commitment of men to their families can be substantially strengthened.

Of course, fathers must choose to change. As David Brooks writes in response to Fukuyama's arguments: "But why, then, have so many of these social indicators turned around (if only slightly in some cases) over the past few years? The answer is that human beings are not merely victims of forces larger than ourselves. We respond. We respond by instinct and by reason."

For those who believe it's already too late, that the nation's slide to degeneracy has proceeded so far that any meaningful rescue becomes impossible, Brooks suggests that the relevant choice would be to turn off the alarming TV news and walk out the front door. "Our cultural pessimists need some fresh air," he wrote, memorably, in *Policy Review*. "They should try wandering around any middle class suburb in the nation, losing themselves amid the cul-de-sacs, the azaleas, the Jeep Cherokees, the neat lawns, the Little Tikes kiddie cars, and the height-adjustable basketball backboards. Is this really what cultural collapse would look like? . . . The evidence of our eyes, ears, and senses is that America is not a moral wasteland. It is, instead, a tranquil place, perhaps not one that elevates mankind to its highest glory, but doing reasonably well, all things considered."

THE KIDS ARE ALL RIGHT

The children of those cul-de-sacs Brooks describes have already begun to surprise the declinists with their improved performance in school (with the National Assessment of Educational Progress reporting steady progress among fourth graders in both math and reading, and with the mean SAT score eight points higher in the twelve years after 1993) and with their reduced rates of drug use, alcohol abuse, smoking, criminal violence, and sexual adventurism. John P. Walters, director of the Office of National Drug Control Policy, succinctly characterized the wide-ranging and encouraging changes: "We have a broad set of behaviors by young people that are going in a healthy direction."

This phenomenon has also produced an increasingly common if unexpected generational contrast: young people (and especially young couples) who embrace a more fervent and rigorous religiosity than their parents or grandparents. The clichéd melodramas in the ancient style of *The Jazz Singer* (1927)—where a youthful, assimilated, show-business-crazy American rejects the pious immigrant orthodoxy of his parents—have given way to distinctive twenty-first-century tales of a new generation renouncing pallid secularism and rediscovering long-forgotten traditions. *USA Today* reported on this new pattern and indicated that "clergy of all stripes say they are seeing a small wave of young adults who are more pious than their parents. And they're getting an earful from boomer moms and dads who range from shocked to delighted."

In other words, religiously as well as morally, Americans refuse to march along a single parade route, even as we find ourselves unable to stand still. All measures of morality show a complex, multifaceted, and, to some extent, turbulent nation. Some Americans (unfortunately concentrated in the media, academia, and other centers of influence) explore decadence and experimental values with more daring or abandon than ever before. At the same time, many others flock to churches and synagogues (where religious services regularly draw four times more participants than all feature films every weekend) and affirm faith-filled values with passion, self-confidence, and dedication that continue to energize the religious conservative movement.

This contribution has already renewed the pro-life cause. Wehner and Levin write: "All in all, not only has the public discussion of abortion been profoundly transformed, but younger Americans seem to have moved the farthest—in September [2007], a Harris poll found that Americans aged eighteen to thirty were the most likely of all age groups to oppose the practice. This trend seems likely to continue."

Wehner and Levin conclude: "In attitudes toward education, drugs, abortion, religion, marriage, and divorce, the current generation of teenagers and young adults appears in many respects to be more culturally conservative than its immediate predecessors. To any who may have written off American society as incorrigibly corrupt and adrift, these young people offer a powerful reminder of the boundless inner resources still at our disposal, and of our constantly surprising national resilience."

Even those young people who may take their time in finding their way cannot be counted as irredeemably lost. As Walter Olson wrote in *Reason* magazine: "Individually, most adolescents who act out do not proceed in a straight line ever downward to crash in early romantic deaths. Something causes most of them to readjust their time horizons in search of longer-term satisfactions, in the mysterious process known as growing up. The thesis of cultural declinists must be that the process of unforced improvement and learning we see take place in individuals all the time couldn't possibly take place writ large."

For society as well as individuals, no passage is final: lifelong skeptics and cynics may embrace biblical truth in their seventies or eighties (as in the controversial case of the British atheist professor Antony Flew), or prominent religious leaders, especially when tainted by scandal or tagged with hypocrisy, may walk away from the faith of a lifetime. Choice remains an option, both nationally and personally—even if you believe that the choice rests ultimately with the Higher Power who directs our ends.

Moreover, in the United States no family story concludes with a single generation. Those raised in strictly religious homes will, on famous occasions, throw over the faith of their fathers with an angry and dismissive attitude. More frequently today, children of unchurched parents will become religious leaders or teachers, and pillars of conventional morality—and even go home to recruit various siblings or elders to the cause of renewal.

No matter how zealous their religiosity, however, these young believers won't take to the streets as wild-eyed prophets of onrushing apocalypse. In all my years of travel to every major city in the country, I've encountered plenty of hirsute hobos but never saw one who actually packed a placard proclaiming THE END IS NEAR. These figures of fantasy fit best in cartoons, since the real nation is focused more fervently on beginnings.

America remains, as always and in all things, on the move. Those who have already written off this great and good society as the victim of unstoppable degeneracy don't understand the eternal national capacity for fresh starts and new life.

Abnormal Nation

"THE HOPE OF MANKIND"

On one essential observation, America haters and committed patriots can emphatically agree: there is nothing normal about the United States.

Our origins, our rise to power, and our present preeminence all set us apart as extraordinary, unprecedented, singular. Alexis de Tocqueville first wrote of America as "exceptional" in 1835, and no one today seriously questions our unique status—to proud citizens, the Republic remains a unique force for good, while astringent critics see it as a unique source of oppression and corruption. Either way, the United States provokes intense emotion; not even the most contemptuous cynic can dismiss the hyperpower (as the French like to call us) as irrelevant or inconsequential. America matters, to its own people no less than to the rest of the world. We inspire love or loathing, devotion or disgust, affection or fear; indifference is not an option.

Lies about America proliferate precisely because no one shrugs off the United States as a nation like any other, with the usual mix of strengths, flaws, and eccentricities. Americans have always claimed more for ourselves ("the land of the free and home of the brave"), and those claims have produced an inevitable polarization. We're either more noble, blessed, and admirable than other states or else more brutal, vulgar, and destructive—rendered especially hateful because of our pretensions of grandeur.

Two Frenchmen set the tone for these opposing views in the early days of the Republic. In 1778 Anne-Robert-Jacques Turgot, the reformist royal finance minister, wrote a famous letter to his English friend Richard Price. The colonies had not even won their long struggle for independence, but Turgot nonetheless described America as "the hope of mankind" because it "must show to the world by its example, that men can be free and tranquil, and can do without the chains that tyrants and cheats of all garb have tried to lay on them. . . . It must give the example of political, religious, commercial and industrial liberty. The shelter which it is going to offer to the oppressed of all nations will console the earth."

A generation later, the great novelist Stendhal (Marie-Henri Beyle) sneered (through one of his characters) at the very notion of a "model country" and denounced America as "vulgar," a "triumph of stupid, egotistic mediocrity."

In the twenty-first century, a far greater number of foreign observers echo the sentiments of Stendhal than those of Turgot. As Peter H. Schuck and James Q. Wilson piquantly summarize these attitudes in their superb 2008 book *Understanding America:* "To them, Americans are exceptional all right: exceptionally vulgar, exceptionally materialistic, exceptionally clumsy, exceptionally unfeeling, and exceptionally self-centered." These skeptics, however, fail to see the obvious contradictions in their hostility. According to Schuck and Wilson, "It is a bit odd for any nation to be deeply divided, witlessly vulgar, religiously orthodox, militarily aggressive, economically savage, and ungenerous to those in need, while maintaining a political stability, a standard of living, and a love of country that are the envy of the world—all at the same time. To do all these things at once, America must indeed be unusual."

Foreigners inevitably feel conflicted in their response to the United States, buffeted and adrift in opposing currents of envy, admiration, and resentment, but Americans should sustain no comparable confusion about their home. If a Spaniard or a Swede won't acknowledge how much he has benefited from the United States and its world leadership for ideals of liberty, free markets, and self-government, he's shallow and stupid. But if a citizen of this favored land can't appreciate his own prodigious good fortune, his limitless opportunities as an American, then it's a case of willful ignorance and ingratitude.

The Lubavitcher rebbe Menachem Mendel Schneerson, the late, great leader of Chassidic Judaism, immigrated to the United States as a Holocaust refugee in 1941 and always marveled at the goodness and decency of his adopted homeland. He referred to America as the *"malchus shel chesed"*—the kingdom of loving-kindness—and that description neatly summarizes the warmhearted, openhanded qualities of our national life for newcomer and native-born alike.

"AN INFORMED PATRIOTISM IS WHAT WE WANT"

President Ronald Reagan (among many others) worried that younger generations of Americans would grow up with limited comprehension of their grounds for gratitude. On January 11, 1989, in his last televised speech from the Oval Office, he noted "a great tradition of warnings in presidential farewells, and I've got one that's been on my mind for some time." He spoke proudly of the "new patriotism" associated with his administration but worried that "it won't count for much and it won't last unless it's grounded in thoughtfulness and knowledge."

> An informed patriotism is what we want. And are we doing a good enough job teaching our children what America is and what she represents in the long history of the world? . . . We've got to teach history based not on what's in fashion but what's important. . . . If we forget what we did, we won't know who we are. I'm warning of an eradication of the American memory that could result, ultimately, in an erosion of the American spirit. Let's start with some

basics: more attention to American history and a greater emphasis on civic ritual. And let me offer lesson number one about America: all great change in America begins at the dinner table. So, tomorrow night in the kitchen I hope the talking begins. And children, if your parents haven't been teaching you what it means to be an American, let 'em know and nail 'em on it. That would be a very American thing to do.

Twenty years after the Gipper's charge, the conversations should continue, at dinner tables and elsewhere. The prevalent slanders against our country offer an especially suitable subject for discussion, and this book means to provide perspective and approaches for responding to those lies.

In the face of scornful assaults from inside and outside the United States, most Americans remain instinctively, incurably patriotic. Josef Joffe, editor-publisher of the leading German weekly *Die Zeit* (and a deeply sympathetic observer of the American scene), writes: "What sets America apart is its enduring identification with flag and country. For all of its multi-ethnicity, America possesses a keen sense of self—and of what it should be. Patriotism scores high in any survey, much higher than in Europe, including France. There is a surfeit of national symbols throughout the land, whereas no gas station in Europe would fly an oversized national flag."

This affirming impulse derives from the visceral understanding that American identity is a matter of will and choice. It didn't emerge organically, slowly evolving from blood ties and prehistoric ancestors who inhabited the homeland from time immemorial. As the French philosopher Bernard-Henri Lévy noted in a 2006 interview with the *Wall Street Journal*: "In France, with the nation based on roots, on the idea of the soil, on a common memory . . . the very existence of America is a mystery and a scandal. . . . The ghost that has haunted Europe for two centuries is America's coming together as an act of will, of *creed*. It shows that there is an alternative to organic nations." No wonder Europeans look with suspicion and resentment at a society that took shape through conscious decisions and willful sculpting by its various founders and builders.

"YOU ARE THE ARTIST"

That tradition continues, with each generation shaping and choosing its own American identity with far more latitude than available elsewhere. My friend Dinesh D'Souza, best-selling author and an immigrant from India, speculated on the direction of his life had he never come to the United States:

> If I had remained in India, I would probably have lived my whole life within a five-mile radius of where I was born. I would undoubtedly have married a woman of my identical religious and socioeconomic background. . . . I would have a whole set of opinions that could be predicted in advance; indeed, they would not be very different from what my father believed, or his father before him. In sum, my destiny would to a large degree have been given to me. . . . In most countries in the world your fate and your identity are handed to you; in America, you determine them for yourself. America is a country where you get to write the script of your own life. Your life is like a blank sheet of paper, and you are the artist. This notion of being the architect of your own destiny is the incredibly powerful idea that is behind the worldwide appeal of America. Young people especially find irresistible the prospect of authoring the narrative of their own lives.

The sense of adventure, of freshness, of D'Souza's "blank sheet of paper, and you are the artist," needs to be recovered from our history and the purveyors of guilt, regret, and apology. The *Wall Street Journal's* Peggy Noonan, President Reagan's onetime speechwriter, longs for a presidential candidate who feels the rollicking American adventure "in his bones"; she asks, "Has he ever gotten misty-eyed over . . . the Wright brothers and what kind of country allowed them to go off and change everything? How about D-Day, or George Washington, or Henry Ford, or the losers and brigands who flocked to Sutter's Mill, who pushed their way west because there was gold in them thar hills? There's gold in that history."

And there is still, perhaps, a golden future—at least according to one of our most distinguished novelists and journalists. In an *Uncommon Knowledge* interview for the Hoover Institution, host Peter Robinson asked Tom Wolfe: "Henry Luce famously called the twentieth century 'the American century.' Will the twenty-first century represent a *second* American century?"

The author responded without hesitation: "I believe we're on the edge of about 800 more years of American centuries. The biggest problem is all the people who see a problem. It's very fashionable to think that the end is near. After the end of the twentieth century, which was unquestionably the American century . . . we were supreme in a way that no country has ever been before. Maybe I have to start giving moral advice, which is, be happy with what you have."

Robinson, another former speechwriter to President Reagan, later commented on Wolfe's response: "Eight hundred years. At that moment, I confess, I could have leaned over and planted a big wet smacker right in the middle of Tom Wolfe's forehead, white suit or no."

Both Robinson and Wolfe clearly understand the import of Lincoln's words (in his Second Annual Address to Congress): "We—even we here—hold the power, and bear the responsibility. . . . We shall nobly save, or meanly lose, the last best hope of earth."

President Reagan loved that phrase, almost as much as he cherished the image of his "shining city on a hill," borrowed from Puritan forefather John Winthrop (who in turn took it from the Bible, of course). Near the conclusion of his deeply moving Farewell Address, Reagan asked, "And how stands the city on this winter night?" and then proceeded to answer his own question, for his time and for ours:

"After two hundred years, two centuries, she still stands strong and true on the granite ridge, and her glow has held steady no matter what storm. And she's still a beacon, still a magnet for all who must have freedom, for all the pilgrims from all the lost places who are hurtling through the darkness toward home."

Resources

Books

Blum, John M., Edmund S. Morgan, Arthur M. Schlesinger Jr., et. al. *The National Experience*. New York: Harcourt, Brace & World, Inc., 1963.

Boot, Max. *The Savage Wars of Peace: Small Wars and the Rise of American Power*. New York: Basic Books, 2002.

Brooks, Arthur. *Gross National Happiness: Why Happiness Matters for America—and How We Can Get More of It*. New York: Basic Books, 2008.

Brown, Dee. *Bury My Heart at Wounded Knee: An Indian History of the American West*. New York: Holt, Rinehart & Winston, 1970.

Buchanan, Patrick J. *A Republic, Not an Empire: Reclaiming America's Destiny*. Washington, D.C.: Regnery Publishing, 1999.

———. *Day of Reckoning: How Hubris, Ideology, and Greed Are Tearing America Apart*. New York: Thomas Dunne Books, 2007.

Butterfield, Roger. *The American Past: A History of the United States from Concord to the Great Society*. New York: Simon & Schuster, 1966.

Caplow, Theodore, Louis Hicks, and Ben J. Wattenberg. *The First Measured Century: An Illustrated Guide to Trends in America, 1900–2000*. Washington, D.C.: The AEI Press, 2001.

Carlson, Allan C. and Paul T. Mero. *The Natural Family: A Manifesto*. Dallas: Spence Publishing Company, 2007.

Chittenden, Hiram Martin. *The American Fur Trade of the Far West*. Stanford, CA: Academic Reprints, 1954.

Chua, Amy. *Day of Empire: How Hyperpowers Rise to Global Dominance—and Why They Fail*. New York: Doubleday, 2007.

Churchill, Ward. *A Little Matter of Genocide: Holocaust and Denial in the Americas 1492 to the Present*. San Francisco: City Lights Books, 1998.

Collier, Christopher and James Lincoln Collier. *Decision in Philadelphia: The Constitutional Convention of 1787*. New York: Ballantine Books, 1986.

Collier, Peter and David Horowitz. *The Race Card: White Guilt, Black Resentment, and the Assault on Truth and Justice*. Rocklin, CA: Forum/Prima Publishing, 1997.

Collins, Robert O. and James M. Burns. *A History of Sub-Saharan Africa*. Cambridge: Cambridge University Press, 2007.

Commager, Henry Steele and Richard B. Morris, eds. *The Spirit of 'Seventy-Six: The Story of the American Revolution as Told By Participants*. New York: Da Capo Press, 1995.

Cox, W. Michael and Richard Alm. *Myths of Rich and Poor: Why We're Better Off Than We Think*. New York: Basic Books, 1999.

Crocker, H. W. III. *Don't Tread on Me: A 400-Year History of America at War, from Indian Fighting to Terrorist Hunting*. New York: Crown Forum, 2006.

Curtin, Philip. *The Atlantic Slave Trade: A Census*. Madison: University of Wisconsin Press, 1969.

Davis, David Brion. *Inhuman Bondage: The Rise and Fall of Slavery in the New World*. Oxford: Oxford University Press, 2006.

Diamond, Jared. *Guns, Germs, and Steel: The Fates of Human Societies*. New York: W. W. Norton and Company, 1999.

DiLorenzo, Thomas J. *How Capitalism Saved America: The Untold History of Our Country, from the Pilgrims to the Present*. New York: Three Rivers Press, 2004.

Dobbs, Lou. *Independents Day: Awakening the American Spirit*. New York: Viking, 2007.

———. *War on the Middle Class: How the Government, Big Business, and Special Interest Groups Are Waging War on the American Dream and How to Fight Back*. New York: Penguin Books, 2006.

Drescher, Seymour and Stanley Engerman, eds. *A Historical Guide to World Slavery*. Oxford: Oxford University Press, 1998.

D'Souza, Dinesh. *The End of Racism: Principles for a Multiracial Society*. New York: Simon & Schuster, 1995.

———. *What's So Great About America*. Washington, D.C.: Regnery Publishing, 2002.

Easterbrook, Gregg. *The Progress Paradox*. New York: Random House, 2003.

Farrow, Anne, Joel Lang, and Jennifer Frank. *Complicity: How the North Promoted, Prolonged, and Profited from Slavery*. New York: Ballantine Books, 2005.

Fenn, Elizabeth A. *Pox Americana: The Great Smallpox Epidemic of 1785–82*. New York: Hill and Wang, 2001.

Flexner, James Thomas. *Washington: The Indispensable Man*. Boston: Little, Brown and Company, 1974.

Folsom, Burton W. Jr. *The Myth of the Robber Barons*. Herndon, VA: Young Americas Foundation, 1991.

Fukuyama, Francis. *The Great Disruption: Human Nature and the Reconstitution of Social Order*. New York: Free Press, 1999.

Furstenberg, Francois. *In the Name of the Father: Washington's Legacy, Slavery, and the Making of a Nation*. New York: The Penguin Press, 2006.

Gartner, John D. *The Hypomanic Edge: The Link Between (a Little) Craziness and (a Lot of) Success in America*. New York: Simon & Schuster, 2005.

Goodrich, Thomas. *Scalpdance: Indian Warfare on the High Plains 1865–1879*. Mechanicsburg, PA: Stackpole Books, 1997.

Gordon, John Steele. *An Empire of Wealth: The Epic History of American Economic Power*. New York: HarperCollins, 2004.

Himmelfarb, Gertrude. *The De-Moralization of Society: From Victorian Virtues to Modern Values*. New York: Vintage Books, 1994.

Hochschild, Adam. *Bury the Chains: Prophets and Rebels in the Fight to Free an Empire's Slaves*. Boston: Houghton Mifflin, 2005.

Hopkins, Donald R. *The Greatest Killer: Smallpox in History*. Chicago: University of Chicago Press, 2002.

Horowitz, David. *Uncivil Wars: The Controversy Over Reparations for Slavery*. San Francisco: Encounter Books, 2002.

Howe, Daniel Walker. *What God Hath Wrought: The Transformation of America, 1815–1848*. Oxford: Oxford University Press, 2007.

Jensen, Robert. *Citizens of the Empire: The Struggle to Claim Our Humanity*. San Francisco: City Lights Books, 2004.

Johnson, Clint. *The Politically Incorrect Guide to the South (and Why It Will Rise Again)*. Washington, D.C.: Regnery Publishing, 2006.

Johnson, Paul. *A History of the American People*. New York: HarperCollins, 1997.

Johnston, James Hugo. *Race Relations in Virginia and Miscegenation in the South, 1776–1860*. Amherst: University of Massachusetts Press, 1970.

Kagan, Robert. *Dangerous Nation: America's Place in the World from Its Earliest Days to the Dawn of the Early Twentieth Century*. New York: Alfred A. Knopf, 2006.

Kaplan, Robert D. *Imperial Grunts: The American Military on the Ground*. New York: Random House, 2005.

Kluger, Richard. *Seizing Destiny: How America Grew from Sea to Shining Sea*. New York: Alfred A. Knopf, 2007.

Koger, Larry. *Black Slaveowners: Free Black Slave Masters in South Carolina, 1790–1860*. Jefferson, NC: McFarland, 1985.

Lind, Michael. *Vietnam: The Necessary War*. New York: Touchstone, 1999.

Macht, Norman L. and Mary Hull. *The History of Slavery*. San Diego: Lucent Books, 1997.

Maier, Pauline. *American Scripture: Making the Declaration of Independence*. New York: Alfred A. Knopf, 1997.

Mann, Charles C. *1491: New Revelations of the Americas Before Columbus*. New York: Vintage Books, 2006.

Mansfield, Stephen. *Ten Tortured Words: How the Founding Fathers Tried to Protect Religion in America . . . and What's Happened Since*. Nashville: Thomas Nelson, 2007.

Marshall, Peter and David Manuel. *The Light and the Glory*. Grand Rapids, MI: Baker Book House Company, 1977.

Martin, Thomas R. *Ancient Greece: From Prehistoric to Hellenistic Times*. New Haven: Yale University Press, 1996.

McDougall, Walter A. *Freedom Just Around the Corner: A New American History, 1585–1828*. New York: HarperCollins, 2004.

Meacham, Jon. *American Gospel: God, The Founding Fathers, and the Making of a Nation*. New York: Random House, 2006.

Meese, Edwin III, Matthew Spalding, and David Forte, eds. *The Heritage Guide to the Constitution*. Washington, D.C.: Regnery Publishing, 2005.

Millard, Catherine. *The Rewriting of America's History*. Camp Hill, PA: Horizon House Publishers, 1991.

Miller, William Lee. *Arguing About Slavery: The Great Battle in the United States Congress*. New York: Alfred A. Knopf, 1996.

Moyar, Mark. *Triumph Forsaken: The Vietnam War, 1954–1965*. Cambridge: Cambridge University Press, 2006.

Murray, Charles. *Losing Ground: American Social Policy, 1950–1980*. New York: Basic Books, 1984.

Novak, Michael. *On Two Wings: Humble Faith and Common Sense at the American Founding*. San Francisco: Encounter Books, 2002.

Olasky, Marvin. *The American Leadership Tradition: Moral Vision from Washington to Clinton*. New York: The Free Press, 1999.

———. *The Tragedy of American Compassion*. Chicago: Regnery Gateway, 1992.

Podhoretz, Norman. *My Love Affair with America: The Cautionary Tale of a Cheerful Conservative*. New York: Simon & Schuster, 2000.

Powell, Jim. *FDR's Folly: How Roosevelt and His New Deal Prolonged the Great Depression*. New York: Crown Forum, 2003.

Rawley, James A. and Stephen D. Behrendt. *The Transatlantic Slave Trade: A History*. Lincoln: University of Nebraska Press, 2005.

Rediker, Marcus. *The Slave Ship: A Human History*. New York: Viking, 2007.

Richburg, Keith B. *Out of America: A Black Man Confronts Africa*. New York: Basic Books, 1997.

Rosebury, Theodor. *Microbes and Morals: The Strange Story of Venereal Disease*. New York: Ballantine Books, 1976.

Scheer, George F. and Hugh F. Rankin. *Rebels and Redcoats: The American Revolution Through the Eyes of Those Who Fought and Lived It*. New York: Da Capo Press, 1957.

Schoen, Douglas E. *Declaring Independence: The Beginning of the End of the Two-Party System*. New York: Random House, 2008.

Schuck, Peter H. and James Q. Wilson, eds. *Understanding America: The Anatomy of an Exceptional Nation*. New York: Public Affairs, 2008.

Shlaes, Amity. *The Forgotten Man: A New History of the Great Depression*. New York: HarperCollins, 2007.

Thernstrom, Abigail and Stephan Thernstrom, eds. *Beyond the Color Line: New Perspectives on Race and Ethnicity in America*. Stanford, CA: Hoover Institution Press, 2002.

Thomas, Hugh. *The Slave Trade*. New York: Simon & Schuster, 1997.

Thornton, Russell. *American Indian Holocaust and Survival: A Population History Since 1492*. Norman: University of Oklahoma Press, 1987.

Tirman, John. *100 Ways America Is Screwing Up the World*. New York: Harper Perennial, 2006.

Utley, Robert M. *The Last Days of the Sioux Nation*. New Haven: Yale University Press, 1963.

Watkins, Richard Ross. *Slavery: Bondage Throughout History*. Boston: Houghton Mifflin, 2001.

Westermann, William Linn. *The Slave Systems of Greek and Roman Antiquity*. Philadelphia: American Philosophical Society, 1984.

Whelan, Robert. *Wild in the Woods: The Myth of the Noble Eco-Savage*. London: The Institute of Economic Affairs, 1999.

Whybrow, Peter C. *American Mania: When More Is Not Enough*. New York: W. W. Norton and Company, 2005.

Winbush, Raymond A., ed. *Should America Pay Reparations? Slavery and the Raging Debate on Reparations*. New York: Amistad/HarperCollins, 2003.

Wood, Betty. *The Origins of American Slavery: Freedom and Bondage in the English Colonies*. New York: Hill and Wang, 1997.

Wood, Peter. *Diversity: The Invention of a Concept.* San Francisco: Encounter Books, 2003.

Woods, Thomas E. Jr. *33 Questions About American History You're Not Supposed to Ask.* New York: Crown Forum, 2007.

Zangwill, Israel. *The Melting-Pot: Drama in Four Acts.* New York: Arno Press, 1975.

Zinn, Howard. *A People's History of the United States: 1492–Present.* New York: Harper-Collins, 1999.

ARTICLES

Adler, Margot. "Behind the Ever-Expanding American Dream House." National Public Radio (NPR.org), November 19, 2007.

"Americans Satisfied with the Lives They Lead." *The Harris Poll, #80,* August 14, 2007.

"America's Pursuit of Happiness." Editorial. *Investor's Business Daily,* January 2, 2008.

Appiah, Kwame Anthony. "A Slow Emancipation." *New York Times Magazine,* March 18, 2007.

Assembly Concurrent Resolution #270. "Apologizing for the Wrongs of Slavery," The State of New Jersey, 212th Legislature, November 8, 2007.

Baker, Al. "New York Homicide Rate Continues to Slow, and May Be Lowest Since 1963." *New York Times,* November 23, 2007.

Banks, Adelle. "'In God We Trust' Inspires, Inflames." *Seattle Times,* September 29, 2007.

Berman, Russell. "McCain Campaign Clarifies 'Christian Nation' Remarks." *New York Sun,* October 1, 2007.

Brooks, Arthur C. "The Left's 'Inequality' Obsession." *Wall Street Journal,* July 19, 2007.

Brooks, David. "Disruption and Redemption." The Hoover Institution, Stanford University, June and July 1999.

Carroll, Joseph. "Most Americans 'Very Satisfied' with Their Personal Lives." Gallup.com, December 31, 2007.

Chavez, Linda. "The Great Assimilation Machine." *Wall Street Journal,* June 5, 2007.

Childs, Craig. "A Past That Makes Us Squirm." *New York Times,* January 2, 2007.

Cholo, Ana Beatriz. "Teachers Emphasize the Indians' Side." Associated Press, November 21, 2006.

Clinton, Hillary. "Remarks on the 40th Anniversary of Dr. King's Death." Memphis, Tennessee, April 4, 2008.

Cost, Jay. "Should We Expect a Third Party Candidate?" Real Clear Politics Horse RaceBlog, October 4, 2007.

Cox, W. Michael and Richard Alm. "The Good Old Days Are Now." *Reason,* December 1995.

Davis, Bob. "Move Over, Che: Chavez Is New Icon of Radical Chic." *Wall Street Journal,* June 16, 2006.

Dobbs, Lou. "Middle Class Needs to Fight Back Now." CNN.com, November 20, 2007.

D'Souza, Dinesh. "10 Things to Celebrate About America." *San Francisco Chronicle,* June 29, 2003.

Evans, M. Stanton. "Faith of Our Fathers." *The American Spectator,* February 2007.

———. "The Christian History of the Constitution." *Insight on the News,* March 20, 1995.

Fletcher, Michael A. "Many Blacks Earn Less Than Parents, Study Finds." *Washington Post,* November 13, 2007.

Folsom, Burton W. "Slim Pickings." *Wall Street Journal*, August 29, 2007.

Fukuyama, Francis. "How to Re-Moralize America." *Wilson Quarterly*, Summer 1999.

Fund, John H. "George Washington, Whiskey Entrepreneur." *Wall Street Journal*, February 21, 2007.

Gelernter, David. "No More Vietnams." *Weekly Standard*, May 8, 2006.

Goldberg, Jonah. "'Empire' Is Such a Loaded Word." *Seattle Times*, December 3, 2007.

Grimes, William. "A New World for Sale, Ocean-to-Ocean View." *New York Times*, August 22, 2007.

Grossman, Cathy Lynn. "Religious Bonds Divide Some Parents, Kids." *USA Today*, July 8, 2007.

Hale, David. "The Best Economy Ever." *Wall Street Journal*, July 31, 2007.

Hampson, Rick. "Along a Brooklyn Avenue, a Melting Pot—and Peace." *USA Today*, August 15, 2007.

Hays, Charlotte. "American Originals." *Wall Street Journal*, May 18, 2007.

Hedges, Chris. "The Christian Right and the Rise of American Fascism." ThirdWorld Traveller.com, April 2, 2008.

Henninger, Daniel. "The Pre-Election Paradox." *Wall Street Journal*, January 3, 2008.

Himmelfarb, Gertrude. "The War Over Virtue." *Wall Street Journal*, March 24–25, 2007.

Hitchens, Christopher. "Imperialism: Superpower Dominance, Malignant and Benign." *Slate*, December 10, 2002.

Hitt, Jack. "The Newest Indians." *New York Times Magazine*, August 21, 2005.

Holt, Jim. "You Are What You Expect." *New York Times Magazine*, January 21, 2007.

Horowitz, David. "Ten Reasons Why Reparations for Blacks Is a Bad Idea for Blacks—and Racist Too." FrontPageMagazine.com, January 3, 2001.

"House Resolution 194: Apologizing for the Enslavement and Racial Segregation of African-Americans." Introduced February 27, 2007.

Howard, Jenna. "Abolishing Columbus Day: USM Student Bound to Make Maine the Fifth State to Say No to Ignorance." *USM Free Press*, October 1, 2007.

Hundley, Tom. "Chocolate, Beer Keep Belgians Together." *Seattle Times*, February 18, 2007.

"Income Mobility in the U.S. from 1996–2005." Report of the Department of the Treasury, November 13, 2007.

Jayson, Sharon. "Teen Survey Shows Virginity Pledges Can Work." *USA Today*, June 10, 2008.

Kagan, Robert. "The End of the End of History." *New Republic*, April 23, 2008.

Koch, Wendy. "Legislators to Push for US Apology for Slavery." *USA Today*, February 28, 2008.

Krugman, Paul. "For God's Sake." *New York Times*, April 13, 2007.

LaSalle, Mick. "The Corporation." *San Francisco Chronicle*, June 4, 2004.

Lewy, Guenter. "Were American Indians the Victims of Genocide?" *Commentary*, November 22, 2004.

Medved, Michael. "Faith and Nationalism Indivisible in America." *USA Today*, July 23, 2006.

Mieder, Wolfgang. "The Only Good Indian Is a Dead Indian: History and Meaning of a Proverbial Stereotype." dickshovel.com, March 11, 2008.

Morris, Stephen J. "The War We Could Have Won." *New York Times*, May 1, 2005.

"Movin' on Up." Editorial. *Wall Street Journal*, November 13, 2007.

Muhlhausen, David B. "Job Corps: A Consistent Record of Failure." The Heritage Foundation. WebMemo #1374, February 28, 2007.

Naimark, Norman. "Germans As Victims: Recovering trom the Third Reich." *Weekly Standard,* November 12, 2007.

"New Study Shows Decline in Teen Drug Use." Associated Press, December 11, 2007.

Newport, Frank. "Religion Most Important to Blacks, Women and Older Americans." Gallup News Service, November 29, 2006.

Noonan, Peggy. "The View from Gate 14." *Wall Street Journal,* April 26–27, 2008.

Noveck, Jocelyn and Trevor Tompson. "Sex and Drugs? Nope." *Seattle Times,* August 20, 2007.

Olasky, Marvin. "Seven Principles from a Century Ago." Acton.org.

Olsen, Walter. "Judge Dread." *Reason,* April 1997.

O'Rourke, P. J. "When Worlds Collide: The American Past Meets Modern Museum Doctrine." *Weekly Standard,* June 9, 2008.

Page, Susan. "Do We Need a Third Party? Most Say Yes." *USA Today,* July 12, 2007.

Parker, Emily. "Weekend Interview with Ang Lee." *Wall Street Journal,* December 1–2, 2007.

Pinter, Harold. "Art, Truth and Politics: Nobel Lecture." The Nobel Foundation, December 7, 2005.

"The Poor Get Richer." Editorial. *The Wall Street Journal,* May 23, 2007.

Rasmussen Reports. "27% of Republicans Would Vote for Pro-Life Third Party." October 4, 2007.

Reagan, Ronald. "Farewell Address to the Nation." January 11, 1989.

Rector, Robert E. "How Poor Are America's Poor? Examining the 'Plague' of Poverty in America." The Heritage Foundation, Backgrounder, August 27, 2007.

———. "Poor Politics." National Review Online, August 27, 2007.

Rieff, David. "America the Untethered." *New York Times Magazine,* July 2, 2006.

Rivlin, Gary. "Las Vegas Proves Immune to Jittery U.S. Economy." *International Herald-Tribune,* December 26, 2007.

Roberts, Sam. "Children's Quality of Life Is on the Rise, Report Finds." *New York Times,* January 11, 2007.

Robinson, Peter. "Tom Wolfe, Patriot." National Review Online, May 9, 2008.

Rochelson, Meri-Jane. "Israel Zangwill 1864–1926." Jewish Virtual Library.

Rose, Stephen. "5 Myths About the Poor Middle Class." *Washington Post,* December 23, 2007.

———. "Class Dismissed: Why the Politics of Class Warfare Won't Work for Democrats." *Blueprint Magazine,* July 22, 2008.

———. "Democrats and the Economy." *Wall Street Journal,* March 25, 2008.

———. "The Myth of the Declining Middle Class." Stats.org, January 2008.

———. "What's the Income of the Typical American?" *The Huffington Post,* May 11, 2008.

Rothstein, Edward. "Captain Smith, the Tides Are Shifting on the James." *New York Times,* March 2, 2007.

———. "Two New Shows Cast Light and Darkness on Early Cultures in the Americas." *New York Times,* March 5, 2008.

Schiller, Brad. "The Inequality Myth." *Wall Street Journal,* March 10, 2008.

Sherk, James. "Upwards Leisure Mobility: Americans Work Less and Have More

Leisure Time Than Ever Before." The Heritage Foundation, WebMemo #1596, August 31, 2007.

Shlaes, Amity. "The Legacy of the 1936 Election." *Imprimis,* September 2007.

———. "The New Deal Jobs Myth." *Wall Street Journal,* December 31, 2007.

———. "The Real Deal." *Wall Street Journal,* June 25, 2007.

Sorman, Guy. "Apartheid à la Française." *Wall Street Journal,* December 4, 2007.

Sowell, Thomas. "Bury the Chains: How the West Ended Slavery." *Capitalism Magazine,* February 8, 2005.

Spalding, Matthew. "How to Understand Slavery and the American Founding." Heritage Foundation, WebMemo #01, August 26, 2002.

Stein, Rob. "Abortions Hit Lowest Number Since 1976." *Washington Post,* January 17, 2008.

Stevenson, Betsey and Justin Wolfers. "Divorced from Reality." *New York Times,* September 29, 2007.

Stoller, Gary. "Gas or Gamble? Economy Forces Some to Choose." *USA Today,* May 7, 2008.

Stone, Andrea. "Poll: Founders Intended Christian USA." *USA Today,* September 12, 2007.

"Treasury Releases Income Mobility Study." U.S. Treasury Department, Office of Public Affairs, November 13, 2007.

"Virginity Pledges May Help Postpone Intercourse Among Youth." *Science Daily,* June 14, 2008.

"Volunteers Gather Money on Portland Streets for Slavery Reparations." Associated Press, October 11, 2007.

Wehner, Peter and Yuval Levin. "Crime, Drugs, Welfare—and Other Good News." *Commentary,* December 2007.

Weyrich, Paul M. "Letter to Conservatives." NationalCenter.org, February 16, 1999.

Wheatcroft, Geoffrey. "The Church in England: Downright Un-American." *New York Times,* November 25, 2007.

Winfree, Paul. "Analyzing Economic Mobility." The Heritage Foundation, WebMemo #1478, May 31, 2007.

Winsman, Albert. "Religion 'Very Important' to Most Americans." Gallup News Service, December 20, 2005.

Wuthnow, Robert. "Myths About American Religion." Heritage Lectures #1049, The Heritage Foundation, October 4, 2007.

Yeagley, David A. "What's Up with White Women?" FrontPageMagazine.com, May 18, 2001.

Thank You

In writing the acknowledgments for a new book, every author faces the temptation of using the occasion to affirm significant relationships with dozens of friends, family members, and business associates. I cheerfully confess to succumbing to that temptation in many (all right, all) of my previous books, but this time I'll confine my thanks to six people directly involved in completing this project.

My intrepid assistant, Stacy Alderfer, helped with research, proofreading, securing photographs and drawings, and general organization, applying her reliable competence and unfailingly sunny disposition to an often wearying and stressful process. I'm not sure how I'll manage without her in the next few months when she takes time off to attend to the twins she's expecting. Meanwhile, my brilliant daughter, Sarah, spent the summer before her final year at Stern College (of Yeshiva University) to work as my intern and made herself utterly indispensable. She helped with research, rewriting, proofreading, source checking, preparing the sidebars accompanying every chapter, and handling the demanding business of finding photographs and other images featured in these pages. Perhaps someday—soon—I'll be able to return the favor by helping her in completing *her* book.

My wonderfully talented radio producers, Jeremy Steiner and Greg Tomlin, offered valuable advice on shaping and organizing this material and took up extra burdens associated with a host distracted by writing demands. Jeremy has worked with me since my first day as a radio host twelve years ago, and without him my whole career would be unimaginable.

My editor, Jed Donahue, deserves especially conspicuous recognition: his single-minded, ferocious commitment to this project kept it on track and brought about its completion in a (relatively) timely manner. Though we worked together previously on *Right Turns*, his participation in this book proved even more consequential and constructive. After I submitted my manuscript, he provided insightful cuts and rewrites and we then spent long hours—days, really—in conference calls going over every line, every word, to reach agreement. It's traditional for authors to say that an editor deserves credit for a book's virtues but no blame for its flaws, but that's not true in this case. Jed was involved in every aspect of this effort, so if you hate this book, you should blame him, too.

Finally, my multitalented wife, Dr. Diane Medved, played a prominent role at every stage in this process. She slaved over research—particularly for the first two chapters, for which she also wrote original drafts several times the length of the final versions here. As the author of five important books of her own, she put her current undertaking (*The Marriage of Opposites*) on hold while she worked with me and continued to run our complicated household. We had previously coauthored four important projects (Sarah, Shayna, Danny, and our book *Saving Childhood*), and she could rightly claim coauthorship here, too. In fact, in nearly twenty-four years of our formal partnership, there's nothing I've attempted or accomplished that hasn't relied on her first and most. Like the sun that provides her inspiration, she lights the life of all in her orbit.

INDEX